AN INTRODUCTION
TO MIDDLE ENGLISH

AN INTRODUCTION

HOLT, RINEHART AND WINSTON, INC.
New York Chicago San Francisco Atlanta Dallas
Montreal Toronto London Sydney

TO MIDDLE ENGLISH

EX LIBRES

CHARLES JONES
University of Edinburgh

AN INTRODUCTION TO MIDDLE ENGLISH by CHARLES JONES
Copyright © 1972 by Holt, Rinehart and Winston, Inc.
All Rights Reserved

ISBN: 0-03-084479-7

Library of Congress Catalog Card Number: 77-155295

Printed in the United States of America

2 3 4 5   038   9 8 7 6 5 4 3 2 1

TO ISLA

ACKNOWLEDGMENTS

I am grateful to the Trustees of the British Museum and to the Keeper of Western Manuscripts, Bodleian Library, Oxford, for their kind permission to reproduce the photographic prints of Middle English manuscript pages. I have also to thank The Council of the Early English Text Society and the Oxford University Press for allowing me to use some extracts from their printed editions. Swets and Zeitlinger N.V., Amsterdam, granted me permission to quote from *English Studies;* Houghton Mifflin Company, Boston, granted me permission to quote from *The Works of Geoffrey Chaucer,* edited by F. N. Robinson; and the Clarendon Press granted me permission to quote from *The Peterborough Chronicle,* 2d ed., 1970, by Cecile Clark. Lastly, my sincere thanks are due to Angus McIntosh and Michael L. Samuels for kindly allowing me to print the two dialect maps.

PREFACE

The writer of an introductory work in any area of historical linguistics faces two large problems. The first of these, and perhaps the most difficult, involves the amount of time he can afford to devote to the exposition of his theoretical model. The historical linguist is concerned more with the methodology of reconstruction than with an attempt to collect the data itself or even to realize his construct; and although this primary concern will at all times be colored by his theoretical bias, he will have little space to propound it to his satisfaction. In addition, there is the recurrent nightmare of theoretical obsolescence. The hypothetical assumptions that underlie many of the statements in this book are those of the transformational-generative models of syntax and phonology as they have been developed up to 1965 and a little beyond. Some knowledge of these models has been assumed throughout the book, although bibliographical reference to some of their principal expositions will be found at the end of each chapter.

The second major difficulty has to do with the amount of Middle English data that has to be omitted in a work of such a limited scope as this. The extant Middle English corpus is vast, and in its own right a collection of it could easily fill many volumes this size, even with the minimum of linguistic comment. This book does not pretend to be a grammar in some of the traditional senses of that word. It in no way attempts to be a data collection or a book of reference from which data information can be acquired or verified. Still less does it claim to be an aid to the translation of Middle English. Rather, the book should be seen as having two principal purposes. The first is to try to show how the data found in Middle English texts can be eminently suitable for the student interested in the nature and extent of changes undergone by the English language in real time. A recurrent concern of the following chapters will be to try to discover the differences underlying the internalized rule systems (or grammars) of the writers of some Middle English manuscripts and the grammars of speakers of Modern English and other historical periods of the language. Simultaneously, there well be several places where it will be possible to show the significance of the Middle English evidence for general theories of linguistic change.

The book's second major issue involves the general methodological procedures involved in the interpretation of data of the kind Middle English presents. Little is known about what a theory of scribal practice should look like, and there are still many difficulties to be overcome concerning the theoretical issues involved in the construction of grammars for languages for which there are no longer any native speakers. Although this attempt to construct historical grammars from purely written sources will be a main concern, it will also be suggested, especially in the chapter dealing with Middle English geographical dialects, that the orthographic marks made by scribes can have an importance in their own right irrespective of the evidence they provide for syntactical and phonological systems.

Traditionally, the linguistic study of Middle English has come off second best to the more popular area of Old English and even in comparison with studies in early Modern English. The reasons for this state of affairs are not difficult to find. The extent of the Middle English data is enormous. Although in itself this does not have to hinder the construction of adequate Middle English grammars, it does mean that even fairly extensive works on the language (for example, Mustanoja [1960], Brunner [1948], and Mossé [1952]) are incomplete in a variety of ways. In addition, there are the familiar problems posed by Middle English; its orthographic system is far from fully understood, resulting in a corresponding uncertainty in proposed phonological reconstructions, while the amount of orthographic variation provides an almost daunting spectacle of idiosyncrasy. Detailed study of the syntax of Middle English has too often been concentrated on very small areas, especially in early Middle English, where there is the traditional concern to show the changes that occurred between Old and Middle English. The result of this is that there are large areas of the period left unexamined and that await research on a considerable scale. Paradoxically, there is also the implicit suggestion sometimes made that Middle English, unlike Old English, is sufficiently similar to the modern language to make linguistic analysis superfluous, despite the fact (among more obvious objections) that some Middle English texts can still defy sensible translation.

In a book of this size only a small amount of such a large and varied corpus as Middle English can be considered. Many areas of the grammar have had to be ignored (notably the semantic component), and in some instances detailed discussion of an individual point will have preference over the demonstration of "overall trends." The general strategy in the chapters that follow will be one of presenting the reader with a small

Middle English sample (together with a rendering of it into Modern English); and the majority of the syntactical, phonological, and orthographic comment will be limited to such a sample. Wherever possible, the Middle English selections will be chosen for their usefulness in highlighting discrepancies between the internalized grammars of their writers. Although discussion of performance factors and their effect on grammatical outputs will be kept to a minimum, largely because little is known about this area in general, the texts chosen will inevitably include some "stylistic" or "variety" differentiation.

Chapter One briefly raises in outline the kind of questions to be discussed as the book progresses, for example, how the Middle English evidence is to be extrapolated and interpreted, what is meant by textual reconstruction, and what appear to be the main obstacles for the historical linguist involved in the construction of grammars for languages that are no longer spoken. Chapter Two deals principally with matters historical, sociological, and paleographic and tries to examine a few traditional ideas about the reasons for the emergence of Middle English from Old English, at the same time bringing to light some of the problems involved in transcribing medieval English manuscripts into a modern form.

Chapter Three centers on Middle English phonology, with special reference to the methodology of constructing sound systems from nonacoustic evidence. It is at this point that some discussion will be found on what scribes meant by what they wrote. This chapter also contains a certain amount of theoretical statement on generative phonologies based upon a distinctive feature framework. There will be a return to some phonological matters, especially in relation to verbal ablaut, in Chapter Five; and in relation to dialectal differences, in Chapter Six.

Chapters Four and Five have as their subjects nominal and verbal syntax respectively. Here will be found some detailed examination of such topics as nominal and pronominal case, number, and gender systems and the verbal characteristics of mood, tense, and aspect among others. It will be obvious that many of the features selected are very often the same ones most frequently dealt with in more traditional Middle English grammars. Part of the reason for this will be the interest in looking at well-documented material in terms of a different grammatical model. At the same time, the wealth of data on such subjects that is present in earlier accounts will enable the reader to verify or reject the conclusions reached in these chapters, as well as to compare the efficacy of the descriptive adequacy of more than one linguistic model on the same sets of data. Chapters Four and Five will also contain some brief mention on current ideas of how children acquire language and the relationship between this phenomenon and linguistic change.

In many respects, the subject of Chapter Six, Middle English geographical dialects, assumes a detailed knowledge of all the points realized and implied in the other chapters. Undoubtedly, the chapter's most interesting feature is the inclusion, for the first time in print, of a complete map from the McIntosh and Samuels *Middle English Dialect Survey*. The detailed information these maps contain (the one here shows the geographical distribution of the spelling variants of *church*) has great importance for the geographical location of Middle English manuscripts, as well as for its as yet unrealized potential in providing data for the study of phonological-graphological correspondences, in other words, for a theory of scribal practice. The author wishes to express his gratitude to both Angus McIntosh and Michael Samuels for their kind permission to reproduce the two maps that appear in this chapter.

Naturally, in a book of this kind, the acknowledgments due are of a very large number. Not only have Angus McIntosh and Michael Samuels provided the author with access to their dialectal materials, but both have been a source of encouragement in his career. Much of the material on the phonology of Middle English reflects the work of John Anderson, Roger Lass, and David Tittensor. The detailed observations on Old English ablaut rely heavily on Anderson's work. I am also indebted to Paul van Buren for his valuable comments on an earlier draft of the manuscript, and to George Leslie for his expert drawing of the two maps. Thanks are also due to Jane Lind, who typed many intermediate and final versions of the book, and to the publishers for their readily given and invaluable assistance at all stages. All remaining inadequacies, and there are doubtless many, are entirely my own responsibility.

C.J.

Edinburgh, Scotland
September 1971

ONTENTS

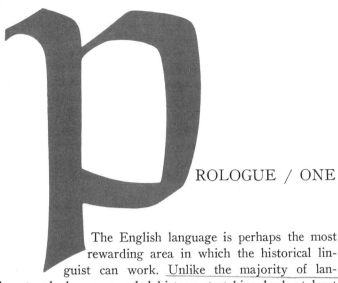

PROLOGUE / ONE

The English language is perhaps the most rewarding area in which the historical linguist can work. Unlike the majority of languages, English not only has a recorded history stretching back at least twelve hundred years, but it is a language that survives in large quantities and in many varieties. The historical linguist working in English is further fortunate in being able to refer to an immense body of research already done in this field, principally in the nineteenth and early twentieth centuries, although, as will be seen, both these facts entail disadvantages as well as advantages. There is little doubt, however, that the historical linguist has received considerable stimulus from the work of present-day theoretical linguistic studies. The fact that most modern linguistic investigation is carried out in terms of Euglish means that the existence of a rather advanced theory for the workings of the modern language implies at least the possibility of more meaningful statements being made with reference to its historical manifestations.

The last point is extremely important, since it has been the lack of a sophisticated grammatical description that has done much to lead to the disinterest in historical studies that has been shown in recent years, as well as to raise considerable misunderstanding both about the nature of the problems involved in historical "reconstruction" and about the processes of linguistic change itself. Middle English studies have perhaps suffered disproportionately from the lack of an adequate grammatical model, and the term *Middle English* can be said to reflect ideas about the nature of language that are now less acceptable. The technique of classifying (albeit for the sake of convenience) the historical "periods" of English into types such as Old, Middle, and Modern (all with the more delicate subdivisions of early and late) is misleading, since, among other things, it fails to ask and define the reasons why such divisions should be necessary in the first place. Middle English, for example, is in traditional scholarship said to begin around the year 1100 and to end around 1500, give or take fifty or so years at each terminus. Statements of this kind (although to be fair they are usually made with various qualifications) are inappropriate on several counts. One of the most obvious of these lies in the fact that it begs a certain status for a linguistic division such as Middle English. There is no easy answer to the question whether Middle and Old English are to be regarded as standing in the same relationship with Modern English as, for example, Modern German, or whether they are to be regarded as temporal dialects with the same status vis-à-vis "standard" English as modern regional and class dialects. Some kinds of linguistic change may be more drastic in their effect on a language than others, whereas others may be of a type that has no important repercussions on the structure of the language at all. The historical scholarship has very often been content to say that language changes slowly, imperceptibly, and in a random fashion, until sufficient differences are accumulated to justify a descriptive break in the historical chain. Leaving aside for the moment the supposition that linguistic change takes place in line with gradualness theories, it is important to know the nature and status of the changes that make it appear that, for example, Middle English is in some sense a different language from Modern English. Despite a considerable amount of scholarly controversy (for example, Malone [1930]), there is probably no empirical basis for deciding where Old English became Middle English, even though it has been said that the earliest Middle English text is the *Sermo in Festis Marie Virginis* (1108–1122) (Clark, C. [1958], "Introduction," p. xl). Recent historical linguists are tending to give a greater emphasis to the search for the underlying linguistic mechanisms that appear to give rise to the variation in output so obvious in texts written at different dates.

Once one accepts the idea of a period such as Middle English, there is a strong temptation to treat it as a homogeneous linguistic set. Traditional works on Middle English, for example, tend to write for that language a number of what are often called "everywhere rules"; that is, it is too often suggested that syntactical or phonological phenomena found in a text written in 1200 are generalizable in the description of texts written at later dates, or even of texts written at the same date in a different geographical dialect, or of texts with different "styles" even when there is a minimum of temporal and geographical discrepancies. There is so much Middle English data that if nonvacuous statements are to be made, they must be restricted to very small parts of the grammars of texts within well-defined areas. Consequently, the reader of this book must bear in mind that by and large the linguistic statements made in it have reference only to the limited data selected.

The very large number of texts written between the *ad hoc* dates of 1100 and 1500 are very well represented in modern printed editions. Every major literary work in the period has been edited (some many times, see Wells [1916]), and there is a reasonably good sample of other nonliterary materials readily available among the many publications of the Early English Text Society. Within the essentially nineteenth-century tradition of textual edition, many Middle English texts have received what appears to be, in the very widest possible sense, a detailed linguistic description. As collections of the data, some of these editions are indispensable, but it must be said that they rarely go beyond this. The grammars they present to us are almost entirely of the taxonomic or item-and-arrangement type, and they say little or nothing concerning the linguistic mechanisms that give rise to the data itself—perhaps one of the best examples of this can be found in Hall (1920), Part II. From the point of view of many modern historical linguists, the sections dealing with linguistic matters in even the best editions (for example, d'Ardenne [1936] and Clark, C. [1958]) have the serious drawback that they are too strongly data-orientated; that is, they are primarily concerned with the output of a linguistic capability, whereas the modern linguist prefers to explore the nature of this capability itself and to formalize as far as possible the internalized system (or set of rules) of which it is comprised. Furthermore, the modern historical linguist tries to make statements that go beyond the level of observational adequacy, endeavoring to reconstruct as far as possible the internalized rule systems or grammars responsible for the written outputs with which he deals, as well as to discover the nature of the grammatical changes, in all their complexity, that give rise to diversification in that output over periods of time. Nevertheless, the modern historical linguist can find a great deal to interest him in the very detailed traditional accounts of Middle English orthographies and phonologies, and to a lesser extent in their descriptions of syntactical patterns.

Some of the shortcomings of traditional descriptions of Middle English arise, of course, from the fact that the bulk of the scholarship in the field is orientated toward a nonlinguistic audience. It is perhaps as much because of the nature of their intended public as well as the inadequacy of their linguistic theories that so many textual commentaries deal with historical syntaxes and phonologies and the processes of linguistic change in an impressionistic and metaphorical fashion: syntactical constructions "die out" because of "the natural processes of decay," inflections "weaken," some dialects are "more robust" than others, and language becomes less "synthetic" and more "analytic," while linguistic change is often supposed to make "inexpressible" or "more difficult" earlier everyday thought patterns. Although such treatments are not characteristic of all accounts of Middle English, they are still, unfortunately, to be found. This is the more to be regretted, since the large amount of Middle English material surviving to us (hardly equaled in quantity or diversity in any other medieval language) makes it an excellent area in which the problems of constructing historical grammars as well as the principles involved in linguistic change can be profitably and fully investigated.

An obvious major difficulty for the linguist trying to reconstruct a grammar for a language like Middle English lies in the absence of native speakers. Without a body of native speakers, it is impossible to test postulated sentences either for grammaticality or acceptability—Chomsky (1962, 1965)—against the intuitions such native speakers will have about their language. Rather than merely list the total number of sentences found in the Middle English period, a grammar for Middle English should try to account for the knowledge speakers then alive in England had about their language, enabling them to produce an infinite and not a finite set of utterances (Chomsky [1965], Jacobs and Rosenbaum [1968]). Rather than contain a list of the sentences a speaker has actually produced, or reproduce the speaker's *performance,* the grammar will try to formalize the internal linguistic processes or rules that enable the speaker to realize all the correct utterances in his language. In other words, the grammar will try to give an account of the speaker's *competence.* Without the insights provided by a native speaker, a grammar of Middle English will, of necessity, suffer from the drawback that at best it will only be able to be formulated in terms of a finite corpus, which despite the bulk of extant Middle English clearly contains nothing like the total possible output of the grammars of its speakers. The consequence of this will be that such a grammar may lead to the realization of utterances that a native speaker may have rejected as ungrammatical. This observation is also true in relation to grammars of languages that are still spoken, since such grammars are only approximations to the competence of their users. As yet grammars of Modern English differ only in their degree of explicitness when compared to those constructed for its historical antecedents.

Unlike some earlier works on the subject of medieval English language that have tended to be performance-orientated, this book will try to place its emphasis on a limited reconstruction of the internalized linguistic competence of Middle English speakers. Its limited extent must, however, be stressed. Since the nature of the data allows only the reconstruction of the competence underlying a scribe's written performance, there may be many instances where the reconstructed grammar would be inadequate as a means of producing acceptable outputs of a nonwritten kind. The competence underlying spoken Middle English performance is beyond our grasp, although, as will be seen, some scribes have apparently endeavored to leave clues to the nature of their phonological competence. Another equally real limitation on the scope of any grammatical study lies in the fact that the present state of linguistic knowledge makes sophisticated description possible only in a very small area of the total grammar. Although it is clear that the hypotheses set up for historical grammars will always be open to severe weaknesses, the more that is known about the workings of synchronic grammars, the less likely this is to be an overriding handicap. An increase in the knowledge of the nature of universal synchronic linguistic phenomena will make it easier to "test" those historical grammars that are reconstructed. Indeed, the process of reconstruction must itself rely on whatever information the linguist has of synchronic grammatical behavior. For example, it might be possible to set up what are known as _naturalness_ conditions in linguistic description; that is, in certain areas' in the grammar (especially in the phonological component) some features appear to be arranged and selected in a nonarbitrary way and appear to exist in what are tentatively suggested to be natural configurations (Postal [1968], pp. 53 ff.). One instance of this might be that features of linguistic sound systems seem to be closely related to the physical, articulatory speech-producing mechanisms, so that some sounds and combinations of sounds are perhaps more "natural" than others. The common phonological feature of assimilation, where there is a tendency for vowels or consonants to "take on" the characteristics of neighboring segments, seems to operate on some conditions of naturalness. At present, little is known about such conditions, but should they prove general in synchronic grammars, they might then profitably be sought in historical grammars as well, with the result that descriptions in the latter that seem to contradict them might either be viewed with skepticism or else lead to a reassessment of the theory of naturalness.

At this point some of the matters to be dealt with in detail in the main part of the book will receive a brief preview. This will be done by means of a comparison between the outputs of a few samples of English at different historical periods together with one "related" Germanic language called Gothic, which was spoken in the Crimea region in the fourth century A.D. The samples are all a rendering of the New Testament passage in Luke 10:3–4:

GOTHIC, A.D. 360
‹Gaggiþ sai. ik ínsandya ιzwis swe lamba in midumai wulfe. Ni bairaiþ pugg, nih matibalg, nih gaskohi, ni mannanhun bi wig golyaiþ.›

ENGLISH, about A.D. 950, glossing seventh-century Latin

‹gaa	heono	ic	sendo	iuih	sua	lombro	bi-tuih	ulfum
ITE	ECCE	EGO	MITTO	UOS	SICUT	AGNOS	INTER	LUPOS

nællað ӡie ӡebeara	seam		ne	posa	ne	sceoe
NOLITE PORTARE	SACCULUM		NEQUE	PERAM	NEQUE	CALCIAMENTA

7	ne ænigne monn	ðerh woege	ӡie groetað ›
ET	NEMINEM	PER UIAM	SALUTAUERITIS. ›

ENGLISH, A.D. 995

⟨Faraþ nu. nu ic eow sende swa swa lamb betweox wulfas. Ne bere ȝe sacc, ne codd, ne ȝescy, ne nanne man be wege ne gretaþ.⟩

ENGLISH, A.D. 1389

⟨Go ȝe lo! I sende ȝou as lambren among wolues. Nyle ȝe bere a sachel, nether scrip, nether schoon, and grete ȝe no man by the weye.⟩

MODERN ENGLISH

⟨Now depart! I send you as lambs among wolves. Do not carry a bag, wallet or shoes with you, and do not acknowledge anyone along the way.⟩

A comparison of the written manifestations of diachronically discrete English forms both with each other and with their cognates in some earlier related language, such as Gothic, can often give some insight into the differences between the grammatical systems that underlie them. Consider, for instance, the way in which in the above samples the plural number is formed in nouns. The forms corresponding to the Modern English ⟨shoes⟩ appear as ⟨gaskohi⟩, ⟨sceoe⟩, ⟨ȝescy⟩, and ⟨schoon⟩. A comparison between these forms and their singular equivalents yields the following set of data:

[+*singular*]	[−*singular*]
⟨gaskohs⟩	⟨gaskohi⟩
⟨sco⟩	⟨sceoe⟩
⟨ȝescu⟩	⟨ȝescy⟩
⟨scho⟩	⟨schoon⟩
⟨shoe⟩	⟨shoes⟩

Leaving aside, for the moment, the significance of such spelling variations as the initial ⟨sk⟩, ⟨sc⟩, ⟨sch⟩, and ⟨sh⟩, and the presence or absence of the prefix ⟨ga⟩ or ⟨ȝe⟩, one can see that at least three rules for the formation of plural nouns appear to underlie these forms. Two of these involve the addition of some kind of suffix to the singular form or a change in an already existing suffix: thus ⟨scho⟩ → ⟨scho + on⟩, and ⟨shoe⟩ → ⟨shoe + s⟩, or ⟨gaskoh + s⟩ → ⟨gaskoh + i⟩. The third, if the spelling evidence is to be accepted at its face value, involves a change in the root vowel of the noun from the singular to the plural: thus ⟨-scu⟩ → ⟨-scy⟩, which, as will be suggested later, involves the change in the pronunciation of a high back vowel, represented by ⟨u⟩, to one that is articulated further forward in the mouth.

A comparison of the English data suggests (in simple terms) that the last, vowel-change rule—still present in such cases as ⟨man⟩/⟨men⟩ and ⟨goose⟩/⟨geese⟩—seems to have been lost, and in this word replaced by the suffix-adding rule involving ⟨on⟩, which in its turn is also lost and replaced by the ⟨es⟩ suffix-adding rule. Thus, <u>since the rules of plural formation involving ⟨on⟩ and vowel change are confined to a small number of rather exceptional nouns in Modern English, it can be deduced that *rule loss* is one characteristic of linguistic change.</u>

If, on the other hand, the English A.D. 995 form is compared with the Gothic, it can be seen that two superficially different processes have a common underlying basis; that is, the change in the English example from a back vowel to one with a more forward degree of articulation does not seem to be unmotivated. The Gothic plural-forming suffix is represented by ⟨i⟩, the spelling, it seems, for a high front vowel. If it is postulated that English too once had this ⟨i⟩ (or similar) plural-forming suffix, then the ⟨u⟩ → ⟨y⟩ change can be said to be the result of an assimilation in frontness between the root and suffix vowels. In this way, it can be seen that external linguistic data are very valuable in the reconstruction process. Since, however, the fronting context is no longer present in the English data, even though its result is still evident, at least two problems are raised that will have to be discussed. The first is whether linguistic change, here rule loss, will take place whenever the context in which the rule applies for some reason disappears. The second, and perhaps the more interesting, is whether different levels of abstraction have to be assumed in grammatical description. In other words, although the suffix front vowel is not superficially present, its existence at a more abstract level in the grammar of the sample English A.D. 995 may have to be postulated if certain regular phenomena in that grammar are to be accounted for satisfactorily. In many instances it will be suggested that the existence of such abstract forms in the grammar of a given language can, as it were, be justified from their presence at a more superficial level in the grammars either of that language's historical precedents or in those of its cognates.

An instance of linguistic change involving a process rather like the loss or the nonapplication of rules in the internalized linguistic system known as the grammar can be seen from a comparison of the way certain aspects of negative sentences are realized in the above English data. The English A.D. 995 and A.D. 1389 selections have respectively:

⟨ne nanne man be wege ne gretaþ⟩
⟨and grete ȝe no man by the weye⟩

whereas those from A.D. 950 and contemporary usage realize:

⟨ne ænigne monn ðerh woege ȝie groetað⟩
⟨and do not acknowledge anyone along the way⟩.

In the first two examples, the indefinite pronoun ⟨someone⟩ or ⟨anyone⟩ is realized as the equivalent of ⟨not one man⟩ rather than some form of ⟨one⟩ (⟨anne⟩ or ⟨a⟩) without a negative particle ⟨ne⟩; that is, the two last examples show ⟨ænig⟩ and ⟨any⟩ without the incorporation of a negative element, whereas the others have ⟨ne + anne⟩ → ⟨nanne⟩ or ⟨ne + an⟩ → ⟨no⟩ before the indefinite ⟨mann⟩ or ⟨one⟩. The rule that incorporated negative elements into certain words in negative sentences is clearly more limited in its application in the grammars underlying the Modern English and the English A.D. 950 outputs.

Although linguistic change can alter the internalized grammatical systems of speakers by means of the deletion of whole sets of rules as well as by a more limited application of others, the opposite process, that is, *rule addition,* can also take place. This can be seen in a comparison of the negative imperative outputs of the grammars underlying the English samples given earlier:

⟨nællað ʒie ʒebeara seam⟩
⟨Ne bere ʒe sacc⟩
⟨Nyle ʒe bere a sachel⟩
⟨Do not carry a bag⟩

also

⟨ne ænigne monn ðerh woege ʒie groetað⟩
⟨ne nanne man be wege ne gretaþ⟩
⟨and grete ʒe no man by the weye⟩
⟨and do not acknowledge anyone along the way⟩

There are at least two differences between the way this construction is realized in the Modern English samples when compared with all the others. The first, a case of *rule deletion,* involves the loss from the superficial structure of the second person pronoun ⟨ʒe⟩ or ⟨ʒie⟩. The second shows the Modern English sentences with an additional element—⟨do⟩—in this syntactic context. It could, therefore, be argued that an extra—*do auxiliary*—rule has at some period been incorporated into the grammar of English. In view of what has been said earlier, however, the possibility should be borne in mind that, rather than representing something completely new added to the grammar, the *do auxiliary* may be a realization at a superficial level of a syntactic feature common to and necessary for all historical stages of English, and always present at a more abstract level of its grammar (Traugott [1967]).

Many theoretical difficulties have to be faced when any attempt is made to comment upon the sound system or phonology represented by a given orthographic system. The reconstruction of much of what Middle English sounded like is impossible, since the evidence that survives is too limited to enable detailed phonetic statements to be made. Even more general theories about scribes' orthographic methods and the relationship they bear to what scribes actually said are limited by the fact that very little is known about orthographic-phonological correspondences even in Modern English (King [1969], Chapter 8). Middle English manuscripts are not written in a national, standard spelling system, since individual scribal training centers seem to have taught their own spelling methods. At present, there is very little information concerning the orthographic theories (if any) underlying these methods, and a great deal of research has still to be done in this area. For example, it is difficult to know how to interpret the near contemporary tenth-century graphic contrasts ⟨eow⟩/⟨iuih⟩, ⟨wege⟩/⟨woege⟩, and ⟨scy⟩/⟨sceoe⟩, which appear in the samples. On the one hand, they may represent attempts to show that different phonological rules were needed to arrive at the sounds of these words in their respective geographical dialects, or they could conceivably be interpreted as mere spelling variants with no phonological significance whatever. A third possibility, which will receive some detailed comment, is that the many spelling variants found for individual words in Middle English can provide valuable evidence in their own right, regardless of whatever clues they provide for the reconstruction of sound systems, as a means of establishing the geographical location of the texts in which they occur. In all, the nonnational, regional, and even personal orthographic systems found in Middle English can provide much data for the scholar interested in the formulation of a general theory of scribal practice.

Although this book will deal in a very limited way with many of the traditional concerns of Middle English scholarship, notably the reconstruction of syntactical, morphological, and phonological features characteristic of English between 1000 and 1450, it will differ from them in at least two ways. In the first place, it makes no claim to completeness, and no lists of paradigms or declensions will be provided, since in general the points raised are selected for the problems they pose for the linguist trying to arrive at a theory of reconstruction and linguistic change, rather than in any attempt to give an all-embracing account of what Middle English looked like. Secondly, the following chapters will leave much unsaid, especially in the area traditionally known as *vocabulary*. One justification for this omission lies in the unfortunate fact that semantic theory can at present add little to what is readily available in textbooks and other sources: Kurath and Kuhn (1954), Luik (1921), Morsbach (1902), Serjeantson (1961), and Weinstock (1969), among many. Again, the description of lexical borrowing from foreign languages such as French, Scandinavian, and Latin into Middle English has been thoroughly enough investigated elsewhere to warrant its omission here (compare Björkman [1900], Mersand [1939]). This area also suffers from the present lack of an adequate theoretical basis for the treatment of "lexical" phenomena. Lastly, little will be said about the great range of diatypic variety found in Middle English texts, even though it would be interesting to include in grammars the features that supply sociolinguistic variation at a given period. Middle English, with its wealth of heterogeneous diatypic material, would be an excellent area for such a study, although its dimensions would have to go far beyond the limited scope of this book (Gregory [1969]).

Middle English studies are overdue for a reappraisal of their traditional concerns and methods in the light of recent developments in general linguistic theory. The next five chapters attempt to encourage further investigation in an area of English studies that has much to offer.

BIBLIOGRAPHY

WORKS RELATING TO GENERAL AND HISTORICAL LINGUISTICS

CHOMSKY, N., "A Transformational Approach to Syntax," *Third Texas Conference on Problems of Linguistic Analysis in English,* Austin, 1962.

———, "Current Issues in Linguistic Theory," in *The Structure of Language,* edited by J. J. Katz and J. Fodor, Englewood Cliffs, 1964.

———, *Aspects of the Theory of Syntax,* Cambridge, Mass., 1965.

GREGORY, M. J., "Aspects of Varieties Differentiation," *Journal of Linguistics,* 4 (1968).

JACOBS, R. A., and P. S. ROSENBAUM, *English Transformational Grammar,* New York, 1968.

KING, R., *Historical Linguistics and Generative Grammar,* Englewood Cliffs, 1969.

LASS, R., *Readings in English Historical Linguistics,* New York, 1969.

LEHMAN, W. P., "A Reader in Nineteenth-Century Historical Indo-European Linguistics," *Indiana University Studies in the History and Theory of Linguistics,* Bloomington, 1967.

———, *Historical Linguistics: An Introduction,* New York, 1966.

———, *Directions for Historical Linguistics: A Symposium,* Austin, 1968.

LYONS, J., *Introduction to Theoretical Linguistics,* Cambridge, 1968.

MALKIEL, Y., "Language History in Historical Linguistics," *Romance Philology,* 7 (1953).

POSTAL, P., *Aspects of Phonological Theory,* New York, 1968.

SMITH, F., and G. A. MILLER, *The Genesis of Language: a Psycholinguistic Approach,* Cambridge, Mass., 1966.

THIEME, P., "The Comparative Method for Reconstruction in Linguistics," in *Language in Culture and Society,* edited by D. H. Hymes, New York, 1964.

WEIR, R. H., *Language in the Crib,* The Hague, 1962.

GENERAL MIDDLE ENGLISH GRAMMARS

BRUNNER, K., *Abriss der mittelenglischen Grammatik,* Halle, 1948; translated by G. Johnston, Oxford, 1963.

CLARK, J. W., *Early English,* London, 1957.

FISIAK, J., *Outlines of Middle English,* part I, Lodz, 1964.

MORSBACH, L., *Mittelenglische Grammatik,* teil I, Halle, 1896.

MOSSÉ, F., *A Handbook of Middle English,* translated by J. A. Walker, Baltimore, 1952.

MUSTANOJA, T. F., *A Middle English Syntax,* part I, Helsinki, 1960.

ROSEBOROUGH, M. M., *An Outline of Middle English Grammar,* New York, 1938.

WARDALE, E. E., *Introduction to Middle English Grammar,* London, 1937.

WEINSTOCK, H., *Mittelenglisches Elementarbuch,* Berlin, 1968.

WRIGHT, J., *An Elementary Middle English Grammar,* Oxford, 1957.

SUPPLEMENTARY READING

BRUNNER, K., *Die englische Sprache,* Halle, 1950–1951.

CAMPBELL, A., *Old English Grammar,* Oxford, 1959.

CRAIGIE, W. A., "The Outlook in Philology," *Transactions of the Philological Society,* 1954.

EINENKEL, E., *Geschichte der englischen Sprache,* volume II: *Historische Syntax,* Strassburg, 1916.

HOENIGSWALD, H., *Language Change and Linguistic Reconstruction,* Chicago, 1960.

KALUZA, M., *Historische Grammatik der mittelenglischen Sprache,* 2 vols., Berlin, 1900, 1901.

LANGENFELT, G., *Select Studies in Colloquial English of the Late Middle Ages,* Lund, 1933.

LUIK, K., *Historische Grammatik der englischen Sprache,* Leipzig, 1913.

MAGOUN, F. P., "Colloquial Old and Middle English," *Harvard Studies and Notes in Philology and Literature,* XIX (1937).

MALONE, K., "When Did Middle English Begin?", *Curme Volume of Linguistic Studies,* Philadelphia, 1930.

MCINTOSH, A. M., "The Analysis of Written Middle English," *TPS,* 1956.

ROBINS, R. H., *Ancient and Mediaeval Grammatical Theory in Europe with Particular Reference to Modern Linguistic Doctrine,* London, 1950.

STURTEVANT, E. H., *Linguistic Change,* Chicago, 1917.

TRAUGOTT, E. C., "Towards a Grammar of Syntactic Change," *Lingua,* 23 (1967).

WYLD, H. C., *A Short History of English,* London, 1927.

DICTIONARIES

BRADLEY, H., *Middle English Dictionary by F. H. Stratmann,* Oxford, 1891.

KURATH, H., and S. A. KUHN, *Middle English Dictionary,* Ann Arbor, 1956.

MIDDLE ENGLISH ANTHOLOGIES

BAUGH, A. C., *Chaucer's Major Poetry,* London, 1963.

BENNETT, J. A. W., and G. V. SMITHERS, *Early Middle English Verse and Prose,* Oxford, 1966.

BOSWORTH, J., and G. WARING, *The Gospels, Gothic, Anglo-Saxon, Wycliffe and Tyndale Versions,* London, 1907.

BRANDL, A., and O. ZIPPEL, *Mittelenglische Sprach- und Literaturproben,* Berlin, 1917.

COOK, A. S., *A Literary Middle English Reader,* Boston, 1943.

DICKENS, B., and R. M. WILSON, *Early Middle English Texts,* Cambridge, 1952.

EMERSON, O. F., *A Middle English Reader,* London, 1916.

HALL, J., *Selections from Early Middle English,* parts I and II, Oxford, 1920.

MORRIS, R., *Specimens of Early English,* parts I and II, Oxford, 1898.

MOSSÉ, F. (1952), pp. 133 ff.

OLIPHANT, T. L. K., *The Old and Middle English,* London, 1878.

ROBINSON, F. N., *The Complete Works of Geoffrey Chaucer,* Oxford, 1933.

SISAM, K., *Fourteenth-Century Verse and Prose,* Oxford, 1922.

SKEAT, W. W., *The Complete Works of Geoffrey Chaucer,* Oxford, 1894–1897.

———, *The Vision of William concerning Piers the Plowman,* Oxford, 1896.

WELLS, J. E., *A Manual of the Writings in Middle English, 1050–1400,* New Haven, 1916, and supplements.

PERIODICALS CONTAINING WORKS ON MIDDLE ENGLISH LANGUAGE
AND LITERATURE AND ON GENERAL LINGUISTIC THEORY

Acta Linguistica Hafniensia (Copenhagen).
American Speech (New York).
Anglia (Tübingen).
Archiv für das Studium der Neueren Sprachen und Literaturen (Braun-schweig).
Beiträge zur Geschichte der Deutschen Sprache und Literatur (Tübingen).
Bulletin de la Société de Linguistique de Paris (Paris).
Canadian Journal of Linguistics (Toronto).
English Language Notes (Boulder, Colorado).
English Philological Studies (Birmingham).
English Studies (Amsterdam).
Essays and Studies (London).
Foundations of Language (Dordrecht).
Indogermanische Forschungen (Berlin).
Journal of English and Germanic Philology (Urbana, Ill.).
Journal of Linguistics (Cambridge).
Langages (Paris).
Language (Baltimore).
Lingua (Amsterdam).
Linguistics (The Hague).
Medium Ævum (Oxford).
Modern Language Notes (Baltimore).
Modern Language Quarterly (Seattle).
Modern Language Review (Cambridge).
Modern Philology (Chicago).
Neuphilologische Mitteilungen (Helsinki).
Neuphilologus (Gröningen).
Notes and Queries (Oxford).
Philological Quarterly (Iowa City).
Publications of the Modern Language Association of America (New York).
Review of English Studies (Oxford).
Romance Philology (Berkeley and Los Angeles).
Studia Linguistica (Lund).
Studia Neophilologica (Uppsala).
Studies in Philology (Chapel Hill, North Carolina).
Transactions of the American Philological Association (Hartford, Conn.).
Transactions of the Philological Society (Oxford).
Word (New York).
Zeitschrift für Deutsche Philologie (Berlin).

Studies in Vocabulary

BJÖRKMAN, E., *Scandinavian Loan Words in Middle English,* parts I and II, Halle, 1901–1902.

FEIST, R., *Studien zur Rezeption des französischen Wortschatzes im Mittelenglischen,* Leipzig, 1934.

KÄSMANN, H., *Studien zum Kirklichen Wortschatz des Mittelenglischen, 1100–1350,* Tübingen, 1961.

LÖFVENBERG, M. T., *Contributions to Middle English Lexicography and Etymology,* Lund, 1946.

RYNELL, A., "The Rivalry of Scandinavian and Native Synonyms in Middle English," *Lund Studies in English,* 13 (1948), Lund.

SANDAHL, B., "Middle English Sea Terms, Parts I and II," in *Essays and Studies on English Language and Literature,* edited by S. B. Liljegren, Uppsala, 1951, 1958.

SCHÖFFLER, H., *Beiträge zur mittelenglischen Medizinliteratur,* Halle, 1919.

SERJEANTSON, M. S., *A History of Foreign Words in English,* London, 1961.

Editions

D'ARDENNE, S. T., *þe Liflade ant te Passiun of Seinte Iuliene,* Liège and Paris, 1936.

CLARK, C., *The Peterborough Chronicle,* Oxford, 1958.

HE SOURCES / TWO

The linguist who is concerned with a description of an extant language, such as Modern English, is in a considerably more fortunate position than his counterpart who deals with "extinct" or historical language data. Above all, the study of a living spoken (and written) language like English has the double advantage of having available large amounts of source material of all kinds as well as native speakers, against whose linguistic intuitions can be tested any predictions set up by the linguist's theoretical apparatus. When he comes to deal with the past stage of a language, neither of these aids, especially the latter, is always available to him. In other words, the sources or data are not always totally reliable as providers of raw material on which a theory can be both based and tested.

In the case of English, the earlier the stage of the language, the less reliable are the predictions as to what can be considered acceptable forms. For this reason, our knowledge of Old English must be of a very limited kind simply because such small amounts of source material remain. Such a limitation in the data means, above all, that a linguistic theory for Old English must be always more tentative than one would like and that its testability is rather limited. In addition to this, it is also possible that a reliance upon such limited sources may mean that the theory and description themselves represent what is really a distorted picture, so that if one had access to a native speaker, a reconstructed grammar might very well produce what for him would be ungrammatical, or at best unacceptable, utterances. Imagine the predicament of a linguist trying to formulate the rules of Modern English grammar without recourse to a native speaker's intuitions and with only a few hundred random and assorted written texts left to him as data. Any predictions he might make about the nature of English in its "totality" would be bound by these two deficiencies, and he could not readily assume his predictions to hold for all the other "lost" texts.

A predictive theory intended to provide the "total" number of rules for Modern English that was based upon a few copies of a popular newspaper, some sports commentaries, a Bible translation, and some history books, would necessarily have only a limited adequacy or power. Any statements one might wish to make about the nature of the utterances in, say, informal conversational, scientific, or "literary" English could, therefore, be only of the most tentative nature.

Fortunately, the sources for Middle English data are considerably more numerous than those for Old English, so that any predictive theory set up for the former can be the subject of a greater degree of testing and verification. Nevertheless, it will still be inadvisable, regardless of the relatively "complete" nature of the data, to make predictions that will be true for Middle English as a whole, since a general, homogeneous Middle English cannot be said to exist.

Middle English sources are to be found in great numbers, are representative of a great many geographical dialects, deal with a multitude of subjects, and range in length from the small inscriptions on monumental brasses to the many-thousand-lined romance poems and religio-philosophical treatises. In fact, this very variety in the subjects covered in the manuscripts is one of the distinguishing characteristics of the Middle English material setting it apart from Old English. Almost every conceivable contemporary topic is to be found in the surviving material, and the geographical distribution of the data is so widespread and detailed (including Scotland, Ireland, and Wales as well as England) that one can draw up with considerable accuracy criteria for the geographical placing of almost any given text. A particular text may appear written in many different dialects at various times. There are, for example, almost one hundred extant versions and part versions of Chaucer's *Canterbury Tales* alone. Unlike his counterpart dealing with Old English, the student of Middle English has clearly no shortage of raw materials.

This wealth of Middle English data is not confined to a subject-matter or geographical proliferation. There are also reasonably large numbers of Middle English sources from almost the entire field of its temporal range. Perhaps, as might be expected, there are fewer manuscripts surviving from the early part of the Middle English period; but even up to the beginning of the twelfth century, they are surprisingly numerous; and certainly there is no shortage in either the thirteenth, fourteenth, or fifteenth centuries. One result of this generous temporal distribution of the data is that it should eventually be possible (once a detailed study of the features characteristic of individual texts has been carried out) to demonstrate a great number of the changes that Middle English underwent at every level of its grammar and also perhaps to discover what prompted such changes.

The high incidence of Middle English texts in all periods within its temporal range is perhaps not something that should be accepted without a good deal of surprise. There are many potentially important political and sociological reasons why English should be a rather rare written product especially before 1300. The most obvious and far-reaching of these were the invasion by the Norman French in 1066 and their subsequent subjugation of the English. If the Norman Conquest of England and Wales was so complete—all serious military resistance dying out within a very short period after 1066—why does one find any written vernacular English texts at all in the eleventh and twelfth centuries? It would perhaps be natural to suppose that the language of the invaders, Norman French, would be adopted for all written purposes at least, so that there would be an overall decline in the production of manuscripts written in the English language. Yet the facts do not wholly support such a view, since in the period immediately following the conquest there is considerable evidence of the survival of a healthy vernacular written tradition that gains in strength with the passing of time.

There has often been considerable controversy among historians as well as linguists as to the nature and extent of the effects of the Norman Conquest upon the spoken and written language habits of the defeated English. The suggestion of one school is that Norman French as the language of the conquerors, and therefore of the ruling classes, became by necessity the primary language of a very large number of the indigenous English population, especially those who came into close contact with, and even joined, the foreign administration of government, court, and church. The knowledge of Norman French was so necessary that it even spread, so it is argued, to certain of the middle classes, especially town traders, knights, and owners of large farms. This view is supported by the important fact that the variety of French spoken by the Normans was almost universally used for as long as three centuries after the invasion as the written language of religious, legal, and governmental texts, from which the use of English seems almost entirely to have been excluded.

However, as a second school of opinion often points out, neither this "universal" use nor influence of the language spoken by the invaders should be overstressed. Any "all-pervasive" theory of French influence must reconcile itself with a number of important facts. In the first place, it seems that not all members of the invading forces themselves spoke the same language. In addition to speakers of Norman French, there were almost certainly many whose only language was either Breton (spoken in the extreme northwest of France and related to the Celtic spoken in Wales and Ireland) or Flemish, a language still spoken today in Belgium. Secondly, the historical evidence strongly suggests that the invading armies were, contrary to what might be expected, rather small in number. Many historians are of the opinion that William the Conqueror brought with him a force of a mere 10,000–15,000 (or less). Even if one allows for an increase in this number by later settlers, it seems that the total number of Norman-introduced foreigners never at any time exceeded 2 percent of the total population of England. Needless to say, the effect of so small a percentage on the language of the majority must have been limited.

On the whole, there is very little to suggest that Norman French could expect to have any chance of seriously affecting, far less of taking the place of, the language spoken by the majority. There was probably as much influence in the opposite direction. Certainly the languages of the conquerors of England in the eleventh century were destined for extinction there almost from the very beginning. Only those who belonged to the highest echelons in the social and administrative hierarchy (men and women of both native and nonnative stock) seem to have been speakers exclusively of Norman French. It is almost certain that those among the middle, and even ruling, classes who had to come into contact with the indigenous population would, of necessity, have some knowledge of English. Some degree of bilingualism, however limited, must be assumed; and in the case of the upper clergy a trilingual Latin-French-English usage may have been widespread and quite long lasting.

There is no doubt whatever that English continued to be spoken by almost the entire population of England throughout the period of the Norman occupation. Indeed, the English language was so strong that it is even used as the linguistic medium of many important written documents from the eleventh to the thirteenth centuries, when the "influence" of Norman French was at its greatest. For example, the *Anglo-Saxon Chronicle* is continued in English, a document (usually referred to in Middle English as the *Peterborough Chronicle,* since it appears to have been written in or near the town of Peterborough) that provides much information about the state of English in the twelfth century and earlier. Also in English are the important literary works the *Ormulum* and the *Owl and the Nightingale.* There seems to have been, throughout the period of greatest Norman contact, a continual process of composition and production in the vernacular language.

Whatever "influence" there was of Norman French on English, it did not result in wholesale changes at every level of the latter's grammatical structure. Since there is no doubt that almost the entire population of England were monolingual English-speakers, there is little likelihood that many of the syntactical or phonological features of Norman French should appear in their language. Yet there seems to have been a considerable English utilization (although perhaps at first only among certain social classes) of many items of French vocabulary, even if it is a difficult matter to be sure whether such a borrowing was the direct result of the conquest, since it could be argued that the prestige of the French language among contemporary European languages was such as to render it a source of technical, literary, and religious terminologies. At any rate, there are grounds for suggesting that this borrowing was in progress before the Norman Conquest had begun and that it came into greatest prominence in a period when the speaking of Norman French was at its lowest ebb. The following statement by William of Nassyngton in his *Speculum Vitae* or *Mirror of Life* (1325) was probably as true for the majority of the English in the eleventh and twelfth centuries as when it was written:

> In English tonge I schal ʒow telle,
> ʒif ʒe wyth me so longe wil dwelle.
> No Latyn wil I speke no waste,
> But English, þat men vse mast,
> Þat can eche man vnderstande,
> Þat is born in Ingelande;
> For þat langage is most chewyd,
> Os wel among lered os lewyd.
> Latyn, as I trowe, can nane
> But þo, þat haueth it in scole tane,
> And somme can Frensche and no Latyn,
> Þat vsed han cowrt and dwellen þerein;
> And somme can of Latyn a party,
> Þat can of Frensche but febly;
> And somme vnderstonde wel Englysch,
> Þat can noþer Latyn nor Frankys.
> Boþe lered and lewed, olde and ʒonge,
> Alle vnderstonden english tonge.
>
> (ll. 61–78).

It is interesting to notice that although William of Nassyngton suggests the possibility of French and Latin speakers, his implication is that (at least by his time) there were none who spoke only these languages. More important even than this is his statement that knowledge of English is not restricted to the lower classes, but that it is known "wel" among the learned as well as the uneducated—"lered and lewed."

Even in the two centuries immediately following the Norman Conquest, the language spoken by the invaders seems to have been on a steady decline. That it survived at all was due to social and political reasons rather than to any increase in use by the bulk of the indigenous population, even despite the introduction of numbers of foreigners into positions of power and wealth in increasing numbers. It is worth stressing again that Norman French seems almost entirely to have been confined in its regular spoken usage to two principal spheres—the court and the clergy. Beyond these, it seems to have had a very limited currency. There are good grounds for believing that even among the powerful administrative and legal hierarchy its use was far from universal, and one can only assume that its popularity in manuscripts surviving from the eleventh to the fourteenth centuries was the result of its status as the appropriate and customary linguistic medium for the written representation of legal and general administrative pronouncements rather than its popularity as a spoken form in the country as a whole.

Its decline was inevitable. One factor in this process was the low status of Norman French in the eyes of French speakers in the native country. By the end of the twelfth century the French of Paris, or Central French as it is sometimes called, was regarded as having the highest prestige, whereas the variety of French spoken and written in England, often known as Anglo-Norman, had come to be regarded as "low" or even "rustic" and "unsophisticated." Whatever the basis of such judgments, they certainly seemed to have caused some embarrassment among speakers of Anglo-Norman French and presumably therefore helped in the process of its extinction. Even Chaucer is somewhat apologetic for the linguistic habits of his Prioress:

And French she spak ful faire and fetisly,
After the scole of Stratford atte Bowe,
For French of Paris was to hir unknowe.
              (*Canterbury Tales, General*
                Prologue, 124–126)

Despite her gracious manner of speaking French, the Prioress, Chaucer seems to suggest, is under some disadvantage in only being able to reproduce the syntactic and phonological features of an English variety of French. Her sophistication stops short of a knowledge of the high-status Central type.

For political reasons, among them King John's loss in 1204 of the English territories in Normandy, the Anglicization of the Norman ruling class was inevitable too. With the loss of their French lands and possessions, many of the nobility were compelled to decide in favor of what remained to them in England; and in doing so they came in time to regard themselves as English and the French as enemies. The mid-thirteenth century also saw a strong upsurge in English nationalism culminating in the Barons' War. The result seems to have been that French came to be regarded more and more as the language not only of foreigners but of foreigners who were hostile to English interests.

In the midst of the almost universal habit of speaking English and with

the existence from earliest times of a very strong tradition of written vernacular manuscripts, the survival of French (and Latin) from the thirteenth
century onward as a written language was in most senses an artificial one.
The social advantages of association with court habits probably helped
toward the retention of some spoken Anglo-Norman. As has been suggested,
its survival as the written language of law, administration, and even religion
was a matter of custom, but one that by the fourteenth century was coming
to be less and less observed. By the late fourteenth century the affairs of
Parliament were being conducted almost entirely in English; likewise,
English was becoming more and more popular as the language of the law
courts and even as the medium of instruction in the schools. In 1385, John
of Trevisa tells how:

> in alle þe gramere scoles of Engelond, children leueþ Frensche and
> construeþ and lerneþ an Englische.

(Interpolation in Trevisa's translation of Higden's *Polychronicon*)

French (and Latin) became increasingly infrequent from the fourteenth century onward, until, by the end of the following century, English
had become by far the most common medium for all written language, rang-
ing from letters (both private and official) to important local and national
government documents.

The result of the tradition of vernacular publication has resulted in a
corpus of medieval written language of an extent having few other equals.
It is, however, a written and not a printed tradition, and one that is at
considerable temporal remove from the modern reader. Confronted by a
Middle English manuscript, an uninitiated reader can be faced with considerable decoding difficulties; the handwriting can often be extremely difficult
to decipher; the punctuation, when it is present, is very unlike contemporary
usage; and many of the alphabet symbols are now obsolete. The remainder
of this chapter will deal with the problems of the availability, accessibility,
and intelligibility of the data, and a brief attempt will be made to discuss
what some Middle English manuscripts look like and the relationship they
bear to their modern printed and edited forms, as well as the technology
involved in their production.

Even if it were possible for the student to have easy access to an
original Middle English manuscript (and such access very often depends
upon the local availability of libraries with manuscript collections), he
would find that its interpretation would be far from an easy or automatic
process. In addition to obvious difficulties, such as divergencies in the spelling and syntactical systems between the language of the manuscript and his

own language, the reader would find that the former employed a very different (and sometimes almost unintelligible) method of writing. The majority of modern editions of Middle and all other historical periods of English tend to "regularize" in various ways the forms of the originals and so, in a sense, to misrepresent them. While in the best editions the main spelling peculiarities of the original manuscript are nearly always faithfully recorded (although even here changes are often made to conform to modern practice), on nearly all occasions the original form of writing employed in the manuscript—its script—will be completely altered, and modern printing symbols everywhere substituted.

Needless to say, until the invention of printing in the fifteenth century, all manuscript composition was of a manual nature. The type face that is used in most modern books has two features that we cannot readily assume for a written medieval manuscript: it is at once very legible and also more or less standardized from book to book. The typescript on this page, for example, is very easy to read and at the same time bears a strong resemblance to that used in other books, articles, newspapers, and so on. When, however, modern practices in handwriting are considered, on many occasions neither legibility nor standardization can be claimed. Handwriting is today very largely, despite fairly rigorous and standardized methods of writing tuition, a matter of personal habit. As can easily be verified, the handwriting of others can often appear at best very strange and at worst can be completely undecipherable. Sometimes individual symbols are hardly formed at all, and punctuation is almost nonexistent.

Since the majority of extant Middle English texts survive to us in a handwritten form, one might perhaps expect to find considerable difficulties in interpretation and much variation between the customs of one scribe and those of another. Surprisingly, this is not necessarily the case. There existed in medieval times centers or schools at which professional writers or scribes were trained in the techniques of manuscript production and handwriting. Once any given scribe was trained in a particular method or style of writing, he tended to adhere to it in a more or less rigorous fashion at all times. As a result, although there may exist differences between the habits of individuals, one can find easily recognizable types or "schools" of writing that are comparatively easy to decipher once their idiosyncratic features have been learned. The handwriting methods of the majority of medieval scribes do not show the wide divergences common between modern hands, but rather slight variations within relatively well-defined and accepted styles. The overall effect is perhaps more like the use of different type faces in printing than the almost free-for-all situation that exists in modern handwriting.

The study of paleography, or the examination of the written symbol and the history and development of individual writing methods, is a most complex one and can, consequently, receive only a very brief treatment here. The science of writing in medieval times was not something that grew up in isolation or that was the invention of any one man or group of men. It can be treated only as a part of a very much larger European tradition. In the so-called Dark Ages (the sixth to the ninth centuries), writing technology in western Europe, especially in England and Ireland, had reached a very advanced degree of sophistication. Indeed, it was under the influence of English and Irish monks and of the monastic settlements and churches that they established in many parts of continental Europe during this period that the science of writing was preserved and improved in such countries as France, Spain, Germany, and Italy.

The script developed by these English and Irish scribes is known as the *insular minuscule*. This script from the British Islands, which survives in English manuscripts till as late as the twelfth century, seems to derive from, or be related to, a capital-letter script popular during the Roman period and often known as *rustic capitals*. One of the important developments of the insular minuscule is that it was able to produce much smaller symbols than the Roman or *majuscule* (large) scripts. This means that pages of insular minuscule have a more compressed appearance than their predecessors and can have more words to the page. The resultant economy was an important improvement at a period when writing materials were in such short supply that vellum pages were often either erased and used again or even contained two separate texts at the same time. The insular minuscule is also important for anyone wishing to study Middle English writing systems, since in it are to be found symbols additional to those of the Roman alphabet that survive into manuscripts of a much later date. The origins and variants of the insular minuscule are of too complex and technical a nature to be profitably pursued further here, but one can perhaps gain some understanding of its nature and importance by a brief look at a small sample (*Text A*)—a reproduction (about life size) of an eleventh-century Anglo-Saxon or Old English rendering of the New Testament Bible.

Making no attempt to edit this piece fully, that is, leaving as many of the original symbols as is typographically feasible and retaining the original's punctuation and abbreviation system, we can transcribe it as on page 25.

7 Ᵽ ið mærsian þa spræce SᚹᏢa þ he ne mihte
openlice ᵒⁿ þa ceastre ȝan. Ac beon ute on
Ᵽestum stoᏢū. 7 hẏo æȝhᏢanon to him comō
7 eft æfter daȝū he eode into capharnaū
7 hit Ᵽæs ȝe hẏred. þ he Ᵽæs on huse 7 mane   5
ȝa toȝadere comon 7 he to heom spræc. 7 hẏo
comon ænne lame man to him berende.
þonne feoᏢer men bæron. 7 þa hẏo ne mih
ton hine in brinȝan for þare meniȝa.
hẏo openedon þonne rof þar se halend Ᵽæs   10
7 hẏo þa in asenden þ bed þe se lama on læȝ.
Soðlice þa se halend ȝe seah heora ȝe leafan
heoᏢað. to þā laman. Sune þe sẏnt þine sinne
for ȝẏféne. þare Ᵽaron sume of þam boceran
sittende 7 on heora heorta þencende hᏢa specð   15
þes þus. he desẏȝað hᏢa mæȝ synna forȝẏfen
buton ȝod ane. Ða se halend þ on his ȝaste
oncneoᏢ. þ hẏo sᏢa betᏢux heom þohton he
cᏢæð to heom hᏢi þence ȝe þas þinȝ on eoᏢrā
heortan. hᏢeðer his eðre to seȝȝanne to þā   20
laman. ðe sind þine sẏnna for ȝẏfene hᏢeðer
ðe cᏢeðen aris nim þin bed 7 ȝa. þat ȝe soðlice
Ᵽiten þ mannes sune hafð anᏢeald on eorðan
Sẏnnan to forȝẏfena. He cᏢæð to þā laman þe
ic seȝȝe aris. nim þin bed 7 ȝa to þinū huse.   25

Even with the small changes that have been made in this transcription, it is clear that alongside many relatively familiar symbols there also exist others that are no longer to be found in the English alphabet. At the same time there are other symbols that, although they still exist in English, are found in our text with rather unexpected shapes. Despite its clear appearance, the manuscript is certainly more difficult to read than the printed transcription; and the symbols, perhaps surprisingly for a handwritten script, are almost always separated and not joined, pointed and not curved.

Two other features clearly distinguish the scribe's methods from modern usage: his punctuation is rather unusual in modern terms, and he regularly uses abbreviation marks to save space. It is worth noting that although very different from a modern printed English text, the specimen does have many similarities to a page of modern printed Irish.

The majority of the minuscule symbols are derived in their shape from the Roman alphabet. The forms of some do, however, appear to be idiosyncratic, for example, the curved form of the ⟨d⟩ and ⟨t⟩ symbols in ⟨daʒū⟩ (4), ⟨eode⟩ (4), ⟨into⟩ (4), and ⟨to⟩ (6). Strange too are the representations of ⟨r⟩ and ⟨f⟩, both easily recognizable, but with their main down strokes going much further than is today acceptable; and in the case of ⟨f⟩, the medial cross stroke also seems exaggerated. The noncapital ⟨s⟩ form used in this text is now extinct, but such "long s" types are common in English, even in printed examples, until as late as the eighteenth century. A great deal of the difficulty in interpreting both Old and Middle English manuscripts can be accounted for by their tendency to use different degrees of height in their up and down strokes (ascenders and descenders) as compared with the modern practice. A good example of this is the symbol ⟨t⟩ in this text, finishing its upward stroke at the cross bar without penetrating it, like the modern capital *T* in printed texts.

More importantly, the text also contains some symbols that have now altogether disappeared from the alphabet: ⟨þ⟩, ⟨Ƿ⟩, ⟨ʒ⟩, and ⟨æ⟩, whose modern equivalents are ⟨th⟩, ⟨w⟩, ⟨y⟩ or ⟨g⟩, and ⟨a⟩ or ⟨e⟩. It is interesting that these four symbols are known to have individual letter names: *thorn* 'a thorn,' *wynn* 'happiness,' *yogh* 'a plough,' and *ash* 'an ash tree.' It is this fact that gives us the clue to their origin. There is some evidence that the primitive precursors of the symbols in the Roman alphabet had such individual names, but this feature seems to have died out long before classical times. Although found in medieval Irish and English manuscripts, two of the above-named symbols—⟨þ⟩ and ⟨Ƿ⟩—seem to have originated in symbol sets that were in use from the earliest times in western Europe. One of these alphabets, in which both ⟨þ⟩ and ⟨Ƿ⟩ were common, was particularly popular in Scandinavian countries and is known as the *runic* alphabet or the *fuþark*. In the same way that the word *alphabet* derives from the first two symbol names of the Graeco-Roman set, so too the term *fuþark* is taken from the combination of the first six symbols in the runic alphabet. The runic alphabet, however, had special properties that distinguish its use from that of its Roman "equivalent." In the first place, this alphabet is rarely found written in manuscripts, its main function being for the carving of inscriptions on wood or stone. As a result, its symbols are formed in a very angular and noncursive fashion. In addition, not every inscription would merit the use of runic symbols; they seem to have been reserved for the representation of particular kinds of language, notably the writing of charms and spells. They appear to have been the symbols of what was probably a kind of black magic, although after the advent of Christianity in Scandinavia and England, they were occasionally put to "acceptable" Christian uses. The Anglo-Saxon Christian poem *The Dream of the Rood,* carved in runes on the cross at Ruthwell in Scotland, is perhaps the outstanding example of this. Even the names of some of the runes were changed to make them appear less pagan: ⟨þ⟩ with its innocuous title *thorn* seems originally to have been associated with the word for a giant or demon.

The influence of the runic fuþárk must have been very strong on the earliest English alphabets since symbols like ⟨3⟩ and ⟨æ⟩, although themselves not originally part of the fuþark, are given names of symbols to be found in it. The symbol ⟨ð⟩ and its capital form ⟨Ð⟩ are not runic symbols as such, but seem to be later innovations found in English, Irish, and Icelandic manuscripts to represent the sound indicated by ⟨eth⟩ in, for example, ⟨Ethelred⟩.

At this point, however, an important qualification must be added to the statements made so far. The selection of manuscript that we have called *Text A* is not a homogeneous or absolute example of the insular minuscule. The significance of this cannot be overstressed because although the majority of scripts in Middle English manuscripts show features that are also to be found in the minuscule, on the whole they are much more related to another great tradition of writing that eventually replaced it. Largely under the impetus of Charlemagne there was developed in continental Europe, especially in France, an extremely influential school of writing that produced what is now known as the *Carolingian script.* The outstanding virtue of this script was its high degree of clarity and legibility, and it spread within a relatively short time over large parts of continental Europe and even to Britain. It is the predecessor of many later medieval scripts, and on it are based most of the symbols found in modern printed texts.

Although a considerable proportion of the English manuscripts were very conservative in their retention of many of the insular and runic forms throughout the medieval period (especially in vernacular contexts), the methods and forms of the Carolingian school had considerable and ever-increasing success. Even in the Anglo-Saxon manuscript one can see evidence of this in the method of formation of the ⟨s⟩, ⟨a⟩, and ⟨æ⟩ symbols replacing their insular equivalents ⟨ſ⟩, ⟨ɑ⟩, and ⟨œ⟩. The Carolingian influence (especially in Latin, but also in English vernacular manuscripts) increases dramatically as the medieval period advances, and it becomes more and more the source from which Middle English manuscripts derive their letter-forming techniques.

These points can be further elaborated by a consideration of a second manuscript extract—*Text B*—which is taken from a fourteenth-century translation of a thirteenth-century original in French. This manuscript was

Herken hi wt gode wille ·
and whils he saies hold ye stille ·
bot answere at temptacionem
sed libera nos amalo amen ·
þit were no nede ye yis to ken
for who con not yis are lewed men ·
when yis is done saye þuely ·
other prayer none y by ·
þat noþ first i laten
and sithen i engliſhe als here is wryten ·
Fader oure þat is i heuen ·
Blessid be þi name to neuen
come to vs þi kyngdome ·
In heuen & ertþ þi wille be done ·
oure ilk day bred grunt vs to day ·
and oure mysdedes forgyue vs ay ·
als we to þm yt trespasus
right so haue merci vpon vs
and lede vs i no foundynge ·
bot shild vs fro al wicked ynge · amen ·
þen eft sone yo pater wil saye ·
stande stille & herken hi al waye
he saies amuis thryse or he cese ·
yo last woode he spekis of pese ·
In ye yt pese may noght be ·
If you be oute of charyte ·
yen is gode of god to craue ·
þat you charyte may haue ·
here when yo prit say wil his ·
knele you & þye yen yis ·

TEXT B

herken hī w^t gode wille·
and whils he saies hold ye stille·
bot answere at temptatōnem·
set libera nos a malo amen·
hit were no nede ye yis to ken·   5
for who con not yis are lewed men·
when yis is done saye p^{r}uely·

other prayer none ẙ by·
pat^r nost^r first ī laten·
and sithen ī englishe als here is wryten·   10
Fader oure yat is ī heuen·
blessid be yi name to neuen·
Come to us yi kyngdome·
In heuen ꝺ erth yi wille be done·
oure ilk day bred g"unt vs to day·   15
and oure mysdedes forgyue vs ay·
als we do hom yt trespasus·
right so haue merci vpon us·
and lede vs ī no foundynge·
bot shild vs fro al wicked yinge· amen·   20

Y̊en eft sone yo p̊ste wil saye·
stande stille ꝺherken hī al waye·
he saies AGNUS thryse or he cese·
yo last worde he spekis of pese·
In ye y^t pese may noght be·   25
If you be oute of charyte·
yen is gode of god to craue·
yat you charyte may haue·

yere when yo p̊st pax wil kis·
knele you ꝺ p"ye yen yis·   30

29

written by an author who identifies himself only as Jeremy, and it is usually called *The Lay Folk's Mass Book,* since its function was to provide non-clerics with prayers for, and information about, the various parts of the Mass ceremony. If we look at the printed transcription, we can see that the script of *The Lay Folk's Mass Book* is clearly a modification and development of that in *Text A.*

Text B is written in what is commonly known as *book hand,* a type of script popular in the period during which Middle English manuscripts were being produced. It incorporates features of both the insular and the Carolingian styles. Its line of descent from the former can be demonstrated by the retention of the runic ⟨þ⟩ symbol as in ⟨þe þis⟩ (5), ⟨þat þou⟩ (28), and many others. It is interesting to notice that on all these occasions this symbol is formed in an identical fashion to that for ⟨y⟩, as in ⟨prayer⟩ and ⟨by⟩ (8). The use in many, although not all, Middle English manuscripts of this one symbol for two separate sounds survived into the era of printed texts and explains why we find the definite article written and printed as ⟨ye⟩ in such pseudoarchaisms as *Ye Olde Inne.* The use of the ⟨y⟩ symbol in such instances is merely the result of its close resemblance in terms of its formation with the runic ⟨þ⟩, although the latter is almost universally replaced by ⟨th⟩ in later Middle English texts and in early printed books.

Even in *Text B* one sees the tendency to avoid the runic ⟨þ⟩ and to use in its place (and in the place of the insular ⟨ð⟩) the symbol combination ⟨th⟩, as in ⟨sithen⟩ (10), ⟨erthe⟩ (14), and ⟨thryse⟩ (23). In the same way, the insular ⟨3⟩ and ⟨æ⟩ have been replaced in this page by ⟨y⟩ or ⟨g⟩ and ⟨a⟩, as in ⟨englische⟩ (10), ⟨for gyue⟩ (16), ⟨saies⟩ (2), and ⟨haue⟩ (18). Runic ⟨Ƿ⟩ has been supplanted by what appears to be a rather strange form of ⟨w⟩, which is Carolingian in origin, as in ⟨wille⟩ (1) and ⟨when⟩ (29). Likewise, a comparison with *Text A* reveals the continuation of the Carolingian ⟨s⟩ symbols: ⟨blessid⟩ (12) and ⟨als⟩ (10), among many others. Unlike the Anglo-Saxon extract, *Text B* no longer retains the insular ⟨r⟩ form, but in its place has what is for the modern reader the more immediately recognizable Carolingian equivalent: ⟨herken⟩ (1), ⟨Fader⟩ (11), and ⟨erthe⟩ (14)—compare these with the ⟨r⟩ symbol in ⟨mærsian⟩ and ⟨spræce⟩ (1) in *Text A.* Other surviving minuscule forms also appear with alterations to their shapes in the Carolingian tradition, with the result that they seem to be more familiar: ⟨f⟩ has come to be raised above the upper line of the majority of other symbols (compare ⟨eft⟩ (21) in *Text B* with ⟨æfter⟩ (4) in *Text A*); and, at the same time, the ascender of the ⟨t⟩ symbol is now made to penetrate its crossbar, as can be seen if the last two examples quoted above are again compared.

Both the insular and the book hand scripts have their legibility impaired by their tendency to form certain symbols by combinations of strokes of *minims.* In the word ⟨AGNUS⟩ (23) in *Text B,* for example, there is some difficulty at first sight in deciding whether one is dealing with a representation of ⟨AGMI-⟩, ⟨AGINI-⟩, or ⟨AGNU-⟩. The reason for this is that the symbols ⟨i⟩, ⟨u/n⟩, and ⟨m⟩ (and even, on some occasions, ⟨w⟩ or ⟨uu⟩) are composed of a single minim stroke or combinations of two or three of them; or in the case of ⟨uu⟩, four. Difficulty in legibility is brought about by the fact that there is not always space between the individual symbols to avoid ambiguity. This technique leads, especially in insular manuscript writing, to a good deal of confusion; for example, in Old English words such as ⟨sunu⟩ one finds ⟨s⟩ followed by a group of six minim symbols, very often with no spaces between individual "letters." One of the important effects of the Carolingian influence upon English handwriting techniques was that it tended to render such forms unambiguous (since ⟨s⟩ + six minims could theoretically represent ⟨s⟩ + ⟨mni/imu/inni/nnu⟩, and so on, as well as ⟨sunu⟩) by replacing a combination of two minims representing ⟨u⟩ by the symbol ⟨o⟩ whenever this appeared before another combination of either two or three minims. Hence one finds such words as ⟨sunu⟩ and ⟨cuman⟩ written as ⟨son-⟩ and ⟨com-⟩ in Middle English texts. It is important to stress that such changes are not made to reflect the pronunciation, but are entirely devices to improve upon what were once confusing methods of notation.

Like the insular example, the book hand also has a tendency to shorthand or abbreviated forms, perhaps even to a greater extent. Abbreviations are, in general, rather complex, but four main kinds can be distinguished. In the first place, one finds the line ⁻ suspended above the symbol ⟨i⟩ denoting the omission of a following ⟨m⟩ or ⟨n⟩, for example, ⟨hī⟩ for ⟨him⟩ (1) and ⟨ī⟩ for ⟨in⟩ (9) in *Text B.* This device of *suspension* is also a feature of the insular *Text A,* where one finds ⁻ suspended above ⟨u⟩ to indicate ⟨um⟩, as in ⟨staᵖū⟩ (3) for ⟨stoᵖum⟩ and ⟨daʒū⟩ for ⟨daʒum⟩ (4). Secondly, there is the fairly common use in the book hand of the *superscripted* symbol, as in ⟨patʳ⟩ (9) for ⟨pater⟩, ⟨wᵗ⟩ (1) for ⟨wit⟩, and ⟨yʳby⟩ (8) for ⟨yerby⟩, among others. Such abbreviations mean that the superscript symbol should be expanded to vowel + symbol or symbol + vowel, as in ⟨pʳuely⟩ for ⟨priuely⟩. Related to this type is the use of the superscripted " (perhaps a conventionalized ⟨a⟩ standing for ⟨au⟩ or ⟨ra⟩) as in ⟨g"unt⟩ (15) for ⟨graunt⟩ and ⟨p"ye⟩ (30) for ⟨praye⟩. Thirdly, medieval manuscripts of nearly all types show a tendency to the *contraction* of certain words, for example, ⟨yt⟩ (17) for ⟨yat⟩ in *Text B,* and ⟨þ⟩ (11) and (5) for the definite article and noun-clause-introducing conjunction—⟨þæt⟩—respectively in *Text A.* Both scripts also show the use of *shorthand* forms, in particular the symbols for the conjunctive ⟨and⟩—⟨7⟩ (*Text A* [1, 4, 5]) and ⟨і⟩ (*Text B* [9, 10, 11]).

It is clear from both the book and insular examples that there is a decided lack of what a modern reader would recognize as the formalities of punctuation. In fact, *Text B* has a mark like the modern full stop almost indiscriminately at the end of most lines, and it is found in places where the present-day system would either omit it altogether or use the comma. The convention in *Text A* is similarly strange. Capitals are used where there is apparently no "sentence beginning," as in ⟨Þіð mærsian þa spræce SÞa þ he ne mihte⟩ (1). The full-stop mark is occasionally found in contexts that correspond more or less to modern ones—lines 3 and 6—but it is also used immediately before the introductory ⟨þ(æt)⟩ in a "noun clause" or "result clause":

> ⟨hit Þæs ᴣe hyred. þ he Þæs on huse⟩ (5)
> ⟨nim þin bed 7 ᴣa. þat ᴣe soðlice Þiten⟩ (22–23)

although this is not true for all cases of this kind. Even though such marks as the comma, period, inverted comma, and semicolon are to be found in vernacular and Latin medieval texts of all dates, their use can be somewhat haphazard or at best different from the conventions found in modern printed texts, which are not realized with any degree of regularity until the middle of the sixteenth century.

From the early part of the thirteenth century onward there was a movement in the direction of a more decorative and elaborate type of book hand. Especially in works of a more costly nature (for example, Bibles and important liturgical and literary works), a tendency developed (originally in France) to accentuate the contrast between the light and heavy strokes of individual book hand symbols. The result is that one starts to find the thick pen strokes becoming heavier and the thin ones developing almost into hairlines. At the same time all the curved forms of the book hand were made angular, and the heads and feet of each of the strokes were often finished off as diamond shapes. The result, the so-called *Gothic* or *littera fractura* script, is considerably more ornate, although, it must be said, less legible. It is presumably the result of this difficulty in legibility, as well as the labor and cost involved in its production, that it has grown out of favor and did not become the basis for the printed word, although it is still found even today (with ever-reducing frequency) in some German printed books.

In *Text C* there is an example of the Gothic script—a leaf from one of the extant manuscripts of *The Cloude of Unknowing,* a religious work written by an unknown author in the middle part of the fourteenth century.

By and large, the symbols in *Text C* are identical to those of the book hand example; it is their method of formation that gives the script its distinctiveness. Perhaps the most confusing practice in this handwriting is the *fusion* of contrary strokes into one. The final and initial strokes of ⟨p⟩ and ⟨o⟩; ⟨b⟩, ⟨o⟩, and ⟨r⟩; ⟨o⟩ and ⟨o⟩; and ⟨b⟩ and ⟨o⟩ are made to join together with a rather compressed result, as in ⟨power⟩ (12), ⟨borowyng⟩ (17), ⟨oon⟩ (22), and ⟨bond⟩ (13). This feature is also found in the book hand example (compare ⟨do⟩ [17]), but its frequency increases considerably in the Gothic. Above all, however, there is the difficulty of distinguishing thin strokes of the pen as well as the high level of occurrence of abbreviation symbols (⟨ppurtie⟩ for ⟨propurtie⟩ [15], ⟨pfytlý⟩ for ⟨perfytly⟩ [9], and ⟨eú⟩ for ⟨euer⟩ [14] being among the more difficult to decipher). The two dots under the second ⟨d⟩ in ⟨dynd⟩ (16) mark that it is canceled or deleted.

The symbols used in modern printing clearly derive from the book, rather than the Gothic, script. The printed word, however, as suggested above, is not the only medium for the written modern language; and there is still in existence today a strong tradition of handwritten language. The question one must now ask is whether there existed in medieval times anything corresponding to this cursive modern handwriting. One must bear in mind the sometimes all-too-obvious fact that modern handwriting is far from standardized and that even one's own handwritten forms can sometimes be unintelligible. Any cursive form of medieval writing, however, will probably not show the same degree of divergence between author and author and between individuals in different contexts, but, as with the book and Gothic varieties, will appear rather more standardized. Cursive writing is found in medieval manuscripts as early as the twelfth century. There is even some evidence for cursive Roman scripts from *graffiti* found in the destroyed cities of Pompeii and Herculaneum. The cursive hand, in Middle English times at any rate, is usually characterized as being the medium used for the recording of the more mundane forms of communication to be found in public and private letters, local government documents, and agreements. It is usually not so common in expensively produced, important texts, although this becomes less true as the period progresses.

The most noticeable feature of the *cursive* hand is its habit of rounding any angular symbols in either the book or Gothic traditions and, most obviously, its tendency to join together, by extending the final and initial letter strokes, the symbols within individual words. The result was almost certainly a much faster, and therefore cheaper, means of writing. Nevertheless, one should stress again that the cursive hand was learned by those who could write in much the same way as the book or Gothic types.

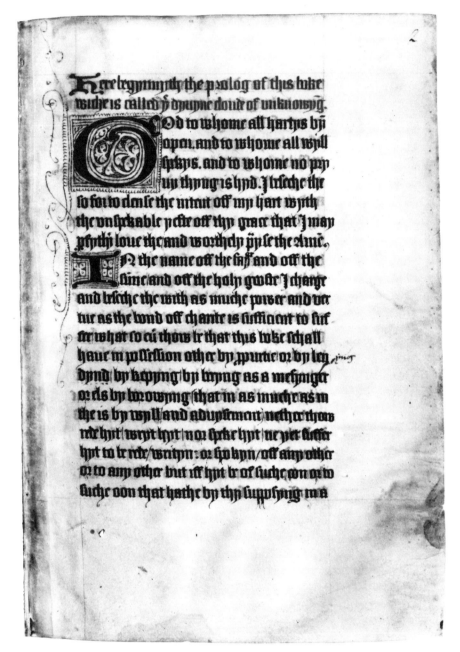

Here begynnyth the prolog of this boke
whiche is called ÿ dyuyne cloude of unknowyng.

Od to whome all hartys byn
open. and to whome all wyll
spekys. and to whome no pry
uy thyng is hyd. I bseche the
so for to clense the intent off my hart wyth
the unspekable preffr off thy grace that I may
pfytly loue the and worthely ÿyi se the Ame.

In the name off the faÿ and off the
sone/and off the holy gwostr I charge
and bseche the wyth as muche powar and ver
tur as the bond off charite is sufficient to suf
fr what so eu thow be that this boke schall
haue in possession other by ppurtue or by len
dyng/ by kepyng/ by beryng as a messingier
or els by borowyng/ that in as muche as in
the is by wyll and adupsement/ nether thow
rede hyt/ wryt hyt / nor speke hyt / ne yet suffar
hyt to be rede/ writtyn : or spokyn / off any other
or to any other but iff hyt be of suche con or to
suche oon that hathe by thy suppsyng in a

TEXT C. *The Cloude of Unknowing.* Bodleian Library, Oxford. Ms. Douce 262, f. 2
(right-hand side only). Edinburgh University Microfilm No. MIC M 477. Reprinted
by permission of the Bodleian Library, Oxford.

TEXT C

Here begynnyth the prolog of this boke

wiche is called ẙ dyuyne cloude of unknowȳg.
God to whome all hartys bȳ
open. and to whome all wyll
spekys. and to whome no pry   5
uy thyng is hyd. I beseche the
so for to clense the intent off my hart wyth
the vnspekable yefte off thy grace that I may
pfytlẏ loue the and worthely p̈yse the Amē.
In the name off the fay^er and off the   10
sūne and off the holy gooste I charge
and beseche the with as muche power and ver
tue as the bond off charite is sufficient to suf
fer what so eú thow be that this boke schall
haue in possession other by ppurtie or by len   15
dynd̠ by kepyng by beryng as a mesynger
or els by borowyng that in as muche as in
the is by wyll and aduysement nether thow
rede hyt wryt hit nor speke hyt ne yet suffer
hyt to be rede writyn : or spokyn off any other   20
or to any other but off hyt be of suche oon or to
suche oon that hathe by thy supposyng in a

Once it was learned, there was apparently little variation in the way it was repeated in use. There were strict rules of symbol formation in cursive scripts; and the documents in which these are rigorously adhered to are usually said to be written in _set hand_. On other occasions, especially in the less expensive manuscript writings, these rules were followed less, although, even in these cases, degrees of irregularity to the extent of those in modern handwritten forms are never found. Such scripts are often referred to as _free hands._

Text _D,_ one of the manuscripts containing Chaucer's _Canterbury Tales_ (Bodley Hatton donat i, f. 119), is really a combination of book and cursive styles.

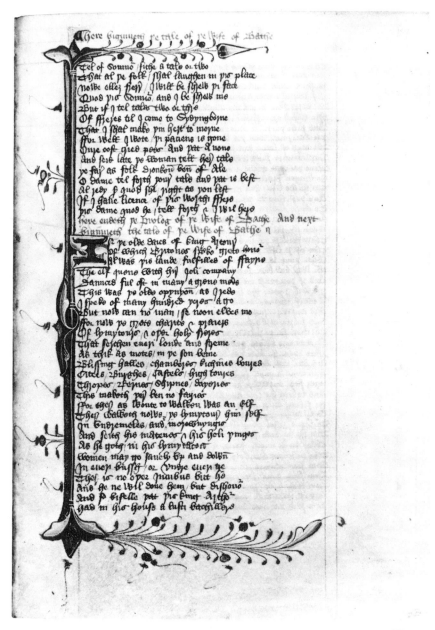

TEXT D. Chaucer's *Canterbury Tales*. Bodleian Library, Oxford. Ms. Hatton, donat. 1, f. 119 (right-hand side only). Edinburgh University Microfilm No. MIC M 1037. Reprinted by permission of the Bodleian Library, Oxford.

TEXT D

Tel of somnᵒʳ siche a tale or two
That al þe folk shal laughen in þis place
Nowe ellez frerr I will be shrew þi face

Quod þis Somnᵒʳ and I be shrew me
But if I tel tales two or thre 5
Of ffreres til I come to Sydyngborne
That I shal make þin hert to morne
ffor well I wote þi paciens is gone
Oure oost cred pees And þat Anone
And seid late þe woman tell her tale 10
ye far as folk dronkeñ beñ of Ale
O dame tel forth your tale and þat is best
Al redy ∮ quod she right as you lest
If I haue licence of þis worthi ffrere
Yis dame quod he tell forth ℭ I wil here 15
Here endeth þe prolog of þe Wife of Bathe and next
biginneth the tale of þe Wife of Bathe
In þe olde daies of king Artour
of which Britones speke grete honoʳ
Al was þis lande fulfilled of ffayre 20
The elf quene with hir Ioli company
Daunced ful oft in many a grene mede
This was þe olde opynyōn as I rede
I speke of many hundred yeres ago
But now can no man se noon elves mo 25
ffor now þe grete charite ℭ preiers
Of lymytours ℭ oþer holy freres
That serchen eueri londe and streme
As thik as motes in þe son beme
Blissing halles chamberes kichénes boures 30
Citees Burghes Castels high toures
Thropes Bernes Shipnes dayeries
This maketh þer ben no fairies
ffor ther as wonte to walken was an Elf

Ther walketh nowe þe lymytour him self   35
In Vndremeles and ⁱ morewnyngis
And seith his matenes ⌢ his holi þinges
As he goth in his lymytacoñ
Women may go sauely Vp and dowñ
Tn eueri bussh or undre eueri tre   40
Ther is no oþer Incubus but he
And he ne wil done hem but dishono͡r
And so bifelle þat þis king Arthoͬ
had in his house a lusti bachiller [flourish]

The development of the cursive from the book hand is quite clear from this text. One sees the rounding of all angular strokes and the attempt at symbol linking; and, in general, the impression is given that one is deal-ing with what must have been a much faster script to produce, albeit rather hard to decipher. Even capitals are rendered in a cursive fashion in the extract, for example, ⟨And⟩ (10), whereas the capital ⟨V⟩, as in ⟨Vndremeles⟩ (36), seems to have been formed with one stroke of the pen. The usually angular minim-formed symbols, such as ⟨m⟩ and ⟨n⟩, also on occasion take on a curved form, especially in the capital ⟨N⟩ example in ⟨Nowe⟩ (3); but such symbols can still cause problems of interpretation—compare ⟨Daunced⟩ (22). An interesting feature, found in other Middle English texts as well, is the practice of making minim clusters disambiguous by adding superscripted "accent" marks: ⟨biginneth⟩ (17). Perhaps the outstanding characteristic of this script is its joining to-gether of symbols. Many of the words seem to have been formed without the pen's having been lifted from the page, for example, ⟨folk⟩ (2), ⟨ffreres⟩ (6), ⟨forth⟩ (12), and many others. It is this feature, however, that tends more than anything else to make the script difficult to read. This is especially true in $r + i$ combinations, as in ⟨eueri⟩ (28) and ⟨charite⟩ (26) as well as in ⟨ch⟩ clusters like ⟨which⟩ (19) and ⟨kichénes⟩ (30). (Note that ⟨kichénes⟩ was probably ⟨kichínes⟩, with the second i altered to e.) In ⟨ellez⟩ (3) one sees a rather unusual forma-tion of the ⟨s⟩ symbol, with a strong resemblance to the ⟨ʒ⟩ shape in Text A. However, the two symbols are different in origin, the one here deriving from the Roman ⟨z⟩ having a tail added. These two forms of ⟨z⟩ still appear in the spelling variants of the proper name ⟨Dalzell⟩ and ⟨Dalyell⟩, with the tailed ⟨z⟩ represented (as is the insular ⟨ʒ⟩ [yogh] symbol) by ⟨y⟩.

   The cursive script relies heavily upon the use of abbreviations of most kinds. Especially common are superscriptions, as in ⟨Somno͡r⟩ (4) and

⟨honoʳ⟩ (19), the superscripted symbol representing the contraction of ⟨ur⟩, as one sees when one compares ⟨Artour⟩ (18) with ⟨Arthoʳ⟩ (43). There are also abbreviations of the by now well-known suspension type, as with ⟨ī⟩ for ⟨in⟩ (36) and ⟨lymytacoñ⟩ for ⟨lymytacion⟩ (38). There may be some inconsistencies in this latter usage, however, since it is difficult to imagine an expanded form for the suspensions ⟨dronkeñ beñ⟩ (11) and ⟨opynyōn⟩ (23). It seems that in these cases one has to interpret the suspended sign as being merely some kind of stylistic flourish added to ⟨n⟩ at the end of a word. Perhaps the suspension mark with ⟨dowñ⟩ (39) should be interpreted in the same way, as the form *⟨dowen⟩ would be rather exceptional and would normally be written as ⟨dowē⟩. A similar flourish or mark of decoration that seems to have no symbolic function is the one after the final ⟨r⟩ in ⟨bachiller⟩ (44). The ⟨and⟩ abbreviations are somewhat different from anything met with so far, and in line 13 is found what is <u>a commonly attested medieval abbreviation</u> $\mathcal{P}$, used in <u>this case to mean *sir* or *sire*.</u>

It is clear that none of the transcriptions of *Texts A, B,* or *C* would be satisfactory for the student as they stand. Certainly, they would not appear in a printed edition in this form. It has been implied throughout the latter part of this chapter that whenever one looks at a modern printed version of a Middle (or, of course, Old) English text, one is, in fact, looking at something that represents a considerable modification of the original data. In order to present his material in an acceptable way, the editor of a medieval text has to perform certain "adjustments" on the raw material. In the first place, he will wish, as far as possible to retain the spelling system of the original, even when this appears to be haphazard and inconsistent. Unfortunately, some editors still tend (especially with Middle English data) to "regularize," and consequently distort, the scribe's spelling conventions. The editor will, however, often be compelled to replace some of the original symbols with their present-day equivalents. This is necessitated by the extreme cost of making up new symbols that do not already exist in printers' fonts. The ⟨þ⟩ and ⟨ð⟩ symbols are usually retained, although some editions have these "regularized" to ⟨th⟩; but other extinct formations, such as some of the ⟨s⟩ and ⟨r⟩ symbols and certainly ⟨ᵽ⟩ (wynn) and ⟨ȝ⟩, are nearly always replaced by modern printed forms. The editor will also cause words to be spaced after the modern convention; he will usually expand all abbreviated forms and supply a form of punctuation that is concordant with modern practice. The degree and extent of such modifications will depend upon the audience for whom the work

* An asterisk before a word, phrase, or sentence means that the form is ungrammatical.

is intended. Very often, textbooks and readers have a high level of "regularization," whereas versions of Middle English texts intended for professional scholars ideally endeavor to be as close to the original as possible.

One cannot always readily assume some perfect "original," however. Occasionally the material from which an edition is being made is of a very low level of reliability. For example, the scribe who copied it may have been working from a poor original and one that he may not have understood very well. At the same time, the techniques of some scribes are poorer than those of others, and we have very often to be on the lookout for obvious mistakes. Yet one must be on one's guard against being too ready to put down as "errors" what one imperfectly understands. Some texts (for example, the manuscripts of the *Canterbury Tales*) exist in a large number of copies. This will involve the editor in a considerable amount of *collation;* that is, he will often find it useful and revealing to include (say, in footnotes to his text) readings from other manuscript versions of the text he is editing. Very frequently this technique will be very helpful in determining what are "mistakes" in a particular original and what are genuine variant and attested forms.

We have continually made the point that the handwriting found in Middle English manuscripts is different from modern handwritten forms in its regular method of production according to various "schools." That such should be the case tells us that those who wrote the manuscripts must have had extensive and highly organized training. This training may have been given either at writing centers usually called *scriptoria* or in the universities. There certainly seem to have been large numbers of people able to write in England in the Middle Ages, and there is no reason to suspect that they were all in monastic orders. The very bulk of the surviving Middle English material itself points to the existence of a class of professional lay writers who could supplement the production of the monastic centers. Indeed, there is evidence to suggest that lay scribes were actually employed by monasteries in the production of manuscripts. In Anglo-Saxon times there seems to have been a rather limited number of centers (and they were all monastic) where manuscripts were produced, for example, Canterbury, Durham, Winchester, and Gloucester. Middle English manuscripts, however, were produced over a much wider geographical area and in establishments other than monasteries alone. There are Middle English manuscripts surviving from centers in every English county and even some originally written in Wales, Scotland, and Ireland.

So far, the question of the materials available to, and used by, the Middle English scribe has been ignored. Unlike now, the medium used for recording the written word was not, till the later part of the period, paper. Paper, or papyrus, was of course known in the ancient world and was widely used as the material upon which written symbols were transcribed. However, largely because of the expense involved in its production, paper is only very rarely found in the Middle Ages; and the favorite raw material for the recording of written language was parchment or *vellum*. Vellum is made from the dried skin of animals, notably the sheep or the goat. It is very fortunate for us that animal skin was preferred in the Middle Ages for the purposes of recording the written word, because, unlike paper, it has a very high tolerance for different levels of humidity and therefore stands a much greater chance of survival. Paper was much more expensive to produce than treated animal skins, and there was no shortage of sheep in England in the Middle Ages.

A scribe would have as his basic writing unit four sheets of vellum. These four sheets would then be folded over to make eight sheets, and this unit is known as the *quire*. The individual sheets could vary considerably in size, but for the smaller manuscripts the skin of aborted lambs was preferred for its fine texture. The four unfolded sheets could be holed or "pricked" through; and then, after folding had taken place, the holes or prick marks would be joined up by means of a sharp point. This was normally some piece of sharpened metal that would be used, in conjunction with a rule, to score lines on one side of the vellum to act as guides for the formation of symbols. The vertical spacing achieved by pricking was often speeded up by the use of a device that consisted of a small wheel with spikes at equidistant points on its circumference. This was attached to a wooden handle and simply run up the side of a sheet of vellum with strong hand pressure. The resultant holes were then joined together by the hard point. In later manuscripts the hard point gives way to the pencil, and even in some cases hard-point marks are gone over with pencil marks. This can often be a means of identifying the temporal provenance of a manuscript, since it is known that the use of the hard point was out of fashion by the very end of the eleventh century and that it had been completely superseded by the pencil by about 1175. Vertical and horizontal pencil lines can be seen clearly in *Text D*.

Vellum was abandoned as the medium for writing only very late in the Middle Ages; and although there are some manuscripts written on paper throughout the period, they can only be said to be extremely rare. Even after the advent of printing, vellum continued to be used for some time in handwritten documents. Vellum, being animal skin, is, of course, characterized by having a hairy and a smooth side. In some cases, although not universally, it was the custom when making up the quire to have the hair side opposite another hair side so that flesh faced flesh. The instrument used for writing itself was either the reed or the goose quill. The former was much more popular in Anglo-Saxon times, but the majority of Middle

English manuscripts seem to have been composed by using the latter. Unlike the modern pen, the nib or writing surface of the goose quill was not cut straight across, but at an angel of forty-five degrees. This has the effect of making down strokes much thicker than upward, diagonal, and horizontal ones, the result of which is obvious in the Gothic script.

The color of the manuscript writing can give some clue to the composition of the writing substance. Many manuscripts retain a black color, which suggests that the inks were made from a carbon (soot) base. Later manuscripts have a brown coloration, which points to a different base, probably gall. Others have a greenish hue, which is the result of copper in the ink compound being exposed to the oxygen in the air.

The bulk of Middle English manuscripts are to be found in collections kept in the United Kingdom. Of these there are three principal centers, the British Museum in London, the University of Oxford, and the University of Cambridge. The main British Museum collections are the Cotton Claudius, Caligula, Caius, Cleopatra, and the Egerton and Harley. The most important collection at the University of Oxford is that in the Bodleian Library, although others are to be found in the separate libraries of the colleges of All Souls, Christ Church, and Jesus. At Cambridge the more important manuscripts are in the college libraries of Corpus Christi, Emmanuel, Jesus, and Kings; and Trinity College Library at the University of Dublin in the Republic of Ireland also holds some important specimens, while a famous source of Middle English documentary material is the Public Record Office in the City of London.

In addition to these, some of the cathedral libraries in England are still the keepers of many excellent texts, especially those at Canterbury, Durham, Hereford, Lincoln, Salisbury, Winchester, and York. Examples of Middle English manuscripts are also to be found in many of the libraries of continental Europe, notably at Paris (Bibliothèque Nationale), Copenhagen (Royal Library), Ghent (University Library), and Brussels (Royal Library).

Since the nineteenth century many important collections of Middle English manuscripts have been gathered in the United States, especially at Princeton (Garrett Collection), Harvard, and the University of Minnesota, as well as at the Huntington Library, California, and the Pierpont Morgan Library, New York. Large private collections are naturally rare, but there are some exceptions, especially that of the Marquis of Bath at Longleat and the A. S. W. Rosenbach Collection, New York.

BIBLIOGRAPHY

THE NORMAN CONQUEST

BAUGH, A. C., *History of the English Language,* London, 1957, chapters V and VI.

BEHRENS, D., "Französische Elemente in Englischen," *Pauls Grundriss der germanischen Philologie, 2* Aufl., Strassburg, 1901, I.2.

BERNDT, R., "The Linguistic Situation in England from the Norman Conquest to the Loss of Normandy (1066–1204)," *Philologia Pragensia,* 8 (1965) : 145–163. Also in Lass, R., *Approaches to English Historical Linguistics, An Anthology,* New York, 1969.

HILL, G., *Some Consequences of the Norman Conquest,* London, 1904.

LEGGE, M. D., "Anglo-Norman and the Historian," *History,* XXVI (1941).

SHELLY, P. VAN DYKE, *English and French in England, 1066–1100.* Dissertation, Philadelphia, 1901.

STENTON, F. M., *Anglo-Saxon England,* Oxford, 1950, chapters 16 and 17.

WILSON, R. M., "English and French in England, 1000–1300," *History,* N.S., XXVIII (1943).

HANDWRITING

BENNET, H. S., "The Author and His Public in the Fourteenth and Fifteenth Centuries," *Essays and Studies* (1938).

CAPELLI, A., *Dizionario delle abbreviature latine ed italiane,* Milan, 1959.

DENHOLM-YOUNG, N., *Handwriting in England and Wales,* Cardiff, 1954.

DESTREZ, J., *La Pecia dans les manuscrits universitaires du xiiie et du xive siècle,* Paris, 1935.

FALCONER, M., "Handwriting," *Mediaeval England,* edited by H. W. C. Davis, Oxford, 1924.

GREG, W. W., *Facsimiles of Twelve Early English MSS. in the Library of Trinity College,* Cambridge, 1913.

GRIEVE, H. E. P., *Some Examples of English Handwriting,* Essex County Council, Chelmsford, 1949.

HECTOR, L. C., *The Handwriting of English Documents,* London, 1958.

JENKINSON, H., *Paleography of Court Hand,* Cambridge, 1915.

———, *The Later Court Hands in England,* Cambridge, 1927.

———, "The Teaching and Practice of Handwriting in England," *History,* 11 (1926).

JOHNSON, C., and H. JENKINSON, *English Court Hand,* Oxford, 1915.

JONES, L. W., "Pricking Manuscripts: The Instruments and Their Significance," *Speculum,* 21 (1946).

LOWE, E. A., "Handwriting," *The Legacy of the Middle Ages,* edited by C. G. Crump and E. F. Jacob, Oxford, 1926.

MAUNDE THOMPSON, E., "The History of English Handwriting," *Transactions of the Bibliographical Society,* 5 (1899).

——, *Introduction to Greek and Latin Paleography,* Oxford, 1912.

NEUMANN, G., "Die Orthographie der Paston Letters von 1422–1461," *Studien zur englischen Philologie,* VII (1904), Marburg.

SCHLEMILCH, W., "Beiträge zur Sprache und Orthographie spätaltenglischer Sprach denkmäler der Übergangszeit," *Studien zur englischen Philologie,* XXXIV (1914), Halle.

STEINBERG, S. H., "Mediaeval Writing Masters," *The Library,* XXIII (1941).

WRIGHT, C. E., *English Vernacular Hands from the Twelfth to the Fifteenth Centuries,* Oxford, 1960.

PELLINGS AND
SOUNDS / THREE

I

This chapter will be concerned with two important aspects of Middle English—the conventions used in spelling its words and the means by which specific sound values can be reconstructed from such spelling. The way in which sound systems are conventionally represented in orthographies is an important study in any language with a written form, but this is particularly true of much Middle English. As briefly mentioned in the last chapter, Middle English texts are not written in a nationally standardized spelling system, and a great amount of orthographic variation can be found between texts written at the same date but in different geographical regions and for different audiences. If any standards of spelling existed, they were regional and not national. Although at first sight this would seem merely to be another complexity in the already difficult study of Middle English, the lack of national orthographic standards has a number of advantages. One of these is that since the spelling systems are regional, they can provide useful evidence for the location of manuscripts. Secondly, variety in orthographic convention can mean (although there are many difficulties involved) that phonological distinctions are more readily recoverable than they would be given a fixed national standard.

Speakers of written languages often display ambivalent views about what the orthographic systems of their languages represent. They often believe that their own orthographic system faithfully reflects the sounds they use, although, when faced with counterexamples, readily admit the need for some kind of more phonetic alphabet. In general, phonetic alphabets are credited with only a limited value by the majority of phonologists, yet in some way orthographic systems do appear to represent some level of phonetic realization; however, in many instances the opposite seems to be the case, and the choice of symbol for sound appears to be quite arbitrary. An obvious example of this in Modern English is the use of the ⟨gh⟩ symbol combination in such contexts as ⟨trough⟩, ⟨thought⟩, and ⟨ghost⟩. Similarly, in the examples the symbol combination ⟨ou⟩ apparently represents two different sounds and, in some British English dialects, in a word like ⟨although⟩, can "stand for" a sound identical to that denoted by the ⟨o⟩ in ⟨ghost⟩. It has recently been suggested that this apparently unmotivated system can correspond to some important phonological phenomena (see Chomsky and Halle [1968], Chapter 2); that is, <u>orthographies may not represent on all occasions the obvious, superficial sounds of language, but the characteristics and structures of these sounds at a more abstract level</u>. At this level superficial differences, such as some of those between cotemporaneous geographical dialects of a given language, are often not expressed. This means that an orthographical system successfully corresponding to an abstract phonological level can be used, as is the case with Modern English, by speakers in all geographical regions as standing for the sounds of their own dialects. For example, Modern English orthography does not attempt to distinguish by means of additional or modified symbols such outstanding regional dialectal features in British English as the uvular [ʁ] (the "back" [r] found in the northeast of England) or the smaller extent of diphthongization in Scottish dialects; and the "loss of final [r]" in such contexts as the final syllable of ⟨father⟩ is not shown in the orthography at all. It is interesting to note, however, that there do exist some "nonstandard" orthographies that try (albeit in a rather inconsistent way) to manifest spoken features, especially of a social and regional dialectal kind, that are otherwise concealed by the accepted spelling conventions—spellings such as ⟨guid⟩ (⟨good⟩) and ⟨hame⟩ (⟨home⟩) for Scottish dialectal forms, as well as such attempts as ⟨comin'⟩ and ⟨runnin'⟩ to denote what are commonly held to be features of the conversational spoken language.

If the general lack of regional, personal, and temporal orthographic diversity can at least partially be explained for Modern English by the suggestion (and at present it is only this) that the spelling system represents abstract and not necessarily realized phonological features, one is faced with the difficulty of deciding how far this is also true for the non-national Middle English systems and to what extent they denote differences at a less abstract level of representation. The following is a list of the graphs, digraphs, and trigraphs that exist in the majority of the orthographic raw material to be found in Middle English texts between 1100 and 1450:

consonantal	vowel and diphthong
hw, wh, ȝ, g, ssh, sc, ss,	a, aa, æ, e, ea, eo, ee, i, y,
s, sch, ssch, þ, ð, f, v,	ii, ey, iy, o, oo, oa, u,
u, y, w, gh, h, ch, b, d,	ou, ow, v, iu, ui, oe, ue,
l, m, n, p, t, z, c, k, cw,	ai, æi, aȝ, æȝ, ay, ei,
qu, kn, x, qh, quh, qw, th,	eu, ew, iw, eou, eow, ag,
gg, dg, j.	agh, oȝ, og, ogh, oy, oi.

It must be stressed that this list does not represent the sum total of graphs available to any scribe at a particular place or in a particular period and that all the graphs are not equally common; but rather, unlike the Modern English alphabet, it represents a collection of forms selected from a wide geographical, temporal, and even idiosyncratic usage. This can best be illustrated by a brief examination of the sometimes extremely diverse appearance of individual lexical items in the spelling systems of much Middle English. If in Modern English one wishes to represent the lexical items ⟨follow⟩, ⟨earth⟩, ⟨near⟩, ⟨not⟩, and ⟨shall⟩, or almost any other, then one will be involved in a particular spelling convention that has been accepted for at least two hundred years regardless of the geographical area of composition. Before 1470 this cannot readily be assumed. One can illustrate this by listing some of the spelling variants found throughout Middle English for the lexical items mentioned above:

⟨follow⟩			⟨earth⟩		⟨near⟩	
folȝhen	volewen	erth	erthe	erðe	neh	neiȝh
folȝen	voluwen	yerthe	erth	erde	nech	nei
folien	folwe	yerþe	herþe	eerþe	næh	nigh
fulien		orþe	orðe	oerþe	neih	
folgen		eorðe	earðe	ierþe	ney	
folwin		eærðe	eorþe	ȝorþe	neȝ	
		yrþe	yerthe	vrthe	neiȝ	
			irthe			

⟨not⟩		⟨shall⟩	
nawiht	nowiht	schal	schalle
nawt	nowt	shall	sall
naut	nowiȝt	xal	scal
naht	nout	scheal	schel
noht	noȝt	scæl	scel
nohht	noght	ssel	sæl
naught	nouth		
nowicht	nocht		

Perhaps the most obvious reaction to such a variety of spellings for individual lexical items would be that the Middle English orthographic system was completely anarchic or even that Middle English scribes were incapable of spelling "correctly." But such judgments must not be made too readily, since there is a high degree of consistency in the spelling habits of individual scribes and, it seems, between scribes trained at the same scriptorium and writing in the same geographical area. Certainly, the situation is not nearly as arbitrary as it appears at first sight, and although there seems to have been no nationally accepted "standard" before the middle of the fifteenth century, there clearly were regionally recognizable, accepted spelling norms. There was definitely no free-for-all situation, and a scribe would not and did not spell according to a purely idosyncratic set of criteria.

Middle English is quite distinct from Modern English in the respect that it employed regional spelling conventions (and it must be stressed that only those standards of a written and *not* a spoken nature are under consideration here). It remains to discover what is significant about this fact for the student of Middle English and what it can tell him about the nature of the spoken versions of that language.

The first problem to be considered is: given regional spelling variation, at what period did the "national" spelling system emerge and on what criteria was it based? Secondly, the different spellings that have been considered above themselves raise special kinds of problems. For example, can one draw the same kind of conclusion from such varieties as ⟨erthe⟩/⟨erþe⟩, ⟨neiʒ⟩/⟨neiʒh⟩, and ⟨sal⟩/⟨sall⟩ as against ⟨yerþe⟩/⟨orþe⟩/⟨eorðe⟩ and ⟨nech⟩/⟨nei⟩? Do all spelling varieties have the same status as information for spoken features? Perhaps it might be suggested that variants such as ⟨erthe⟩/⟨erþe⟩ are of no significance, since only a paleographical difference is involved. However, it depends very much on how one treats the evidence provided by spelling systems. It is often too readily assumed that spelling evidence is useful only as a means of arriving at clues to pronunciation and that therefore scribal variants of the types ⟨erthe⟩/⟨erþe⟩ or ⟨sal⟩/⟨sall⟩ should be ignored, since it is unlikely that they represent differences in phonological representation. It is true that spelling systems may shed some light upon their phonological "equivalents," and this will be investigated at some length in this chapter. At the same time, however, as we shall see especially in the chapter on "Middle English Dialects," spellings that are apparently unmotivated from a phonological point of view can provide important evidence of another kind, in particular as a means of manuscript localization.

Although "standard" regional forms of written English are not unknown before modern times, no one orthographic system seems to have been acceptable on a national scale, at least in England and Wales, before the fifteenth century. In later Old English times, the written form of the West Saxon dialect, in which perhaps the majority of surviving Old English manuscripts are written, had a very wide currency, owing probably to the great social, economic, and military status of the kingdom of Wessex. Other writing systems, however, existed in Old English at the same time or in earlier times, although their localization and influence have never been fully investigated. At the time of the Norman Conquest there was probably no *single* standard orthographic system widely enough accepted to form the basis of a large number of manuscripts composed in a variety of geographical regions. This situation seems to have lasted for almost four hundred years, and it is only after 1430 that one can see the beginnings of something that can be considered a national vernacular spelling norm, although its use is at first restricted to important documents of a legal or administrative nature.

The best account of the origins and development of the fifteenth-century written standard is that given by Samuels (1963). Samuels shows that at the beginning of the fifteenth century several important regional standards existed side by side, none of which had a wide national currency. Perhaps the most important of these was the orthographic system used as the written standard in the manuscripts connected with the Wycliffite movement. The spelling system in these secular and religious works is based upon the Central East Midland regional standard, especially that found in documents localized in the counties of Northamptonshire, Huntingdonshire, and Bedfordshire. The great popularity of these works meant that they had a wide currency in the whole country, and, most importantly, the spelling system from the Central East Midland area often came to be used in their composition regardless of the geographical area in which the scribe happened to be writing. The result was that Wycliffite manuscripts written or copied outside the Central East Midland area still used the original's system of spelling. The acceptability of the Central East Midland written standard was no doubt enhanced by what appears to have been the high status of the Midland *spoken* dialect:

> Also of þe forseyde Saxon tonge, þat ys deled a þre, and ys abyde scarslych wiþ feaw vplondysch men, and ys gret wondur, for men of þe est wiþ men of þe west, as hyt were vnder þe same party of heuene, acordeþ more in sounyng of speche þan men of þe norþ wiþ men of þe souþ. Þerfore hyt ys þat Mercii, þat buþ men of myddel Engelond, as hyt were parteners of þe endes, vndurstondeþ betre þe syde longages, Norþeron and Souþeron, þan Norþeron and Souþeron vndurstondeþ eyþer oþer.
>
> (John of Trevisa, Translation of
> Higden's *Polychronicon* [1387])

[In the same way English is divided into three (regional varieties) and survives among a few rustic people. It is an incredible fact that people living in the east and west regions (sharing a common [middle section] of the country) sound more alike in their speech than do people living in the northern and southern regions with each other.

As a result, the Mercians, that is those who live in the Midland region of England, since as it were they share boundaries with both extremities, better understand the languages of the Northerners and Southerners than these can understand each other.]

The Central Midland written standard was so popular that it lasted almost unchanged for more than fifty years and came to be by far the most important among other smaller regional spelling varieties.

However, even this important regional standard seems to have had only a limited currency, since the orthographic systems used in such important literary manuscripts as those of Chaucer and Gower are in many ways different from the Wycliffite standard and certainly do not show the same degree of regularity or consistency. What is interesting is that despite the differences in their spelling systems, the manuscripts of Chaucer and Gower were acceptable at the London court; the implication to be drawn from this seems to be that there was no orthographic norm or standard yet in existence in London itself around 1400. After 1430, however, manuscripts produced in the London area begin to show a high degree of conformity in their spelling; and there emerges what is at first a new regional standard, often called the *Chancery Standard,* since most of the manuscripts composed in it belong to a collection known as the *Early Chancery Proceedings* at the Public Record Office in London. From this time onward the great bulk of manuscripts produced in the London area are written in the orthographic convention of the Chancery Standard, and it is this system that gradually gains popularity as a national and nonregional orthographic method. One consequence of this was that on many occasions letters addressed to the Lord Chancellor in London, but written in regions like Yorkshire or Cornwall, would use, not the regional spelling standard of their area of composition, but the London Chancery Standard. The change from regional to national standard was not immediate, and for a time at least many manuscripts are to be found written in a mixture of regional and Chancery systems.

The Chancery Standard itself is rather different from the orthographic method found in Chaucer and Gower manuscripts of London and cannot be said to have derived directly from that source. The evidence suggests that the Chancery Standard is primarily based upon the Central East Midland Wycliffite system mentioned earlier, together with the addition of features from local London types. With the immigration into the London area of a large group of people from the Central East Midland area in the early and mid-fifteenth century, and with them the import of scribes accustomed to the Central East Midland standard orthography, it is not surprising (especially when one takes into account the wide currency of the

Wycliffite spelling system) that this spelling system should form the basis of the Chancery Standard itself. Indeed, the Modern British English (and, in part, international English) spelling system owes a heavy debt to the Central East Midland/Chancery types, since it was on these that the orthography used in early printed books was based, and it is from the last mentioned that all Modern English systems derive.

We have stressed several times so far that we have been concerned solely with a written, and not a spoken, standard of English. Indeed, there are few references to the notion of a standard English pronunciation with all its attendant sociological and value-judgment features before 1500. It is only when the sixteenth century is reached that one begins to find reference to such ideas of "better," "correct," or "proper" forms of the spoken language's syntax, phonology, or vocabulary:

> speke none englisshe but that which is cleane, polite, perfectly and articulately pronounced, omittinge no lettre or sillable, as folisshe women oftentimes do of a wantonnesse, whereby diuers noble men and gentilmennes chyldren (as I do at this daye knowe) have attained corrupt and foule pronunciation.
>
> (Elyot, *Gouernour* [1531])

However, value and sociolinguistic judgments may be implicit in another of Trevisa's comments:

> Al þe longage of þe Norþhumbres, and specialych at ȝork ys so scharp, slyttyng, and frotyng, and vnshape, þat we Souþeron men may þat longage vnneþe vndurstonde. Y trowe þat þat ys bycause þat a buþ nyȝ to strange men and aliens, þat spekeþ strangelych, and also bycause þat þe kynges of Engelond woneþ alwey fer from þat contray; for a buþ more yturned to þe souþ contray, and ȝef a goþ to þe norþ contray, a goþ wiþ gret help and strengthe.
>
> (Translation of Higden's *Polychronicon* [1387])

[The speech of the Northern English, and especially the type heard at York, is so harsh, piercing, grating and formless, that we men of the South can hardly understand it. It seems to me that the reason for this lies in the fact that those parts lie alongside areas occupied by foreigners where an alien language is spoken, and also because kings of England have always resided far from the North. The reason for this is that they are more fond of the South and whenever they do go to the North they are always accompanied by large and powerful forces.]

II

There are several ways of reconstructing the sound system of a language like Middle English that exists only in a written form. The most important of these lies in the interpretation of the orthographic systems and the relationship their writers thought they bore to the phonologies of the language. As mentioned earlier, some recent research in phonology has made the suggestion that in many instances the orthography of Modern English represents its sound system at an abstract and not a superficial level (Chomsky and Halle [1968], page 49). Consider the underlined vowels in the pairs ⟨serene⟩/⟨serenity⟩, and ⟨divine⟩/⟨divinity⟩. The symbols ⟨e⟩ and ⟨i⟩ are each used for two quite different phonetic shapes, [i]/[e] and [aj]/[ɪ]. But given one word of each pair, a native speaker of English can automatically derive the other—the variation in vowel quality is entirely predictable in the given context. The orthography does not show the predictable variants, but rather represents the vowel sounds underlying the alternants at the superficial level, thus:

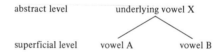

Thus, for the pairs ⟨divine⟩/⟨divinity⟩:

<u>The denotation of abstract phonological levels will be seen to be a very important characteristic of some of the Middle English orthographic systems to be studied.</u>

This feature of orthographic systems is important when one comes to consider the treatment given in spelling to Modern English geographical dialects. The word ⟨book⟩, for example, is pronounced differently by speakers of both British and American English, yet both sets of speakers think of it as unambiguously standing for their own pronunciation. Since different dialects may utilize a similar underlying vowel system, there is no need for their orthographies to represent their superficial differences, which can be predicted from general dialect-specific phonological rules. One orthographic system can be used for several geographical dialects. In Middle

English, however, a scribe copying a manuscript written at some other regionally distinct center was prone to translate what confronted him into the conventions of his own regional orthographic system. For instance, a manuscript containing the word ⟨bane⟩ could be transcribed as ⟨bone⟩ by a scribe trained in the system of another scriptorium. This change can mean several things. It might suggest that the Middle English spelling methods were more intent than their modern counterparts to show superficial differences:

Alternatively, there is always the possibility to be borne in mind that although for some dialects ⟨bane⟩ and ⟨bone⟩ may have shared the same abstract vocalic segment, phonological *restructuring* (King [1969], Chapter 4) may have taken place in these items in others, so that this orthographic presentation may show a vocalic contrast at an abstract level.

In a rather special sense, native speaker information is available to the historical phonologist and can often provide him with his most valuable evidence. From the sixteenth century onward, there is a great deal of comment upon the nature of English sound systems by contemporary phoneticians, who often give phonetic transcriptions of their pronunciations as well as the position and shape of their vocal organs in the production of their own speech sounds. Very often, the information so provided can cast much light on the medieval situation as well. There is little systematic comment on phonological matters relating to English among writers in the medieval period, although there is one indirect exception—the *Ormulum*—whose material will form a large part of the discussion to follow.

Another source of information is provided by the evidence of phonetic equivalences—rhymes, puns, and metrical devices. Rhyming evidence can obviously be important in showing historical homophony, although it is limited in that the mere fact of vocalic correspondence says little about the nature of the equation involved. The same is true for the information given by punning devices, for instance, Shakespeare's "Now it is Rome indeed and room enough" (*Julius Caesar,* act 1, scene 2), although puns have the added complexity in that the vocalic equivalences they show may only have been approximate, even at the time they were written.

The remainder of this chapter makes no claim to give a comprehensive description of the Middle English sound system, but will be restricted to three main concerns. In the first place, there will be a short outline of the basic characteristics of the phonological model to be utilized, as well as more detailed comment upon the methodology of historical reconstruction. Secondly, a brief sketch will be given of some of the principal features of the Middle English vowel, diphthong, and consonantal system mainly with reference to one text. Lastly, there will be an examination of some of the more important sound changes that have taken place between Middle English and the linguistic periods preceding it and following it, and there will be a proposal of some principles upon which a theory of such changes might be founded.

VOWEL SOUNDS

Principles of Description

Unlike consonantal [+consonantal] sounds, vowels (and diphthongs) do not involve any complete closure at any point in the vocal tract (that is, the oral and nasal cavities). In describing vowel sounds one will primarily wish to know the relative position of the principal organ involved in their production—the tongue. Two features will be of prime importance: (1) the relative _horizontal_ position of the part of the tongue most actively involved in the production of the vowel, the _front, center,_ or _back,_ and (2) the relative _vertical_ position of the tongue, that is, whether it is _high, low,_ or _non-high_ and _nonlow_ (_mid_).

According to these criteria, one can classify the following Modern English vowels:

+high +front	⟨seat⟩	+high +back	⟨look⟩
—high —low +front	⟨bait⟩ (Scottish)	—high —low +back	⟨go⟩ (Scottish)
+low +front	⟨sat⟩	+low +back	⟨bath⟩ (Southern British)

To include within this framework many other Modern English vowels, one must introduce another descriptive feature of vowels in general—whether they are _tense_ or _nontense_ (_lax_). Tense vowel sounds are produced with a much more distinct and tense muscular effort, but lax vowel sounds are produced more rapidly, relaxedly, and less distinctly. This feature can be used to account for the difference between the vowels in ⟨seat⟩ (tense) and ⟨sit⟩ (nontense), ⟨bait⟩ and ⟨go⟩ in Scottish English, and ⟨bet⟩ and ⟨top⟩ in other forms of British English, as well as ⟨blue⟩ and ⟨put⟩ in most varieties of English. One can, therefore, expand the description of Modern English vowels to:

	Front		Back	
	+*tense*	−*tense*	+*tense*	−*tense*
+high	⟨heat⟩	⟨hit⟩	⟨full⟩	⟨such⟩
−high −low	†⟨bait⟩	⟨bet⟩	†⟨low⟩	⟨stop⟩
+low		⟨man⟩	⟨father⟩	

The items marked † are taken from Scottish English dialects, since such words often appear with a diphthong in other regional varieties.

As well as being able to classify vowels in terms of such features as [±back], [±high], and [±tense], one can also add a fourth—[±long]. The feature involving length is an important one, especially in the history of English vowel sounds, and is very closely associated with the feature of tenseness, since on very many occasions tense vowels also share the feature [+long]. This is not always the case, however, since one finds in British English an interdialectal contrast between those vowels that are [+tense, +long] and those that are [+tense, −long]; compare some Southern British pronunciations of the verb ⟨see⟩ having a high, front, tense vowel of long duration [ii] with its Scottish "equivalent," which, although high and tense, has a much shorter duration [i].

Initially, our attempt at a recovery of some aspects of the Middle English vowel system will be concerned only with one text—the *Ormulum* (Bodleian, Junius 1). The reason for this is that this text is unique in Middle English. It is very early, written about the year 1200. The manuscript itself is probably an autograph (that is, it seems to have been written by the author himself), and it can be localized almost exactly at Stanford, Lincolnshire, in the East Midlands. But the feature in which it is unique, and the one most interesting to the student of Middle English phonology, is that its author, variously called Orm, Orrm, or Ormin, seems to have used a system of orthographic representation designed to characterize, in a very systematic way, many features of his phonological system. Before a look at this manuscript is taken, however, there will follow a short examination of one of the earliest attempts by a phonetician at a formal description of the sounds of English, and the evidence provided by his comments and phonetic transcriptions will be used to draw a comparison with the sounds of Modern English and to interpret the more indirect evidence provided by the *Ormulum*. The phonetician whose evidence will be studied is John Hart, especially as regards the material provided by his two best known works, *Orthographie* (1569) and *Methode* (1570). The advantage to this procedure will be that Hart's work will provide a halfway point of reference, as it were, between whatever sound system can be constructed from the *Ormulum* and the phonological characteristics of contemporary English. The result will be that the process involved in historical change will clearly be visible to the student. In his description of both vowel and consonant sounds, Hart uses a script rather like a "phonetic alphabet" in an endeavor to characterize as unambiguously as possible their distinctive features. His classification of vowel sounds, for example, separates those with the features [+tense, +long] from those with [−tense, −long] by means of a superscript(ed) bar above the relevant symbol. Compare the following:

	+tense +long		−tense −long	
	Hart	Modern	Hart	Modern
+high −back	hī uī nīd	he we need	kirk sit intu	kirk sit into
−high −low −back	sē spēk mēt	see, sea speak meet, meat	beter els send	better else send
+low +back	lāt māk tāk	late make take	man that ran	man that ran
+high +back	dū sūn gūd	do soon good	under sun but	under sun but
−high −low +back	hōm gō stōn	home go stone	for oftn ov	for often of

Hart's vowel system shows both similarities to, and differences from, that of Modern English. Perhaps the most obvious difference is that in his phonology the [−high, −low, +back] vowel is common, whereas in many modern dialects (with certain exceptions, notably Scottish English) these appear as diphthongs, for example, <home>, <grow>, and <know>. At the same time, the lexical items (such as <sē> and <spēk>) with the

[+long, +tense, —high, —low] vowel have all become [+high] in Modern Standard English. A third difference is the existence of the[3] [+high, +back, +tense] vowel in such items as ⟨under⟩, ⟨sun⟩, and ⟨but⟩, where Modern English now has a [—front, —back, +low, —tense] vowel. The [+high, +back] vowel in these words still exists in many (especially Midland and Northern—but not Scottish) dialects of Modern English.

Before we look in more detail at the kind of changes involved between these two systems, it will be interesting to compare Hart's system with that found in the *Ormulum:*

| | +tense | | —tense | |
	Hart	Orm	Hart	Orm
+high —back	hī uī nēd	he we ned	kirk sit intu	kirrk sittenn innto
—high —low —back	sē spēk mēt	sæ spekenn mete	beter els send	bettre elles senndenn
+low +back	lāt māk tāk	lăte măkenn tăkenn	man that ran	mann tatt rann
—high —low +back	hōm gō stōn	ham gan stan	for oft ov	forr offte off
+high +back	dū sūn gūd	don sone god	under sun but	unnderr sunne butt

Perhaps the most obvious conclusion to draw from this comparison is that the [—tense] vowels seem to be identical in both Orm and Hart and that the former appears to use the orthographic device of doubling the postvocalic consonant as a means of marking this feature. Indeed, in the dedication to his work, Orm is quite emphatic about the value of his orthographic system as a means of marking phonological features:

Annd whase wilenn shall þiss boc efft oþerr siþe writen
Him bidde icc þat hët wríte rihht, swa summ þiss boc him tæcheþþ
All þwerrt üt affterr þatt itt iss vppo þiss firrste bisne
Wiþþ all swillc ríme alls her iss sett, wiþþ all-se fele wordes

Annd tatt he loke wel þatt he an bocstaff wríte twiȝȝess
Eȝȝwhær þær itt uppo þiss boc iss writenn o þat wise
Loke he wel þatt hët write swa, forr he ne maȝȝ nohht elless
Onn Ennglissh wríten rihhte te word þatt wite he wel to soþe
                          (*Ormulum,* "Dedication," *95–110*)

[I command anyone who will want to write this book over again at
some other time to copy it exactly, just as this copy guides him. (He
must copy it) precisely as it is done in this first copy, keeping every
rhythm intact and representing every word. He must also pay particular attention to writing double consonants everywhere they so appear
in the book. Let him be sure that he follows these instructions, for
he must realize it is true that he cannot otherwise correctly represent
the word which he knows to be true in the English language.]

The assumption can perhaps be made (and this would seem to be
borne out by the corresponding forms in Hart) that whenever one finds
the segments $V + C_2^2$ (where C_2^2 represents a geminate or double consonant), then the V has the features [−tense] and [−long]. The corollary of
this rule will be that in the context of $V + C_0^1$ (where C_0^1 is a notation for
one consonantal segment or a zero segment), that V has at least the feature
[+tense], although, as will be seen later, it is hardly yet likely to have the
feature [+long]. It is interesting to note in this last respect that Orm
uses the diacritic mark ˘ in the cases ⟨lăte⟩, ⟨măkenn⟩, and ⟨tăkenn⟩.
There is some controversy over the significance of this, but it seems
possible that it is a marker of the feature [−long] for the vowel, since
Orm also seems to use the symbol ʺ or ′ to mark [+long], for example
⟨ȝẽt⟩, ⟨mõt⟩, and ⟨nẽt⟩.

Perhaps the most obvious difference between Hart's vowel system
and that in the *Ormulum* hinges upon the discrepancies between the relative heights of individual elements. For instance, vowels that are [+high,
+front] in Hart appear as [−high, −low, +front] in Orm. Compare
⟨hí/he⟩, ⟨dū/don⟩, and ⟨hōm/ham⟩. The presentation of the vowels in
Orm (given on p. 57 above) might lead to the conclusion that there were
no [+high, ±front] vowels at all in his phonology. This is not the case,
since one can find such spellings as ⟨time⟩ and ⟨lif⟩ as well as ⟨hus⟩ and
⟨dun⟩. When these spellings are compared, however, with their equivalents
in Hart, one discovers there the forms ⟨teim⟩, ⟨leif⟩, ⟨hous⟩, and ⟨doun⟩.
There has been no raising of Orm's [+high] vowel since no further raising
is possible. Rather, two things happen—a glide element, [j] or [w], is
formed after both the front and back high vowel, and this vowel itself is
then lowered by one degree in height. The process of vowel shifting and

glide development between the time of Orm and Hart can be diagrammatically represented as follows:

1. Vowel-raising

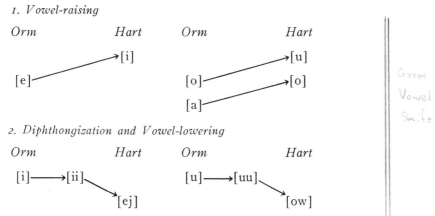

2. Diphthongization and Vowel-lowering

The symbols [e], [i], and [o], and so forth, are not meant to represent maximally discrete units, but rather are to be seen as a shorthand way of displaying bundles or matrices of vowel segment distinctive features. For a complete discussion of these features, see Chomsky and Halle (1968), Chapter 7. It should be noted too that the glides [j] and [w]—respectively the front and back glides—are found attached to vowels with the same coefficient of frontness.

The forms in Hart are arrived at by the addition of several rules to a phonological system like Orm's. Principally these rules (given here only in an approximate form) are three in number, and must, for reasons that cannot be gone into here (see Chomsky and Halle [1968]), pp. 264 ff., and King [1969]), apply in the order given:

1. Glide Addition

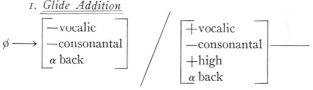

This rule states that an additional glide element [—vocalic, —consonantal] is added (the place where the addition is made being denoted by the line ———) whenever it is in the context (represented by whatever appear to the right of the slash) of coming after a high vowel. The symbol α is used, rather than either + or —, as a variable over both these values. Whenever + appears on the left hand side of the rule, + will also appear on the right side, so:

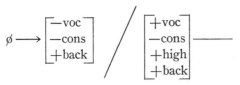

$$\emptyset \longrightarrow \begin{bmatrix} -voc \\ -cons \\ +back \end{bmatrix} \Big/ \begin{bmatrix} +voc \\ -cons \\ +high \\ +back \end{bmatrix} \underline{\quad\quad}$$

and so with minus. This notation captures the fact that the new glide agrees in backness with the vowel it follows. The $\emptyset$ (zero) symbol is misleading, since it implies that an empty slot is filled by a vocalic segment matrix. As the notation shows, however, vowel-lengthening involves the addition of another segment to that of the short vowel ([u] ⟶ [uu]), a segment identical to it in every respect except in the feature of syllabacy. Instead of $\emptyset$ one could have [+voc, —cons, +high, ±back, —syllabic], so that the change of this segment to a glide involves only the alteration of the feature [+voc] to [—voc]. See Anderson and Lass (forthcoming).

2. *High Vowel-lowering*

$$\begin{bmatrix} +voc \\ -cons \\ +high \end{bmatrix} \longrightarrow \begin{bmatrix} -high \\ -low \end{bmatrix}$$

i.e. mid.

Thus, [i] ⟶ [ii] ⟶ [ij] (*Glide Addition*) ⟶ [ej] (*High Vowel-lowering*).

3. *Vowel-raising*

Because of the limited nature of the data used, it is only in the back vowel series that all the nonhigh vowels are raised one degree of height. Consequently two, related rules are required:

(a)

$$\begin{bmatrix} +voc \\ -cons \\ -high \\ -low \\ -back \end{bmatrix} \longrightarrow [+high]$$

i.e. mid

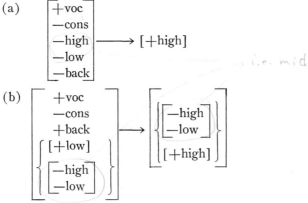

(b)

$$\begin{bmatrix} +voc \\ -cons \\ +back \\ \left\{ \begin{array}{l} [+low] \\ \left[\begin{array}{l} -high \\ -low \end{array}\right] \end{array} \right\} \end{bmatrix} \longrightarrow \left[\begin{array}{l} \left\{ \begin{array}{l} \left[\begin{array}{l} -high \\ -low \end{array}\right] \\ [+high] \end{array} \right\} \end{array} \right]$$

That is, by (a), [e] ⟶ [i], and by (b), [a] ⟶ [o], and [o] ⟶ [u].
Two further points have to be made. There are in the data some ex-

ceptions to both rules 3 (a) and (b), since forms such as ⟨spēk/spekenn⟩ and ⟨lāt/latenn⟩ appear. It is beyond the scope of this book to discuss how exceptions should be treated within the grammar, but it could be suggested that in Hart's grammar such words were marked as [—Rules 3(a) and (b)] (see Chomsky and Halle [1968], pp. 172–176). Between Hart's time and contemporary English, such words have, however, undergone raising of their root vocalic segment. The whole series of rules roughly outlined above is part of a process traditionally known as the Great Vowel Shift.

It should be noted that the addition of rules 1–3 to Orm's phonology in no way changed its vocalic makeup, since it does not involve the development of any new vowels. It merely appeared to have contributed two new diphthongs, if one assumes for the moment that the last did not exist in Orm's phonology:

Orm		*Hart*	
[i]	[u]	[ii]	[uu]
[e]	[o]	[ee] [ej]	[oo] [ow]
	[a]	[aa]	

As will be seen below, the rules adding the feature of length to the (tense) vowel series of Orm occur at a later period in Middle English.

So far, all the vowels dealt with have been those that occur in syllables that have a relatively high degree of stress. In Modern English, the vowel of the unstressed syllable, for instance, the second vowel in words like ⟨father⟩, ⟨mother⟩, and ⟨Cuba⟩, are in many dialects [—high, —low, —back, —front]. Although it is difficult to put forward convincing evidence either way, nevertheless there seem to be at least some grounds for thinking that vowels in "unstressed" contexts had a similar feature configuration in Middle English; examples of this might be the second vowel segments in the items ⟨unnderr⟩, ⟨senndenn⟩, and ⟨writenn⟩ in the *Ormulum*.

i.e. /ə/

"Nonvowel" Sounds

It was suggested above that one of the criteria distinguishing vowels and consonants is that there is no complete obstruction involved at any point in the mouth when the former are being produced. Although this is a useful working definition, there are several important refinements that must be made to it. Rather than include only restricted or nonrestricted features of the vocal tract in one's description, one must think in terms of degrees (instead of polarity) of restrictiveness or obstruction. For this reason, we shall introduce the universal distinction in phonologies of *resonant vs. obstruent ?*

Manner of Articulation

sonorant and *nonsonorant* sounds. Sounds that have the feature [+sonorant] are those in which no complete obstruction is utilized in the vocal tract; in this group one can therefore include not only vowels, diphthongs, and glides, but also liquids, nasals, and retroflex sounds. These latter types will be dealt with more fully later. Segments having the feature [−sonorant], and therefore involving some more complete closure of the vocal tract, are what are often referred to as *stops* and *fricatives.*

Let us look in a little more detail at the sounds that have the feature [−sonorant]. Although they share this feature, it would seem natural to treat the group of sounds including [b, d, t, and g] rather differently from the group including [f, s, z, and ð], since although both involve some kind of blockage of the vocal tract, the degree or extent of the blockage is not the same for the two groups. It seems, therefore, that at this point it would be useful to introduce yet another feature. In the first group of sounds mentioned above, the blockage of the vocal tract is complete at some point, but in the second it is only partial. This distinction between total and partial obstruction one can classify in terms of the features [±continuant]. Sounds classified as [−continuant] are those in which a partial (or no) blockage of the vocal tract is involved, whereas their [+continuant] counterparts involve a momentary total obstruction. In Modern (and, as will be seen, Middle) English, sounds such as [k, t, d, g] have the feature [−sonorant, −continuant], and others like [s, ð, f, v] have the features [−sonorant, +continuant].

Vowel and diphthong sounds are, of course, characterized as [+sonorant, +continuant], since there is no restriction of the vocal tract involved. There is, however, another group of sounds that, although they too share these features, are classified as consonants rather than vowels because some obstruction of the vocal tract is involved. This group, comprising principally liquids, nasals, and retroflex sounds, share the characteristics of both the vowel and the consonant. Unlike consonantal sounds, the group under discussion do not involve any blockage of the midsection of the vocal tract, and they are rather like vowels in having the feature [+sonorant]; that is, the vocal tract is not completely blocked off. In nasal sounds the air is allowed to pass through the nose cavity, whereas in the case of the liquids and retroflex sounds, air escapes at the sides and over the top of the tongue respectively.

So far this description of consonantal sounds has dealt only with the degree of obstruction involved in the vocal tract. There are, however, two other important characteristics of the consonant that have yet to be taken into account. We will want to know not only whether some kind of blockage is involved in the production of a consonant, but also where in the vocal tract that blockage takes place. To this end we shall introduce the feature *place of articulation* [±anterior]. According to this, sounds are divided into two main groups on the basis of their position of stricture. <u>Consonantal sounds produced at, or in front of, the hard ridge behind the upper teeth (the alveolar ridge)</u> are classified as [+anterior], and those involving <u>a stricture at some position behind the alveolar ridge</u> are [—anterior]. Consonants such as [s, p, t, f] are therefore [+anterior], but [k, g, ç, n] are [—anterior].

Secondly, like vowel and diphthong sounds, consonants involve the tongue in relative degrees of movement both in its height and its horizontal position. They can, therefore, be described in terms of such features as [±high] and [±back]. <u>High and low consonantal sounds</u> (like vowels) involve the <u>raising or lowering of the body of the tongue in relation to a neutral position.</u> For example, consonantal sounds that can be classified as [+high] are [k and g], but [t, d, l, b, p] can be described as [—high]. On the other hand, [+back] sounds involve <u>a retraction along the horizontal plain from a neutral position</u> and include [k, g], the sound represented as <ch> in Scottish English <loch>, and the nasal sound spelled as <ng> in such words as <singing> and <bringing>.

The last feature to be used in this description of consonantal sounds is [+voice]. Sounds that are [+voice] involve the <u>vibration of the vocal cords;</u> all vowel and diphthong sounds are therefore [+voice], as are many consonants—consider the Modern English voiced and voiceless pairs [g/k, z/s, d/t, b/p].

Using these features, one can now attempt a simplified account of the consonantal system in the *Ormulum,* and one can see that the consonantal segments in this text are represented by an orthography that is at pains to keep certain distinctions clear in a way reminiscent of its treatment of the vowel system. We shall begin by postulating certain general feature values ([±sonorant] [±continuant]) for the consonants in Orm's language and then progress to a more detailed description, at the same time making mention of the main differences in this early Middle English system from contemporary usage.

	Orm's Spelling	*Examples*
[—sonorant	<p>, <pp>	<preost> <uppon>
—continuant]	<b>, <bb>	<broþer> <sibb>
	<t>, <tt>	<treo> <sittenn>
	<d>, <dd>	<dede> <biddenn>
	<k>, <c>	<king> <kirrke>
		<seoc> <clene>
		<kinges> <ɡann>

[—sonorant +continuant]	⟨f⟩, ⟨ff⟩	⟨feorr⟩ ⟨offrenn⟩ ⟨ofer⟩ ⟨ofne⟩
	⟨þ⟩, ⟨þþ⟩	⟨muþ⟩ ⟨moneþþ⟩ ⟨broþer⟩ ⟨muþess⟩
	⟨s⟩, ⟨ss⟩	⟨hus⟩ ⟨missdede⟩ ⟨chesen⟩
	⟨sh⟩, ⟨ssh⟩	⟨shame⟩ ⟨nesshe⟩
	⟨ʒh⟩, ⟨h⟩, ⟨hh⟩, ⟨hʒh⟩	⟨sahh⟩ ⟨nahht⟩ ⟨ʒho⟩ ⟨lahhʒhenn⟩ ⟨hus⟩ ⟨hallf⟩
	⟨ch⟩, ⟨cch⟩	⟨chesen⟩ ⟨racchess⟩
	⟨ɡ⟩, ⟨ɡɡ⟩	⟨ɡyn⟩ ⟨biɡɡenn⟩
[+sonorant +continuant +consonantal]	⟨m⟩, ⟨mm⟩	⟨mihht⟩ ⟨kemmpe⟩
	⟨n⟩, ⟨nn⟩	⟨nett⟩ ⟨sinnfull⟩
	⟨l⟩, ⟨ll⟩	⟨libbenn⟩ ⟨follʒhenn⟩
	⟨r⟩, ⟨rr⟩	⟨riche⟩ ⟨þurrh⟩
	⟨ʒ⟩, ⟨ʒʒ⟩	⟨ʒe⟩ ⟨seʒʒde⟩

Orm's orthographic system seems to be one that both conflates and keeps distinct important consonantal phonetic distinctions. He takes care regularly to keep distinct the symbols ⟨ʒ⟩, ⟨ɡ⟩, and ⟨ʒh⟩, since they represent, as can be seen below, consonantal sounds that have a rather different feature makeup from each other. On the other hand, there is evidence to suggest that other feature distinctions, especially that of voice, are not kept apart in the orthography. Although it is true that the sounds [k] and [g], which differ only in their voice feature, are given distinct orthographic representation, this is not true for other similarly distinct segments. For example, the symbols ⟨s⟩ and ⟨ss⟩ are apparently ambiguous as markers of voice, since Orm will use the same symbol in the words ⟨hus⟩ and ⟨þise⟩, even though there is every reason to suppose that two sounds distinguished by the feature of voice existed in his language, as in Modern English. Hart too has the distinction reflected in his orthography—⟨hous⟩, ⟨ðez⟩. Likewise, the symbol ⟨f⟩ is used by Orm to represent both voiced (⟨ofer⟩) and voiceless (⟨for⟩) segments. There seems also to be a rather similar inconsistency in his use of the symbol ⟨h⟩. On some occasions this symbol seems to represent a sound that is voiceless and with the body of the tongue in a neutral position of height, rather like the sound represented by the symbol ⟨h⟩ in some Modern English manifestations of ⟨here⟩ or ⟨her⟩. Instances of this in Orm are ⟨hus⟩ and ⟨hallf⟩. On other occasions, however, the same symbol is used by Orm as an apparent equivalent to ⟨ʒh⟩ or ⟨hʒh⟩, as in

⟨sahh⟩ or ⟨nahht⟩. In these cases the symbol represents a sound that is still to be heard in certain Modern English dialects, especially in Scottish English in such words as ⟨loch⟩ and ⟨Balloch⟩; that is, it is a consonant with the features [+continuant, +high, +back].

On the whole, however, the consonantal spelling system in the *Ormulum,* with the exception of the greater tendency to gemination, is not unlike that found in Modern English. Where there are differences, there seems also to be reason to suspect a corresponding phonological discrepancy. For example, the Modern English words ⟨loud⟩ and ⟨roof⟩ are spelled ⟨lhud⟩ and ⟨rhof⟩ in the *Ormulum.* Since in one of its manifestations the symbol ⟨h⟩ can represent a consonant with the features [+high, +back] (for example, ⟨sahht⟩), it is possible that Orm is trying to indicate that the lateral and retroflex sonorants (which are [−high, −back] in most dialects of Modern English) are to be considered as [+high, +back]. There are, in fact, some British English dialects, especially Northeast English, that still retain such a back or uvular [ʁ] in their phonological systems. It is interesting to note also that Orm uses the symbol [ŋ] in such words as ⟨king⟩ and ⟨brinngenn⟩. This suggests that he did not have the modern sound value for the symbols ⟨ng⟩ in such contexts, the nasal being considerably more fronted than it is today and no assimilation having yet taken place to the position of the following [+high, +back, +voiced, −continuant] consonant.

At this stage a fuller specification of the consonantal sounds in the *Ormulum* can be given based upon the feature convention set out above:

[+sonorant
 +consonantal]

	r	l	m	n
Anterior	−	−	+	+
High	+	+	−	−
Back	+	+	−	−
Nasal	−	−	+	+
Lateral	−	+	−	−

[−sonorant
 +anterior]

	p	b	t	d	f	v	θ	ð	s	z
High	−	−	−	−	−	−	−	−	−	−
Back	−	−	−	−	−	−	−	−	−	−
Voiced	−	+	−	+	−	+	−	+	−	+
Continuant	−	−	−	−	+	+	−	+	−	+

[—sonorant
—anterior]

	k	g	x	h	s	č	ǰ
High	+	+	+	+	—	—	—
Back	+	+	+	+	—	—	—
Voice	—	+	—	—	—	—	+
Continuant	—	—	+	+	+	—	—

There is also another group of sounds that, although they often occur in positions filled by consonants (for example, the initial sounds in the words ⟨yes⟩ and ⟨west⟩), nevertheless share many of the features of vowels; they are sonorants and involve no total stricture in the vocal tract. This group, called *glides,* most often occurs as the second element in diphthongs, that is, combinations of two vowel sounds involving a movement (in the same syllable) from one vowel position to another, as in words like ⟨house⟩, ⟨sight⟩ and ⟨toy⟩. Glides have the following (simplified) feature composition:

[—consonantal
+sonorant]

	w	j
Anterior	—	—
High	+	+
Back	+	—

However, see Anderson and Lass (forthcoming), chapters 1 and 2.

III

Even a brief survey of the kind given above is enough to demonstrate that there have been considerable changes in the English sound system from the time of the *Ormulum.* Many of these changes, especially those involving vowel-heightening and glide addition, seem to have occurred not long before the time of John Hart, but there are others that appear to have come about at a much earlier date. One has only to compare the evidence of the spelling system (supported by information from rhymes) found in many of the Chaucerian manuscripts with that of the *Ormulum* to realize that between 1200 and 1400 many important developments occurred in the English vowel system. Compare, for instance, the following root vocalic variation in data taken from Orm and Chaucer:

Orm	Chaucer
lukke	loke
wuke	wowke
ploh	plough
þohht	thoughte
seȝȝen	seyen

At the same time, there are other important differences between early and late Middle English texts with respect to their phonologies, especially those involving changes in the nature of the vowel in the various syntactic contexts of the "strong" verb (see pp. 77–86). How is one to account for the differences in vowel form in the following examples taken from various periods in Middle English?

Present	Past Singular	Past Plural	Participle
helpe	halp	hulpen	holpen
	help	holpen	hulpen
	holpe	helpen	help
	hulpe	halpen	

The solution to such problems will very much depend on the particular view one takes of the processes involved in both syntactic and phonological changes in language as a whole. Very many suggestions have been put forward in an attempt to account for the phenomenon of sound change. Perhaps the most popular of these has been based upon the idea that phonetic variation is an unconscious process and is brought about by the inability of children to imitate correctly the sounds they hear spoken by their parents. Indeed, owing to differences in the size and shape of the human vocal organs, it is argued, exact reproduction of some "correct" sound system is impossible, so that an infinite variation is set up. The result of this is that there is some unconscious phonetic drift set in progress such that eventually the original system is altered, and some new one takes its place. It has often been proposed that as a result of this drift a chain reaction of change is begun, causing gaps left in the original pattern by the drifting away of certain elements to be filled by other sounds, with the result that the overall nature of the system is retained. For instance, if there is a system of "completely distinct" sounds A, B, and C, then any move or drift by A would allow a corresponding shift in B and C for the sake of preserving the uniqueness of the system. In other words, the sound changes brought into play by the initial movement of A may be motivated by a desire to preserve the symmetry of the original phonological pattern. See Martinet (1955) and King (1969).

This "functional" motivation of sound change has not, however, always readily been accepted, and among alternative theories have been those that suggest the process of sound change to be the result in some way of an (b) articulatory principle involving "ease of articulation." The consequence of this principle is that all "unnecessary" distinctions in the system are dropped, with the result that it becomes more "simple." It is difficult, however, to discover what is meant by terms like "ease" or "necessary" in this context, and the logical conclusion to theories of this type would be the elimination of distinctions of all kinds.

The strongest argument that can be brought to bear against all these theories is that they do not seem to take into account the (small) amount that is known about how language is acquired by children. Notions of phonetic drift caused by some inability to learn sounds precisely are difficult to reconcile with what appears to be the process by which children are able to produce language. It seems that one must not think in terms of language being learned wholly by a process of imitation (perfect or otherwise), but rather note that every child is capable of *constructing for itself* a set of rules that will enable it to produce the set of sounds, as well as the syntax, that it hears uttered by its parents and others, including children. The important thing is that one is dealing with some kind of inductive, rather than purely imitative, process and that the set of rules developed by the child may well be different from that utilized by the adult. In addition, it seems that the child will produce or generate utterances acceptable to others by the simplest possible set of rules. Indeed, there are rules in the parents' grammars that he may not possess in his own. It is by means of this process (or a similar one) that language seems to be acquired and therefore changed. The best summary of this position is Halle's (1962):

> It has been suggested by Chomsky that language acquisition by a child may best be pictured as a process of constructing the simplest (optimal) grammar capable of generating the set of utterances, of which utterances heard by the child are a representative sample. The ability to master a language like a native, which children possess to an extraordinary degree, is almost completely lacking in the adult. I propose to explain this as being due to deterioration or loss in the adult of the ability to construct optimal (simplest) grammars on the basis of a restricted corpus of examples. . . . Since every child constructs his own optimal grammar by induction from the utterances to which he has been exposed, it is not necessary that the child and his parents

have identical grammars, for . . . a given set of utterances can be generated by more than one grammar.   (pp. 64–65)

Although some alterations and additions to these ideas will appear when some of the aspects of linguistic change as it is manifested in Middle English are dealt with, nevertheless Halle's views represent one of the most satisfactory bases so far devised for characterizing the processes of linguistic evolution.

The understanding of these events as they affect the phonology of a language is also helped by a decision to consider sound systems as being composed of "distinctive feature" matrices rather than of units that are completely separate and distinct in themselves. Some of the advantages of this principle in the description and explanation of phonological change can be illustrated by the following hypothetical case. Suppose that a language A has the consonants [p], [f], [s], and [k] at a period Y in its history, and that at some later period Z these consonantal sounds appear in the same contexts as [b], [v], [z], and [g]. It can be said, therefore, that the sound change

$$
\begin{bmatrix} p \\ f \\ s \\ k \end{bmatrix} \longrightarrow \begin{bmatrix} b \\ v \\ z \\ g \end{bmatrix}
$$

has taken place. However, to present the sound change in this way is not only uneconomical (involving four separate statements), but it also obscures an underlying generalization. Let us consider (in a simplified way) the distinctive feature composition of the sounds involved.

	p	b	f	v	s	z	k	g
Anterior	+	+	+	+	+	+	−	−
Back	−	−	−	−	−	−	+	+
Voiced	−	+	−	+	−	+	−	+
Continuant	−	−	−	−	−	−	−	−

What is immediately obvious from this kind of approach is that the sounds of period Y do not undergo some "complete" or "total" change by the time of period Z. Nor, perhaps more important, do they each undergo a different kind of change. To treat these sounds other than as feature complexes obscures both these points. The change involved from period Y to period Z in language A can, therefore, be stated as follows:

$$\begin{bmatrix} -\text{voc} \\ +\text{cons} \\ -\text{sonorant} \end{bmatrix} \longrightarrow [+\text{voice}]$$

This rule shows that far from there being four separate sound changes involved in language A, there is merely the addition of one rule to its grammar, namely, that nonsonorant voiceless consonants acquire the feature of voice. At the same time, it is possible to state the environments in which phonological rules occur. Were the voicing addition rule sensitive to the context *between vowels* (that is, the given consonants become voiced only when they appear between two vocalic segments), then the rule could be expanded to:

non-sonorant consonant adds voice / *between consonants*

$$\begin{bmatrix} -\text{voc} \\ +\text{cons} \\ -\text{son} \end{bmatrix} \longrightarrow [+\text{voice}] \Bigg/ \begin{bmatrix} +\text{voc} \\ -\text{cons} \end{bmatrix} \underline{\hspace{2cm}} \begin{bmatrix} +\text{voc} \\ -\text{cons} \end{bmatrix}$$

This *context-sensitive* (CS) rule will be referred to again below under the name *intervocalic consonantal voicing*.

Utilizing as far as possible the principles of generative phonology, the rest of this chapter will examine some of the more important sound changes associated with Middle English. It must be stressed that, as before, the account given here will fall far short of the fully detailed and will therefore be of only a limited descriptive adequacy. Consider the following data:

Orm	Chaucer	Hart	Modern English
fend	feend	——	fiend
feld	feeld	——	field
findenn	finde	feind	find
kinde	kinde	keind	kind
child	child	tʃeild	child
bundenn	bounden	bound	bound
grund	ground	ground	ground
hund	hound	hound	hound

A comparison of the forms in the *Ormulum* with those in either Chaucer or Hart shows that one or more things are happening. Either the Orm vowel is represented in these later texts by a double vowel or it is manifested by what looks from the orthography to have been a diphthong. Although the spelling is not always explicit, one might suggest that two major developments take place between the above root vocalic segments. The first is that the feature of [+long] seems to be added to some of the *Ormulum* vowels, while in other cases this lengthening seems already to have taken place and (since high vowels are involved) *glide addition* and *vowel-lowering* rules applied (see pp. 59–60 above). As suggested earlier, the two sets of changes are related and the rules for vowel-lengthening not only preceded the other two, but, when high vowels were involved, were a necessary condition for their application. It should be noticed that the short vowels in the *Ormulum* data become long in the same kind of phonological contexts, that is, before the segment clusters represented by and orthographic ⟨nd⟩ and ⟨ld⟩. In short, lengthening takes place in the following context:

$$
\underline{\hspace{2cm}} \left[\begin{array}{l} -\text{voc} \\ +\text{cons} \\ +\text{son} \end{array} \right] \left[\begin{array}{l} -\text{voc} \\ +\text{cons} \\ -\text{son} \\ -\text{continuant} \end{array} \right]
$$

Since all vowels are automatically sonorant, it may be the case that the addition of a [+length] feature stems from the proximity of two segments carrying a [+sonorant] feature. It is also interesting to point out that this lengthening is restricted to those vowels in the *Ormulum* that are [+tense]. Compare, for example, the Modern English equivalents of Orm's ⟨hund⟩ and ⟨hunndred⟩. This scribe's orthographic method is usually careful to distinguish those vowels that later undergo lengthening from those that do not by the absence with the former of any following geminate consonantal symbols. In other words, Orm's orthographic method in this instance does not reflect the superficial phonetic difference between the tense and lax vowels, since both have the identical symbol ⟨u⟩. Rather, Orm appears to be representing the shape of these words at a more abstract level in the grammar, in other words, the shape they would have in its *lexicon* (Chomsky and Halle [1968], pp. 43–50). If the rules for tensing and lengthening occur only in special phonological contexts, simplified here to the environment of preceding only certain kinds of consonantal clusters, and failing before geminate consonant segments, then one has to propose an abstract representation of ⟨hound⟩ as [hund] and ⟨hundred⟩ as [hunndred], to ensure that tensing and lengthening rules will not apply to the latter. Compare the following derivations:

Input	[hund]	[hunndred]
1. Tensing rule	ū	inoperative
2. Lengthening rule	ūu	inoperative
3. Glide-addition rule	ūw	inoperative
4. Vowel-lowering	ōw	inoperative
Output	[ōw]	[u]

The output of this derivation corresponds to the situation in Hart's time; rules 3 and 4 had not been added to the grammar of English in Chaucer's lifetime. There would, of course, have to be a further rule deleting one of the geminate consonants of [hunndred], as well as a later, modern rule to effect the change from [u] to [ʌ]. In such instances as the above, Orm's spelling system appears to denote something that corresponded to the lexical representation of words, rather than the way they superficially appear as output of a derivation, once general phonological rules have been applied to their elements.

Another indication that the *lengthening rule* had not taken place in Orm's grammar is his frequent use of a superscripted single or double accent mark that seems to denote vowel length, as in ⟨ʒet⟩ and ⟨mót⟩. This symbol does not appear with reference to vowels lengthened by Chaucer's time before the consonant clusters described above. It is also worth mentioning that the feature of tenseness characteristic of the vowels that later undergo changes in their length seems itself to have been added to the grammar of English not long before 1200. Certainly, the majority of these vowels appear to have been [—tense] in Old English. A tentative statement of this first of the *lengthening rules* to be considered is as follows:

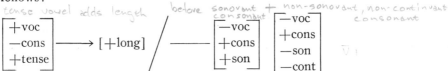

$$
\begin{bmatrix} +\text{voc} \\ -\text{cons} \\ +\text{tense} \end{bmatrix} \longrightarrow [+\text{long}] \Bigg/ \underline{\hphantom{xxx}} \begin{bmatrix} -\text{voc} \\ +\text{cons} \\ +\text{son} \end{bmatrix} \begin{bmatrix} -\text{voc} \\ +\text{cons} \\ -\text{son} \\ -\text{cont} \end{bmatrix}
$$

This rule states that the feature of length is added to vowels whenever they occur in the context (/) of coming before two consonants ($\underline{\hphantom{xx}}C_2^2$) with the given feature makeup. There are, however, some restrictions as well as possible additions that one must impose upon this rule. In the first place, the rule is operative only when the context is $V + C_2^2$; that is, two, and only two, consonants with the above feature pattern can follow the vowel for lengthening to take place. One can see this by comparing the vowels in the Modern English words ⟨child⟩ and ⟨children⟩. It is perhaps likely also that the vowel has the feature [—tense] in contexts where it is followed by more than two consonants, since Orm gives a spelling ⟨chilldre⟩ (involving a geminate letter for the sonorant, which probably implies lack of tenseness in the preceding vocalic segment) in the possessive plural of the noun ⟨child⟩. At the same time, the rule is rather more general in its application than the examples that have so far been provided. It states that *all* sonorant consonants after the vocalic segment will fulfill the context requirements for lengthening to take place, and not merely the nasal and the lateral. There may, in fact, be some justification, at least in the case of some Middle English dialects, for leaving the rule in this rather general form, since Modern English words such as ⟨climb⟩ and ⟨forth⟩ (Orm's ⟨climben⟩ and ⟨forrþ⟩) have vocalic segments apparently derived from underlying tense and long forms.

On the other hand, Orm's spelling ⟨king⟩, with a tense [i], would suggest that this segment should undergo the later lengthening and other rules—compare the spelling ⟨brinngenn⟩ also in the *Ormulum*. Either the scribe's spelling habits are inconsistent, or the first lengthening rule must be emended to exclude second consonantal segments with a [+back] feature, since the vowel in Modern English ⟨king⟩ is lax and short in nearly all dialects. Alternatively, but less likely, it could be suggested that ⟨king⟩ be allowed to develop a tense vowel, later lengthened, but at some later stage in English these rules are then deleted for this and other similar lexical formatives.

There is also evidence that a second lengthening rule was added to the grammar of Middle English. Compare the following spellings of Orm and Hart—⟨tăkenn/tāk⟩, ⟨lăte/lāt⟩, ⟨măkenn/māk⟩. The first vocalic segments in the samples from Orm appear to have the feature [−long], overtly marked by the superscripted accent ˘. Hart, on the other hand, uses a mark that signifies both length and tenseness, and the latter is also characteristic of the vowels in Orm's phonology, since he does not write geminate consonants after them. The context of this second lengthening rule is well-defined. Unlike the first rule adding length, the environment is not of the type ———C_2^2, but one where the lengthened vocalic segment appears preceding a single consonant followed by another vowel. The second lengthening rule:

$$\begin{bmatrix} +\text{voc} \\ -\text{cons} \\ +\text{tense} \end{bmatrix} \longrightarrow [+\text{long}] \Big/ \underline{\quad} \begin{bmatrix} -\text{voc} \\ +\text{cons} \end{bmatrix} \begin{bmatrix} +\text{voc} \\ -\text{cons} \end{bmatrix}$$

$\bar{V} + CV \rightarrow \bar{V}: + CV$

It is important to stress that these rules will only function in the given contexts, since in environments where the tense vowel is followed by C_2^2 not fulfilling the stipulations for consonant clusters of the first lengthening rule, or where the C_2^2 is a geminate, no lengthening takes place. A good example of the rules and the restrictions upon them, as well as of some of the principles of orthographic representation, can be had from a comparison of the derivations of the [±singular] ⟨staff⟩ and ⟨staves⟩ in contemporary English. In the grammar of Modern English, the root vowels of these words are derived from the same underlying vowel in different phonological contexts:

Input	[stæff]	[stæfe]
1. Tensing rule	inoperative	ǣ
2. Lengthening rule	inoperative	ǣæ
3. Glide-addition rule	inoperative	ǣj
4. Vowel-raising	inoperative	ēj
5. Intervocalic consonantal voicing (p. 70 above)	inoperative	v
Output	[stæf]	[stējv]

The final output also assumes the operation of two other rules, one delet-ing the second of two identical consonantal segments, the other deleting the final [e] necessary in the abstract representation for the functioning of rule 5. The presence of two underlying forms in the singular and plural of this formative for some modern dialects probably reflects the existence in distinct geographical dialects in Middle English of two separate formatives [stæff] and [stæfe], each with its respective singular and plural outputs.

As they stand, however, both lengthening rules will still fail to ac-count for some important differences between the phonology of the *Or-mulum* and that of later Middle English. For example, one finds that vowels which are [+high] will behave rather differently, *in the same kind of context,* from their nonhigh counterparts. Consider, for instance, the spellings ⟨luke⟩, ⟨wuke⟩, and ⟨bule⟩ in the *Ormulum* against their mani-festation in Chaucer—⟨loke⟩, ⟨wowke⟩, and ⟨bole⟩. At the same time, the high front vowel in Orm's spelling of the word ⟨wicke⟩ (Modern English ⟨weak⟩) appears in Hart as ⟨uēk⟩, and Orm's ⟨ifell⟩ can be realized in later Middle English spellings as ⟨euel⟩. In these instances the second lengthening rule must have an additional feature added to it, in order to assign one degree of lowering to high vocalic segments:

$$
\begin{bmatrix} +\text{voc} \\ -\text{cons} \\ +\text{high} \end{bmatrix} \longrightarrow \begin{bmatrix} -\text{high} \\ -\text{low} \\ +\text{long} \end{bmatrix} \Big/ \underline{\qquad} \begin{bmatrix} -\text{voc} \\ +\text{cons} \end{bmatrix} \begin{bmatrix} +\text{voc} \\ -\text{cons} \end{bmatrix}
$$

This rule, however, may have a different distribution from the length-ening rules involving nonhigh vocalic segments, since it seems to have been introduced at a later date than the latter and was at first apparently re-stricted to specific geographical dialects, notably those in the North and East Midlands. The significance of temporal and dialectally conditioned rules and the relationship they bear to the "more general" type of rules will be discussed in more detail in Chapter Six.

The last rule given above is often referred to in textbooks as *length-ening in open syllables.* This nomenclature is very often misleading, since it can conceal the fact that more than vowel length is involved in the change. At the same time, lengthening in a context such as ———$V + C_1^1$ $+ V$ appears to be different in kind from that in which vowels added a length feature in the environment of two specified consonantal segments. Nevertheless, such a difference may be only superficial, since the necessity of including in a phonological theory such suprasegmental features as the syllable and even apparently nonsegmental features as the word boundary will be further illustrated in Chapter Five.

It was suggested above (p. 61) that the sound system we find in the *Ormulum* may have contained no diphthongs. Bearing this in mind, let us consider the following items in the *Ormulum* and those that correspond to them in Chaucer and in some Southern British English dialects of the present day:

Orm	*Chaucer*	*Modern English*
draȝhen	drawen	draw
laȝhe	lawe	law
aȝhenn	owe	owe

In the examples from the *Ormulum* there would appear to be a $V + C$ combination with segments having the following feature makeup:

whereas, in the Middle and Modern English examples, we have a post-vocalic segment with a set of features as:

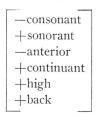

In other words, the nonsonorant back consonant in the *Ormulum* has, by the time of Chaucer (and probably some considerable time before), changed into a nonconsonantal sonorant, that is, a *glide*. It is interesting to notice too that this glide shares the feature of [+back] with the consonant it has "displaced," so that <u>all that is involved in the change from</u> <u>vowel + consonant to vowel + glide in these words is the feature of</u> [±sonorant]. One can, therefore, write the following rule to account for this Middle English sound change:

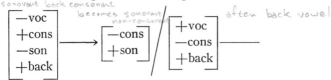

$$\begin{bmatrix} -\text{voc} \\ +\text{cons} \\ -\text{son} \\ +\text{back} \end{bmatrix} \longrightarrow \begin{bmatrix} -\text{cons} \\ +\text{son} \end{bmatrix} / \begin{bmatrix} +\text{voc} \\ -\text{cons} \\ +\text{back} \end{bmatrix} \underline{\quad\quad}$$

(handwritten annotations: non-sonorant back consonant / becomes sonorant, non-consonant / after back vowel)

The situation is, however, further complicated when one compares the following examples in the *Ormulum* with their equivalents in later Middle English and Modern English:

Orm	Later Middle English	Modern English
fleȝhenn	fleyen	fly
tweȝȝen	tweien	"poetic" twain
weȝȝe	wey	way

Here one has vowel and consonantal segments in the *Ormulum* with a feature makeup:

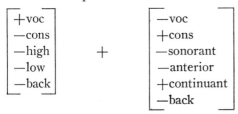

$$\begin{bmatrix} +\text{voc} \\ -\text{cons} \\ -\text{high} \\ -\text{low} \\ -\text{back} \end{bmatrix} \quad + \quad \begin{bmatrix} -\text{voc} \\ +\text{cons} \\ -\text{sonorant} \\ -\text{anterior} \\ +\text{continuant} \\ -\text{back} \end{bmatrix}$$

whereas the later postvocalic segment seems to be the glide

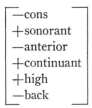

$$\begin{bmatrix} -\text{cons} \\ +\text{sonorant} \\ -\text{anterior} \\ +\text{continuant} \\ +\text{high} \\ -\text{back} \end{bmatrix}$$

Therefore, one can say, as with the earlier set of examples given above, that <u>the postvocalic segment has changed to [+sonorant]</u>, but one can add that <u>in both cases the degree of backness of the glide is the same as the degree</u> <u>of backness of the vocalic segment itself.</u> In consequence, one can account for both sets of examples by means of a single rule, which will state that <u>in the Middle English period nonsonorant consonants in postvocalic</u> <u>segments became sonorant and nonconsonantal and that the resultant</u> <u>glide was in backness harmony with the preceding vocalic segment.</u> This rule might take the form:

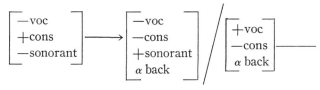

The result of this rule is that there are no longer two unrelated segments made up of V + C, but rather two almost identical segments—V + glide.

It must be remembered, however, that such rules are, if anything, an oversimplification of the sound changes involved in the Middle English period. It is possible that spellings such as ⟨dæwe⟩, ⟨daȝȝ⟩, and ⟨maȝȝden⟩ (with their apparent contradiction of the backness harmony principle) suggest that, at least in some contexts, diphthongs were already a feature of the phonology of the *Ormulum*.

The last issue to be discussed in this chapter concerns certain aspects of the phonology of the Middle English verb and the changes that it underwent. This topic is again an ideal one, since a consideration of it will not only illustrate the phonological principles so far utilized, but it will also enable some additional characteristics to be added to those principles. Also, the aspect of verb phonology chosen is an excellent example for the student concerned with the description, direction, and motivation of linguistic change.

As will be seen again in Chapter Five, tense can be marked in the English verb at all periods in its history by means of a contrast between the root vowel of the present and past forms. <u>The variation involved often</u> <u>takes the form of an opposition between vocalic segments with the features</u> <u>[+high, +front], and those that are [−high, −front] or [−high, −low,</u> <u>−front].</u> Examples are the contrasting vowels in such verbs as ⟨sit/sat⟩, ⟨see/saw⟩, ⟨sing/sang⟩, and many others. Verbs forming tense distinctions in this way are traditionally referred to as *strong* verbs, as against *weak* types that show past-nonpast contrasts by the addition of a dental inflection to the verb "stem," as in ⟨look/looked⟩ and ⟨touch/touched⟩. In the majority of Middle English grammars, verbs of the strong variety are classified into types or classes according to the nature of the vowel change involved between present and past tenses. For example, in Middle English the following five (out of as many as seven) classes are often distinguished:

Class	Pres	Pret$_1$	Pret$_2$	Part
_1_	dryve	dro(o)f	dryve(n)	ydryven
_2_	chese	ches	chusen	chosen
_3_	binde	band	bunden	bunden
	helpe	halp	hulpen	holpen
_4_	bere	bar	beren	boren
_5_	bidden	bad	beden	ibede

[margin note: ME strong verbs cf. 171 ff.]

A number of points can be briefly made here about this deliberately very mixed set of forms. It is unlike many instances in Modern English, for there is a tendency toward vowel variation in three, rather than two, distinct contexts. Indeed, there are examples where four vocalic contrasts are used. Consequently, we shall examine the behavior of the vocalic segment in the contexts *Pres*(ent) tense (although this will have to be made more explicit later) ; *Pret*(erite)$_1$, the past tense in the singular ; *Pret*(erite)$_2$, the past tense in the plural ; and the *Past Part*(iciple). A modification must now be made of the earlier statement to the effect that this vowel variation was only a means of realizing tense differences, since it is also used (in the case of *Pret*$_1$ and *Pret*$_2$) to indicate a number contrast. It must also be mentioned at this point, and this will prove to be very important, that the forms given above for the five strong classes are in an extremely generalized and even oversimplified form. Later in the discussion it will be seen that, especially in later Middle English, and particularly in its geographical dialects, there are many instances where vowels, restricted in the above data in a given class to *Pret*$_1$, can also appear in *Pret*$_2$ and *Part,* and vice versa.

From almost any point of view, the multitude of vowel alternants in the Middle English strong verb system look quite haphazard and do not seem to bear any systematic resemblance to each other. For instance, the vowel of the *Pres* form can be spelled either as ⟨y⟩, ⟨e⟩, or ⟨i⟩ ; of *Pret*$_1$ as ⟨o⟩, ⟨e⟩, or ⟨a⟩ ; of *Pret*$_2$ as ⟨y⟩, ⟨u⟩, or ⟨e⟩ ; and of *Part* as ⟨y⟩, ⟨o⟩, ⟨u⟩, and ⟨e⟩. To all intents and purposes, the chosen vowel in any given case appears to be quite arbitrary, and there seems little point in trying to predict which one will occur by means of a rule. The situation, however, looks rather more arbitrary than it actually is ; and although there appears to be a considerable amount of variation in the superficial manifestation of the vowels, they may in fact all derive from one underlying form that undergoes predictable changes in appearance in specified contexts. In other words, it is possible to dispense with the traditional idea of five or seven different classes of strong verbs entirely and to suggest instead that only one vowel is involved and that this will be given a surface or superficial appearance according to the surroundings (both syntactic and phonological) in which it appears. In this way, instead of having to deal with what seem to be rather random vowel variations, one can say that the same vowel is involved in each case, that this vowel undergoes changes in its feature composition that one can describe by means of a set of *context-sensitive* (CS) rules, and that these rules will enable one (and presumably the Middle English native speaker) to generate or predict the appropriate and "grammatical" superficial form of the underlying common vowel.

Although it is not possible to give anything like a fully detailed account of these phenomena here, one can attempt at least a very simplified reconstruction of some of the major principles that are involved. Let us assume, for example, that the underlying vocalic segment common to all the so-called classes and tense and number types is

$$\begin{bmatrix} +\text{vocalic} \\ -\text{consonantal} \end{bmatrix}$$

and nothing else. One can now propose the following rule, which will generate some of the appropriate surface or superficial vowel forms in the *Pres:*

$$\begin{bmatrix} +\text{voc} \\ -\text{cons} \end{bmatrix} \longrightarrow \begin{bmatrix} -\text{high} \\ -\text{low} \\ -\text{back} \end{bmatrix} \Big/ \begin{bmatrix} \quad\quad \\ Pres \end{bmatrix}$$

This rule states that the underlying vocalic segment will appear in its superficial or surface manifestation as front and mid whenever it is found in the syntactic context of present tense in strong verbs. (For a discussion of the role of *readjustment rules* in incorporating "features" such as the *strong verb* into the lexicon, see Chomsky and Halle [1968], pp. 10–11; and for the underlying vowels in ⟨chese⟩ and ⟨dryve⟩, see Chapter Five, pp. 173–174, below.) But, if this is indeed the case, how is one to account for such present tense forms (for example, in the traditional Class 3 verbs) as ⟨binde⟩ and ⟨finde⟩? The ⟨i⟩ spelling of the underlying vowel only occurs, however, when certain phonological conditions are fulfilled; that is, when the root vowel segment is immediately followed by a nasal sonorant. To account for the realization of the superficial root vowel in this context, the following rule must be added to the grammar:

$$\begin{bmatrix} +\text{voc} \\ -\text{cons} \\ -\text{high} \\ -\text{low} \end{bmatrix} \longrightarrow [+\text{high}] \Big/ \underline{\quad\quad} [+\text{nasal}]$$

As will become evident, this *nasal-raising rule* has a rather wide application in the grammar as a whole, so that at this point no reference is made to either the backness coefficient or the syntactic context of the root vowel.

The implication of what has been said so far (see Anderson [1971]) is that at an abstract level of representation in the grammar of Middle English, the root vowel of strong verbs was *unspecified* or *neutral* as regards features height, backness, and others, and that all its superficially complex realizations are the result of later, general phonological rules. As a very simple case, consider the derivation of the *Pres* forms of the Middle English verbs for ⟨to bind⟩ and ⟨to carry⟩. The symbol V stands for the unspecified vowel as it appears in the lexicon:

Input	[bVnd-]	[bVr-]
1. Present-tense rule	e	e
2. Nasal-raising rule	ɪ	inoperative
Output	[bɪnd-]	[ber-]

A more sophisticated grammar might also be able to dispense with syntactic-type rules like 1, and to replace them with phonological rules like 2. The above rules must clearly apply in the order given if the correct derivation is to be achieved.

A discussion of the other present-tense forms with root vowels orthographically represented by ⟨i⟩, but not occurring in a prenasal context, such as ⟨driven⟩ and ⟨writen⟩, must wait until Chapter Five. The $Pret_1$ vowel segment forms can, however, be produced by means of the following (simplified) syntactical rule:

$$\begin{bmatrix} +\text{voc} \\ -\text{cons} \end{bmatrix} \longrightarrow \begin{bmatrix} +\text{low} \\ +\text{back} \end{bmatrix} \Big/ \begin{bmatrix} \rule{1.5em}{0.4pt} \\ Pret_1 \end{bmatrix}$$

that is, in the past tense singular of the strong verb, the root vocalic segment is realized superficially as low and back. To this rule also, of course, there are apparent exceptions, such as ⟨chose⟩ and ⟨drof⟩, but, as will be seen, these surface forms can also be generated by the application of general phonological rules to an unspecified vocalic abstract segment.

The rules that will realize the correct superficial vowel in the stem of the $Pret_2$ and *Part* forms are rather complex, and the following remarks have reference only to the traditional Classes 2 and 3—⟨chusen/chosen⟩ and ⟨hulpen/holpen⟩. The variation between [u] and [o] in these syntactic contexts can be predicted by the inclusion in the grammar of the two rules:

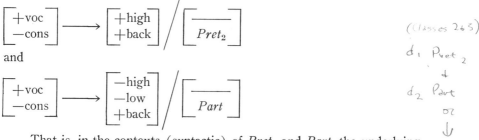

$$\begin{bmatrix} +\text{voc} \\ -\text{cons} \end{bmatrix} \longrightarrow \begin{bmatrix} +\text{high} \\ +\text{back} \end{bmatrix} \bigg/ \begin{bmatrix} \underline{\hspace{1em}} \\ Pret_2 \end{bmatrix}$$

and

$$\begin{bmatrix} +\text{voc} \\ -\text{cons} \end{bmatrix} \longrightarrow \begin{bmatrix} -\text{high} \\ -\text{low} \\ +\text{back} \end{bmatrix} \bigg/ \begin{bmatrix} \underline{\hspace{1em}} \\ Part \end{bmatrix}$$

That is, in the contexts (syntactic) of *Pret₂* and *Part*, the underlying, unspecified vowel will be characterized as [+back] and either as [+high] or [−high, −low]. It may be possible, however, to express the vocalic variation in terms, not of a syntactic, but of a phonological context that is no longer apparent at the superficial level of the language. If the *Pret₂*- and *Part*-forming suffixes ‹on› and ‹en› are taken as having the (simplified) underlying shapes [un] and [on] respectively, then a phonological motivation for the root vowel preceding these suffixes can be postulated. There is, in fact, evidence from languages such as Gothic suggesting that these underlying representations are correct. If they are, then the variation [u]/[o] in the back vowel root configuration can be predicted according to the shape of the vowel following them—a process of vowel-height assimilation. Thus

$$\begin{bmatrix} +\text{voc} \\ -\text{cons} \end{bmatrix} \longrightarrow \begin{bmatrix} +\text{high} \\ +\text{back} \end{bmatrix} \bigg/ \longrightarrow C_2^2 \begin{bmatrix} +\text{high} \\ +\text{back} \end{bmatrix}$$

and

$$\begin{bmatrix} +\text{voc} \\ -\text{cons} \end{bmatrix} \longrightarrow \begin{bmatrix} -\text{high} \\ -\text{low} \\ +\text{back} \end{bmatrix} \bigg/ \longrightarrow C_2^2 \begin{bmatrix} -\text{high} \\ -\text{low} \\ +\text{back} \end{bmatrix}$$

Alternatively, these two rules can be collapsed into the single *vowel-height-assimilation* rule:

$$\begin{bmatrix} +\text{voc} \\ -\text{cons} \end{bmatrix} \longrightarrow [\alpha\text{high}] \bigg/ \underline{\hspace{2em}} C_2^2 \ [\alpha\text{high}]$$

The coefficient of backness is omitted on purpose, since it will be shown that this rule has a wider degree of application than only to back vowels.

If, as the *vowel-height-assimilation* rule suggests, the degree of height of the root vocalic segment can be predicted from the height of the vowel in the following suffix, it is at first puzzling to find such an obvious counter-example as the *Part* ‹bunden›. The failure of this *Part* vowel to be manifested as the expected [−high, −low] height can, however, be easily explained in terms of a wider application of the *nasal-raising* rule. Before the nasal segment in *Part,* the mid-vowel [o] is raised to [u] and can then, like its *Pret₂* counterpart, undergo lengthening, glide addition, and vowel-lowering, to give the later Middle English ⟨bounden⟩ form. A much simplified derivation of the following Class 3 *Pret₂* and *Part* forms demonstrates the phonological rules that relate to the production of their root vowels:

Input	[hVlpun]	[hVlpon]	[bVndun]	[bVndon]
Rule 1.				
Vowel-height-				
assimilation	u	o	u	o
Rule 2.				
Nasal-raising	inoperative	inoperative	inoperative	u
Output	[hulp-]	[holp-]	[bund-]	[bund-]

Other rules are, of course, needed to give an appropriate Middle English shape to the vowels of the suffix; and the above outputs can act, where appropriate, as inputs to such rules as lengthening, glide addition, and vowel-raising and vowel-lowering.

This brief account still leaves, of course, many features of the five strong verb class samples totally unexplained, although more details will be added in Chapter Five. Before going on to consider typical Middle English "modifications" to the vowel variation in strong verbs, one can try to account for yet one other rather obvious exception to the rules so far given. In Class 5, unlike its equivalents in Classes 2–4, the vocalic segment of the *Part* form is characterized by its having the features [−high, −low, −back], for instance, ⟨ibede⟩. At first sight, there seems no motivation for this unique feature composition, but, in fact, verbs of Class 5 do have a first-syllable vowel in an idiosyncratic context, and correspondingly its superficial shape can be predicted from the phonological features of its environment. In this class, the first-syllable vowel occurs before a segment that is a "true" consonant. In all other classes, the root vowel is followed either by a nonvowel sonorant (a liquid or a nasal), for example, ⟨bunden⟩, ⟨holpen⟩, or as will be seen in Chapter Five, by another vowel, as in ⟨chesen⟩:

Classes 1 and 2:   root V + [+voc, −cons]
Classes 3 and 4:   root V + [−voc, +cons, +son]
Class 5:   root V + [−voc, +cons, −son]

Perhaps one of the best reasons for a study of vowel variation in the Middle English strong verb lies in the light it can shed upon the processes involved in sound change. It was suggested above that at present the most acceptable account of sound (and syntactic) change was that which was closely allied to such theories as exist about language acquisition. Since children do not (at least on all occasions) seem to "learn by rote" the language to which they are subjected, it would seem that they can make up their own grammar to account for the material they hear; and, it is argued, this grammar will be the *simplest* grammar possible and may therefore contain fewer rules than the different grammars of the child's parents. It is difficult to test directly the validity of these notions by the examination of one or two sound changes in a given language, but nevertheless one can perhaps show that at least something like this process will be the best way of accounting for some of the differences between early and later Middle English phonologies.

As already stressed, the examples given above of Middle English strong verb classes represent a greatly oversimplified picture. This is especially true if one looks at examples from texts that come after 1300, for strong verbs in these often show vowel variation rather different from equivalent forms in earlier texts. Let us consider, for example, some examples of Classes 2, 3, and 4 (again in a simplified form) in later Middle English:

Class	Pres	Pret₁	Pret₂	Part
2	chese	ches	chosen chusen	chosen
3	helpe	halp	hulpen holpen	holpen
4	bere	bar	boren	boren

What seems to be happening here is that there is no longer any distinction being made between the vowels of the *Pret₂* and the *Part* forms. It seems that some process of rule simplification may have taken place. In other words, the grammar of native speakers for the language in which these forms are to be found does not contain one of the rules

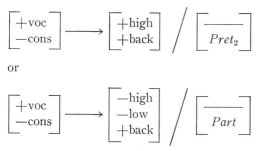

or

nor, by definition, does it contain the vowel-harmony rule that, as suggested above, underlay these two syntactically context-sensitive rules:

$$\begin{bmatrix} +\text{voc} \\ -\text{cons} \end{bmatrix} \longrightarrow [\alpha\text{high}] \ \Big/ \ \underline{\hspace{1cm}} \ C_2^2 \ [\alpha\text{high}]$$

In the later Middle English examples, there is a situation where one can say either that the vowel-harmony rule has been deleted from the grammar (and this is a point to be returned to) or that the CS $Pret_2$ and $Part$ rules have been collapsed into one:

$$\begin{bmatrix} +\text{voc} \\ -\text{cons} \end{bmatrix} \longrightarrow \begin{bmatrix} -\text{high} \\ -\text{low} \\ +\text{back} \end{bmatrix} \ \Big/ \ \begin{bmatrix} \underline{\hspace{1cm}} \\ Pret_2 \\ Part \end{bmatrix}$$

or

$$\begin{bmatrix} +\text{voc} \\ -\text{cons} \end{bmatrix} \longrightarrow \begin{bmatrix} +\text{high} \\ +\text{back} \end{bmatrix} \ \Big/ \ \begin{bmatrix} \underline{\hspace{1cm}} \\ Pret_2 \\ Part \end{bmatrix}$$

One must add, however, that the collapsed rules given above are not used indiscriminately in later Middle English. The rule collapse in favor of the [+high] solution is a feature of Northern Middle English dialects, but the other, which has [−high, −low] vowels in these two syntactic contexts, is more common in Midland and Southern geographical areas. The question might be asked at this point as to why people acquiring Middle English and using the same simplification process should choose to select one rule deletion in one area of the country and another in a different area. To this question there is as yet no satisfactory answer, although there is no reason to suppose that the choice was a completely random one. It may have been that the selection of the [+high] vowel in Northern dialects was motivated by the contrast that this feature provided in the phonology as a whole, whereas in the context of the vowel systems of other dialects, it may be that the features [−high, −low] were regarded as more marked.

The deletion from the grammar of the *vowel-height-assimilation* rule, a process perhaps begun as an idiosyncratic feature of isolated speakers, and only become more general over several generations, has important consequences in other areas as well. When this rule was formulated for the first time (see pp. 80–81 above), it was made sufficiently general not to be restricted to the environments of $Pret_2$ and $Part$. In fact, the same rule can be used to account for a vowel alternation in the Middle English verb system that at first sight seems to be completely unrelated to the vocalic contrasts involved in verbal ablaut. It is characteristic of Middle English, especially in manuscripts written during its early stages, that there is a contrast in height between the vowel segment in the root of the *Pres* first- and other-person singular forms. Compare, for example, the stem vowel in the following early Middle English forms:

Pres first	*Pres* third
bere	birð
breke	brikith
fle(e)	fliþ

Here, as well as in those instances involving second-person forms, is a situation employing the rule:

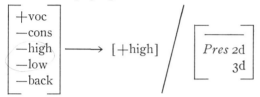

The raising rule seems, at first sight, to be unrelated to any kind of vowel-height assimilation, until one realizes that the inflectional endings of the *Pres* second and third (variously spelled in Middle English as ⟨est⟩, ⟨ist⟩, ⟨st⟩, and ⟨eth⟩, ⟨ith⟩, ⟨eþ⟩, or ⟨iþ⟩) have an underlying [+high, +front] vowel, and were apparently [ist] and [iθ] at some stage of English prior to Anglo-Saxon. The result is that in those instances where a root vowel precedes an (underlying) inflectional vowel with a [+high] feature, vowel-height assimilation occurs; and the stem vowel takes the feature of [+high] also. On the other hand, the presence of a [−high] underlying inflectional vowel acts to block this assimilation. This process, part of a larger tendency traditionally referred to as *i-mutation,* was very widespread in early, especially Old, English. Compare, for example, the difference in root vocalic segments between such pairs as ⟨man/men⟩, ⟨goose/geese⟩, and ⟨foot/feet⟩ in both Middle (with different orthographic representation) and Modern English. Underlying such plurals are (simplified) configurations such as [mæniz], [gosiz], and [fotiz], so that, in the context of coming before a following high front vowel, the singular stem vowel alternates as:

$$\ddot{u} \leftarrow u$$
$$e \longleftarrow o$$
$$\uparrow$$
$$æ$$

The fronting of the high back vowel [u] to [ü] is attested in such an Old and Middle English third-person singular present indicative spelling as ⟨cymð⟩ of the verb ⟨cuman⟩ or ⟨comen⟩, ⟨to come⟩.

Such spellings as

Pres first	*Pres* third
breke	breketh
bere	bereth
flee	fleþ

found in late Middle English suggest that there has been a rule collapse or deletion of the type already suggested for the *Pret₂* and *Part* forms. Indeed, there is evidence to suggest that the rule deletion or simplification may have taken place in the first instance in the *Pres* context only. The question remains as to why such a rule deletion should have taken place at all and at these particular points in the grammar and not at others; for example, why not also in the [±singular] contrast in words like ⟨man/men⟩, ⟨foot/feet⟩?

Totally convincing answers to these questions are difficult to find; nevertheless, one can tentatively suggest two possible motivations. The first is that phonological change may be more likely to occur in contexts where a phonologically context-sensitive rule no longer can be recovered from the superficial structure. In other words, the motivation for a vowel-harmony rule, for example, may have been clear to a child acquiring a language when the distinction between [+high] and [—high, —low] vowels was still present in the surface inflectional forms; that is, when *Pret₂* and *Part* were realized as *⟨hulpun⟩ and *⟨holpon⟩. However, by the time of Middle English, such "motivation" is no longer present (⟨hulpen/holpen⟩), so that a child acquiring the language may see no "reason" to retain the distinction. One, of course, begs the question by talking about motivations and "reasons"; but, and this may be a second motivation for rule deletions of this kind, a child making for itself a grammar on the basis of rather random information may feel that the syntactic distinction between *Pret₂* and *Part* or *Pres* first and *Pres* third is sufficiently marked by other devices in the grammar (for example, by the use of distinct pronouns for number and person) to warrant the deletion of what seems an "unnecessary" redundancy. Still, it is difficult to know on what basis such judgments as "unnecessary" and "redundant" are made; and at the same time there appears to be evidence for a countertendency to have such elements retained in the grammar regardless of any "logic" that might suggest their deletion.

BIBLIOGRAPHY *

Spellings and Sounds

ABERCROMBIE, D., "The Visual Symbolization of Speech," *Proceedings, International Shorthand Congress,* 1938.

BERRY, J., "The Making of Alphabets," in *Readings in the Sociology of Language,* edited by J. A. Fishman, The Hague, 1968.

BOLINGER, D., "Visual Morphemes," *Language, 22* (1946).

BRADLEY, H., "On the Relations between Spoken and Written Language," *Proceedings of the British Academy,* vol. VI.

CRAIGIE, W. A., "Some Anomalies of Spelling," *S.P.E. Tract,* LIX (1942), Oxford.

EDGERTON, W. F., "Ideograms in English Writing," *Language, 17* (1941).

PULGRAM, E., "Phoneme and Grapheme," *Word, 7* (1951).

VACHEK, J., "Some Remarks on Writing and Phonetic Transcription," *Acta Linguistica, 5* (1945–1949).

General Accounts of Middle English Orthographic and Sound Systems

ANDERSON, J., and R. LASS, *Studies in Old English Phonology* (forthcoming).

BENNETT, J. A. W., and G. V. SMITHERS (1966), "Introduction," pp. xxxvi–xlvi.

BRUNNER, K. (1948), chapter II, *Lautlehre.*

CLARK, J. W. (1957), chapter II, pp. 117 ff.

EMERSON, O. F. (1948), "Introduction," pp. xviii–lxxvii.

JESPERSEN, O., *A Modern English Grammar on Historical Principles,* I, Copenhagen, 1909.

JORDAN, R. (1934), vol. I, *Lautlehre.*

KÖKERITZ, H., *A Guide to Chaucer's Pronunciation,* Uppsala, 1954.

LUIK, K. (1913), paragraphs 203–206, 352, and 479 ff.

MCINTOSH, A. (1956). Also in Lass (1969), pp. 35 ff.

MOORE, S., and A. L. MARCKWARDT, *Historical Outline of English Sounds and Inflections,* Ann Arbor, 1964.

MORSBACH, L. (1896), pp. 25 ff.

MOSSÉ, F. (1952), pp. 16 ff.

SISAM, K. (1959), pp. 276–283.

* If a book appears in the Bibliography that follows an earlier chapter, subsequent references will be to the author, date, and pages (or chapters) only.

SWEET, H., *History of English Sounds,* Oxford, 1888.

WARDALE, E. (1949), pp. 46 ff.

WEINSTOCK, H. (1968), pp. 31–145.

WRENN, C. L., "The Value of Spellings as Evidence," *TPS,* 1943.

WRIGHT, J. (1957), chapters I–VI.

WORKS OF A MORE DETAILED NATURE THAT DEAL WITH MIDDLE
ENGLISH PHONOLOGY, ORTHOGRAPHY, AND RELATED MATTERS

ALLÉN, S., *Grafematisk Analys Som Grundval för Textedering,* Gothen-
burg, 1965.

ANDERSON, J. M., " 'Ablaut' in the Synchronic Phonology of the Old English Strong Verb," *Indogermanische Forschungen,* 1971.

BHAT, D. N. S., "Is Sound Change Gradual?", *Linguistics,* 42 (1968).

BLISS, A. J., "Vowel Quantity in Middle English Borrowings from Anglo-
Norman," *Archivum Linguisticum,* 4 (1955).

———, "Quantity in Old French and Middle English," *Archivum Linguisticum,* 7 (1955).

BRIGHT, W., and A. K. RAMANUJAN, "Sociolinguistic Variation and Language Change," *Proceedings of the Ninth International Congress of
Linguists,* The Hague, 1964.

CARROLL, J. B., "Language Development in Children," in *Psycholinguistics:
A Book of Readings,* edited by S. Saporta, New York, 1961.

CLARK, C. (1958), "Introduction," pp. xxxv–xlix.

DOBSON, E. J., *English Pronunciation 1500–1700,* Oxford, 1957.

———, "Middle English Lengthening in Open Syllables," *TPS,* 1962.

FLASDIECK, H. M., "Die sprachliche Einheitlichkeit des *Ormulums,*" *Anglia,*
XLVII (1923).

FRANCIS, W. N., "Graphemic Analysis of late Middle English Manuscripts,"
Speculum, XXXVII (1962).

HALE, E. E., "Open and Close e in the *Ormulum,*" *MLN,* VIII (1893).

KING, R. (1969), chapters 8 and 10.

KUHN, S. M., and R. QUIRK, "Some Recent Interpretations of Old English
Digraph Spellings," *Language,* XXIX (1953).

KURATH, H., "The Loss of Long Consonants and the Rise of Voiced Fricatives in Middle English," *Language,* 32 (1956). Also in Lass (1969),
pp. 142 ff.

LEHMANN, W. P., "Types of Sound Change" in *Proceedings of the Ninth
International Congress of Linguists,* The Hague, 1964.

———, *Proto-Indo-European Phonology,* Austin, 1962.

LEOPOLD, W. F., "Patternings in Children's Language Learning," in *Psycho-*

linguistics: A Book of Readings, edited by S. Saporta, New York, 1961.

LIBERMAN, A. S., "On the History of Middle English ă and ā," *Neuphilologische Mitteilungen,* 67 (1968).

LYONS, J. (1968), chapter 3.

MCLAUGHLIN, J. C., *A Graphemic-Phonemic Study of a Middle English Manuscript,* The Hague, 1963.

MCNEILL, D., "The Creation of Language by Children," in *Psycholinguistics Papers,* edited by J. Lyons and R. J. Wales, Edinburgh, 1966.

RUBIN, S., "The Phonology of the Middle English Dialect of Sussex," *Lund Studies in English,* XXI (1951), Lund.

SAMUELS, M. L., "Some Applications of Middle English Dialectology," *English Studies,* 44 (1963). Also in Lass (1969), pp. 404 ff.

STOCKWELL, R. P., "The Middle English 'Long Close' and 'Long Open' Mid Vowels," *Texas Studies in Literature and Language,* 2 (1961). Also in Lass (1969), pp. 154 ff.

————, and C. W. BARRITT, "Scribal Practice: Some Assumptions," *Language,* 37 (1961). Also in Lass (1969), pp. 133 ff.

————, and C. W. BARRITT, "Some Old English Graphemic-Phonemic Correspondences—*æ, ea* and *a*," *Studies in Linguistics; Occasional Papers,* 4 (1951), Washington.

TAYLOR, J., "Notes on the Rise of Written English in the Late Middle Ages," *Proceedings, Leeds Philosophical and Literary Society, Literature and History Section,* VIII (1956), Leeds.

VOYLES, J., "Simplicity, Ordered Rules and the First Sound Shift," *Language,* 43 (1967).

WAGNER, K. H., *Generative Grammar Studies in the Old English Language,* Heidelberg, 1969.

PHONOLOGICAL THEORY

CHOMSKY, N., *Current Issues in Linguistic Theory,* The Hague, 1964.

————, and M. HALLE, *The Sound Pattern of English,* New York, 1968.

————, and M. HALLE, "Some Controversial Questions in Phonological Theory," *Journal of Linguistics,* 2 (1965).

HALLE, M., "Phonology in a Generative Grammar," *Word,* 18 (1962).

HARMS, R. T., *Introduction to Phonological Theory,* Englewood Cliffs, 1968.

HOUSEHOLDER, F. W., "On Some Recent Claims in Phonological Theory," *Journal of Linguistics,* 1 (1965).

JAKOBSON, R., and M. HALLE, *Fundamentals of Language,* The Hague, 1956.

KING, R. D., "Push Chains and Drag Chains," *Glossa,* 3 (1969).

KIPARSKY, P., "Linguistic Universals and Linguistic Change," in *Universals in Linguistic Theory,* edited by E. Bach and R. T. Harms, New York, 1968.

MARTINET, A., *Economie des changements phonétiques,* Bern, 1955.

POSTAL, P., *Aspects of Phonological Theory,* New York, 1968.

NOUN MORPHOLOGY AND SYNTAX / FOUR

I

One of the major difficulties for the student of Middle English lies in the often unfamiliar grammatical and syntactical usages to be found in texts of the period. Some of these differences, in fact, appear to be so great and the usage so strange that it is often difficult at first sight to see how the modern forms of English could possibly be related to them, and to a great extent it is grammatical usage that makes Middle English appear to the modern reader very much like a foreign language. Yet one must stress that these differences can often seem more extreme than they really are and that, in fact, compared to earlier forms of the English language, Middle English is very modern in its grammar and shares a great many features common to present usage, many of which can be said to appear for the first time in Middle English itself. In this area, as in so many others, the era of Middle English appears to be one of great innovation and invention, although, as usual, one must always be on guard against supposing either that the changes to be discussed took place overnight or uniformly or that some of them did not exist at a still earlier stage of the language disguised by a conservative orthographic system or suppressed owing to the nature of the surviving data.

In this chapter, the reader will find a discussion of certain of the aspects of the noun phrase in Middle English. A principal concern will be the shapes the noun and pronoun take as they enter into number and case relationships with other parts of the sentence, since many important changes have taken place between Middle, Old, and Modern English in this area of the grammar. Other "parts of speech" traditionally associated with the noun, such as the articles and adjectives, will also be included in the discussion and, as with the conclusions reached in the part of this book dealing with phonology, remarks made here are to be construed as being relevant only to the small amounts of datum provided.

In the syntactical, as well as the phonological component of the gram-

mar, one must be prepared to recognize <u>different levels of structural ab-</u>
<u>straction</u>. The particular way such features as case and number are realized
in the grammar of English represent the working of the language at a rather
superficial level. At a higher level of abstraction, these features may take on
a shape not found at the surface level, and it is the surface shapes that give
the impression that considerable and far-reaching changes have taken place
between the historical periods of English. <u>With a few exceptions, the under-</u>
<u>lying representation of syntactical relationships has remained unaltered</u>
<u>throughout the history of the language, and it is the surface shape, and the</u>
<u>rules that determine it, that have changed most in the course of time</u>. Both
Middle and Modern English clearly have nouns and pronouns, and the
functional case relationships such as subject and object into which they
could enter are shared by both languages. <u>In Modern English, for instance</u>
(see Chomsky [1965] and Jacobs and Rosenbaum [1968]), the case func-
<u>tions in which these "parts of speech" could partake are determined by</u>
<u>the hierarchical structural relationship they bear to other syntactical cate-</u>
<u>gories such as the N(oun) P(hrase) and the V(erb) P(hrase) in the</u>
<u>S(entence)</u>. Thus for ‹John likes Bill› :

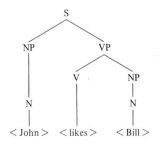

or, in terms of *labeled brackets:*

[[[John]]   [[likes] [[Bill]]   ]   ]
 S NP N   N NP VP V   V NP N   N NP VP S

the function of *subject* is defined not as N or NP, but by the structural
configuration :

or [[[
   S NP N

while *object,* although it involves the same category N, is structurally defined as:

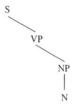

or, in terms of the bracketing configuration,]   ]   ]   ] .
                                            N NP VP S

These abstract functional relationships are in all probability shared by both Middle and Old English, but there can be considerable differences in the rules to which these abstract configurations act as input, resulting in many discrepancies between the superficial shapes of sentences (especially as regards their word order and inflectional forms) in the two languages.

Both Middle and Modern English have identical as well as different rules that will realize the above underlying structures into acceptable surface word orderings. In Middle English, however, even once these superficial orderings had been arrived at by general rules of syntax, the resultant case relationships at this level were further márked by the attachment of suffixes to individual nouns. Such case-indicative suffixes are introduced by an even later set of rules, almost completely absent in Modern English, and these rules were the object of considerable change in the period with which this book deals.

Rather like the suffix case markers are the superficial manifestations of the abstract category of *number.* At an underlying grammatical level, nouns will be inherently marked for the feature (analogous to feature in the phonological sense) of [±singular]. The surface shape of this feature will, among other things, be determined by a series of rules applied late in the grammar, and, in Modern English, mainly of the suffix-adding type. This type of rule, too, has undergone considerable alteration and deletion both during and since Middle English. Two things should be noted. The first is that sometimes very great superficial discrepancy between Middle and Modern English is just this—superficial. The reasons for the variant surface structures are often not the result of abstract grammatical changes, but rather of change in, addition to, or deletion from the lower level rules that give the abstract configurations a superficial shape. Secondly, it is not altogether surprising that these rules, which come late in sentence derivations, are the ones that should be liable to the greatest change, since their effect on the "meaning" of the sentence is comparatively small. Even without their application, the speaker is generally able to recover the abstract structure of sentences.

In a Middle English sentence such as ⟨þe eorles heolden þa lambren⟩ (⟨the earls kept the lambs⟩), the nouns ⟨eorles⟩ and ⟨lambren⟩ enter into the same functional relations of subject and object respectively as their modern counterparts. Even the rules that assign them a surface position in the sentence are the same:

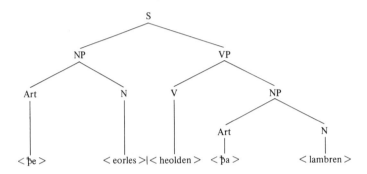

or:

```
[ [   [ þe] [ eorles]  ]   [   [ heolden] [   [ þa]
 S NP A   A  N       N NP VP V       V NP A   A
[ lambren]  ]   ]   ]
 N          N NP VP S
```

There are, however, many well-attested instances, to be discussed immediately below, where the superficial ordering is quite different between the two languages. For instance, the presence of a temporal adverb (⟨when⟩ = ⟨þa⟩) would represent an environment for the operation of a Middle English rule giving the surface appearance:

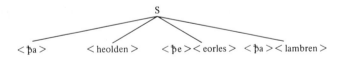

Word order variation is still possible in the contemporary language, but not necessarily in the same contexts or with the same meaning as Middle English. For example, in Modern English, reversal of subject and object can often mean that the latter is being topicalized or emphasized, although the same interpretation of reordering phenomena need not apply to Middle English.

The reader will notice too that both nouns in the above sentence have the feature [—singular] and that both, as today, employ a late rule to realize this by suffix addition:

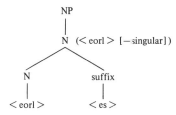

In the instance of the object noun, however, the suffix has a shape no longer appropriate to this word, although still found in others. The linguistic change involving the switching of nouns from one suffix type to those of another is a very common phenomenon in the history of English. Again, there is no change in the underlying feature of plurality, merely in the rules that determine its surface shape.

The strategy of this and the following chapter will be to concentrate on two principal areas in the grammar, to describe them, and to show how they have changed within the terms of a limited set of datum. The chapters will be divided into two parts, both containing a Middle English sample, the first from an early stage of the language, the second from a later. The syntactical features under discussion will be taken almost entirely from these samples, and the material they provide will be compared. This chapter will be involved with a more detailed look at some of the features briefly discussed above: that is, the way in which presumably shared abstract syntactical patterns come to be differently manifested (with the greatest emphasis on suffix affixation and word order) and what changes they can undergo in the course of time.

In order to compare the respective surface-structure manifestations of noun features in Middle and Modern English, we shall examine in some detail two short extracts from the former language. Examples will be chosen that, although they were composed in approximately the same geographical area, are relatively well-separated from each other on the temporal scale. One shall, therefore, be able to have as clear a picture as possible of the direction as well as the nature of any differences from contemporary usage.

The first passage to be considered (see *Text I*) is taken from the annal for the year 1129 in the manuscript commonly referred to as the *Peterborough Chronicle*. This piece of early Middle English is of particular interest for a number of reasons, principally because it was written at a time almost contemporary with the events it describes, with the result that one is able to date its linguistic usage with some certainty. It is also inter-

TEXT I. PETERBOROUGH CHRONICLE: ANNAL 1129

On ðis gear sende se kyng to Englaland æfter þone
eorl Walderam 7 æfter Hugo Gerueises sunu ; 7 þær
hi gisleden hem ; 7 Hugo ferde ham to his agen land.
to France, 7 Walderam belaf mid þone kyng 7 se kyng
him geaf eall his land buton his castel ane. Siððon   5
þa com se kyng to Englaland innon heruest, 7 se eorl
com mid him ; 7 wurðon þa alswa gode freond swa hi
wæron æror feond. Ða sone be þes kynges ræd 7 be his
leue, sende se ærcebiscop Willelm of Cantwarabyrig ofer
eall Englaland 7 bead biscopes 7 abbotes 7 ærcedæcnes   10
7 ealle þe priores, muneces 7 canonias þa wæron on
ealle þa cellas on Englaland, 7 æfter ealle þa þet
Cristendome hæfdon to begemen 7 to locen, 7 þet hi
scolden ealle cumen to Lundene at Michaeles messe 7
þær scolden sprecon of ealle Godes rihtes. Þa hi   15
ðider comen, þa began þet mot on Monendæig 7 heold
onan to ðe Fridæig. Þa hit eall com forð, þa weorð
hit eall of earcedæcnes wifes 7 of preostes wifes,
þet hi scolden hi forlæten be Sanctes Andreas messe,
7 se þe þet ne wolden done forgede his circe 7 his   20
hus 7 his ham 7 neframa nan clepunge þærto na hafde
mare. Þis bebæd se ærcebiscop Willelm of Cantwarabyrig
7 ealle þa leodbiscopes ða þa wæron on Englalande.
7 se kyng hem geaf ealle leaue ham to farene ; 7 swa
hi ferdon ham. 7 ne forstod noht ealle þa bodlaces ;   25
ealle heoldon here wifes be þes kynges leue swa swa
hi ear didon.

[In this year the king (Henry I) sent to England for earl Waleran and the son of Hugo Gervase, and hostages were given in exchange for them. Hugo went back to his own estate in France, while Waleran remained with the king, who gave him back all his estates with the exception of his castle. Then in the autumn the king came to England, and Waleran came with him, and from that time they were as good friends as they had before been enemies. Soon after this, William, the archbishop of Canterbury, sent, at the king's suggestion and with his permission, (messages) over the whole of England commanding bishops, abbots, archdeacons, as well as all the priors, monks, and canons in all the cells in England, and all those who had the duty of protecting and looking after Christendom, that all of them must come at Michaelmas to London, where it was intended that they should discuss all the rights ordained by God. When they had come there, the meeting began on a Monday and lasted until the next Friday. When it all came out, it was realized that it had been all about the wives of priests and archdeacons, who had to be got rid of by Saint Andrew's day. Anyone not willing to do this would have to give up his church, house, and home and have no further claim to them at any time. This was the decree of the archbishop William of Canterbury and of all the next most senior bishops in England. The king gave them his permission to return to their homes and they did so. But none of the decrees had any effect, and all of them kept their wives with the permission of the king as they had done before.]

esting not only because it clearly appears very much like Modern English despite its very early date, but especially since, compared with earlier linguistic usage, the changes that have already taken place in the grammar of the sample are quite considerable, especially in the placement of subject and object nouns in relation to the verb in the sentences. The superficial ordering difference between subject nouns does not appear from the evidence to be context free, but rather context sensitive, especially to those environments where there is a temporal adverb in the sentence and where this adverb (⟨þa⟩, ⟨on ðis gear⟩, for instance) is in initial position. In such a context, a sentence like [[[se] [kyng]] [[com]]]
S NP A A N   N NP VP V   V VP S
has a surface shape:

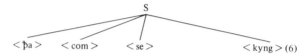

It is, however, interesting to observe that the rule that gives this surface ordering of elements after temporal adverbs, fails to operate in several instances, notably, ⟨þa hit eall com forð⟩ (17) and ⟨þa hi ðider comen⟩ (15–16). These failures may themselves not be random but tied to contextual phenomena of a kind too detailed to appear in this small sample. It is perhaps more likely, however, in view of the evidence from later Middle English texts where sentence initial temporal adverbs have no such reordering consequences, that in the *Peterborough Chronicle* the rule has only, or is coming to have, a minor and not a general status (see Chapter Six, p. 189).

At the same time, the syntactic function of *object of* appears in shapes both recognizable and strange to the modern reader. The rules underlying such orderings as ⟨forgede his circe⟩ (20), and ⟨se kyng . . . geaf ealle leaue⟩ (24) are clearly those applied in the majority of instances in contemporary English. Yet Middle English appears to have additional rules for word ordering that have subsequently come to be deleted. Compare the abstract configuration:

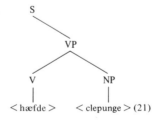

(simplified to omit the negative forms), with its superficial realization, ‹clepunge hæfde›, and similarly, the sentence ‹ealle þa þet Cristendome hæfdon› (12–13). The following examples are interesting because they seem to show environments where one can predict certain surface positions for object nouns: the abstract configuration

```
[ [   [    hi]    ]   [   [      sceolden]      [  forlæten]
  S NP PRO    PRO NP VP MOD          MOD V          V
[   [    hi]    ]    ]    ]
  NP PRO    PRO NP VP S
```

is input to some ordering rule that produces the superficial shape:

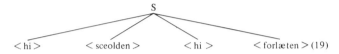

where the ordering direct object + verb may be sensitive to environments where modals or other verbal auxiliaries are present. It has often been suggested too (Bacquet [1962]) that the realization of an object (direct or indirect) noun as a pronoun is another context where the main verb is relegated to a postobject position. See, for instance, ‹se kyng him geaf eall his land› (4–5) and ‹se kyng hem geaf ealle leaue› (24).

CASE INFLECTION

Nouns

The forms of all the nouns in the singular in the *Peterborough Chronicle* extract are presented below according to their surface case shapes.

The Noun in the Singular

SUBJECTS
‹se kyng› (1) (4) (6): ‹se ærcebiscop› (9) (23): ‹se eorl› (6) ‹þet mot› (16)

OBJECTS
‹eall his land› (5): ‹Cristendome› (13): ‹circe› (21): ‹hus› (21): ‹ham› (21): ‹nan clepunge› (21): ‹leaue› (24).

POSSESSIVES
‹þes kynges› (8) (26): ‹Godes› (15): ‹Michaeles› (14): ‹Sanctes Andreas› (19).

LOCATIVES

(a) *Spatial* ⟨to Englaland⟩ (1) (6) : ⟨æfter þone eorl⟩ (2) : ⟨æfter Hugo
Geruesis sunu⟩ (2) : ⟨to his agen land⟩ (3) : ⟨to France⟩ (4) : ⟨ofer
all Englaland⟩ (6) : ⟨on Englaland⟩ (12) : ⟨to Lundene⟩ (15) : ⟨on
Englalande⟩ (23) : ⟨ham⟩ (25) : ⟨mid þone kyng⟩ (4).
(b) *Temporal* ⟨On ðis gear⟩ (1) : ⟨innon heruest⟩ (6) ⟨at Michaeles
messe⟩ (14) : ⟨on Monendæig⟩ (16) : ⟨to ðe Fridæig⟩ (17).

INSTRUMENTALS
⟨be þes kynges ræd⟩ (8) : ⟨be his/þes kynges leue⟩ (8)/(26).

In the discussion, and the rules that follow, the syntactic features, such as
[+agent, +object, +locative], and so on, are to be interpreted not as
functional symbols, but merely as representing superficial case relationships.
For instance, in a sentence like ⟨þe abbot wæs gyuen ðone castel be þæm
kynge⟩ (⟨the abbot was given the castle by the king⟩), the surface-structure
locative ⟨be þæm kynge⟩ represents an underlying subject function, which
can also be superficially represented as ⟨þe kyng geaf þæm abbode ðone
castel⟩. The rules that realize the above list of case forms must be rather
like those for Modern English, since there are so few inflectional differences between the two languages on the basis of the above data. The suffix
representing nouns with the feature [+possessive] has an orthographic
form rather like the one still used—compare ⟨kynges⟩ (8) and ⟨Godes⟩
(15) among others, although the text contains no example of another possible contemporary realization of possession, the preposition *of*. There are,
however, some instances where the extract shows nominal case marked by
a preceding preposition, as in ⟨be þes kynges ræd⟩ (8), ⟨on Monandæig⟩
(16), although in some places a form of preposition, now regarded as inappropriate, is to be found : ⟨on Englaland⟩ (12), and ⟨on ðis gear⟩ (1) ; yet
others have no modern realization ⟨innon heruest⟩ (6).

The sample does show, nevertheless, that the grammar of early
Middle English contained rules of case-sensitive suffix addition that since
then appear to have been deleted. Compare, within a short space of each
other, such postprepositional forms as ⟨on Englaland⟩ (12) and ⟨on Engla-
lande⟩ (24). If the spelling evidence, in fact, means that (24) has a vocalic
segment suffixed to it, then the grammar of the text would have to contain
the rule :

$$\text{inflectional suffix} \longrightarrow \begin{Bmatrix} ⟨e⟩ \\ ⟨\emptyset⟩ \end{Bmatrix} \Big/ \begin{bmatrix} \text{N} \\ ⟨\text{Englaland}⟩ \\ +\text{locative} \end{bmatrix} \underline{\quad\quad}$$

a choice of suffix that appears to be quite arbitrary as to its application or
not. However, if one looks up a dictionary of Old English, one would find

that for this noun in this case environment there would be the compulsory rule:

inflectional
suffix $\longrightarrow$ ⟨e⟩

(Note that throughout this book only orthographic realizations of inflectional suffixes are considered, since the question of their phonetic values is too complex and too little understood to warrant a detailed discussion.) To be noted also in the *Peterborough Chronicle* extract are such forms as ⟨to Lundene⟩ (14) and ⟨be leaue⟩ (9), although the majority of nonpossessive case slots show nouns without suffixation, leaving one to suspect some kind of widespread, and perhaps environmentally predictable, rule deletion to have taken place. To appreciate fully the nature of these changes, as well as their extent, it will be necessary for us to look briefly at the situation found in West Saxon Old English usage of the late tenth and early eleventh centuries. At this period, as in Middle and Modern English, the case features of nouns could be shown by (among other things) the addition to the noun of an inflectional suffix:

N[+case] $\longrightarrow$ N + inflectional suffix

In Old English, however, the variety of inflectional suffix types was considerably greater than it has been in any other period since. The following set of rules represents (in a much simplified form) some of the case-sensitive inflectional possibilities in Old English:

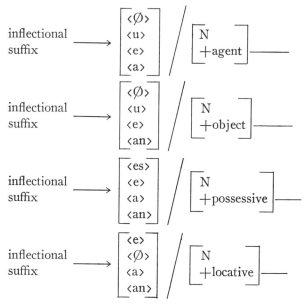

But the matter is even more complex than this in Old English. How, for example, did a native speaker know which set of inflectional suffixes to select for any given noun? Was the selection arbitrary? These questions are difficult to answer; for example, a noun such as ⟨ʒief-⟩ (a gift) would involve in the singular the following selectional rules:

$$\text{inflectional suffix} \longrightarrow \langle u \rangle \ \Big/ \ \begin{bmatrix} +\text{agent} \\ \langle \text{ʒief} \rangle \end{bmatrix} \underline{\hspace{2cm}}$$

$$\text{inflectional suffix} \longrightarrow \langle e \rangle \ \Big/ \ \begin{bmatrix} \langle \text{ʒief} \rangle \\ -\text{agent} \end{bmatrix} \underline{\hspace{2cm}}$$

On the other hand, a noun such as ⟨dæd⟩ (a deed) would select singular inflectional suffix forms according to a different set of CS rules:

$$\text{inflectional suffix} \longrightarrow \langle \varnothing \rangle \ \Big/ \ \begin{bmatrix} \langle \text{dæd} \rangle \\ +\text{agent} \\ +\text{object} \end{bmatrix} \underline{\hspace{1.5cm}}$$

$$\text{inflectional suffix} \longrightarrow \langle e \rangle \ \Big/ \ \begin{bmatrix} \langle \text{dæd} \rangle \\ +\text{possessive} \\ +\text{locative} \end{bmatrix} \underline{\hspace{1.5cm}}$$

Two of the most common types of noun found in Old English took their case-sensitive inflectional forms, again in the singular, after the rules:

$$(1) \ \text{inflectional suffix} \longrightarrow \langle \varnothing \rangle \ \Big/ \ \begin{bmatrix} \langle \text{stan} \rangle \\ +\text{agent} \\ +\text{object} \end{bmatrix} \underline{\hspace{1.5cm}}$$

$$\text{inflectional suffix} \longrightarrow \langle es \rangle \ \Big/ \ \begin{bmatrix} \langle \text{stan} \rangle \\ +\text{possessive} \end{bmatrix} \underline{\hspace{1.5cm}}$$

$$\text{inflectional suffix} \longrightarrow \langle e \rangle \ \Big/ \ \begin{bmatrix} \langle \text{stan} \rangle \\ +\text{locative} \end{bmatrix} \underline{\hspace{1.5cm}}$$

$$(2) \ \text{inflectional suffix} \longrightarrow \begin{Bmatrix} \langle a \rangle \\ \langle e \rangle \end{Bmatrix} \ \Big/ \ \begin{bmatrix} \begin{Bmatrix} \langle \text{nam} \rangle \\ \langle \text{tung} \rangle \end{Bmatrix} \\ +\text{agent} \end{bmatrix} \underline{\hspace{1.5cm}}$$

$$\text{inflectional suffix} \longrightarrow \langle an \rangle \ \Big/ \ \begin{bmatrix} \begin{Bmatrix} \langle \text{nam} \rangle \\ \langle \text{tung} \rangle \end{Bmatrix} \\ -\text{agent} \end{bmatrix} \underline{\hspace{1.5cm}}$$

It is difficult to explain how rules of this kind were acquired by a native speaker of Old English. It seems that in a sense they were "unmotivated" for him, so that as a child he would have had to learn that different sets of nouns would provide the contexts in which the rules of selection for case-sensitive inflectional suffixes would operate. Perhaps the process was rather similar to the way in which speakers of Modern French "learn" the appropriate form of the definite article (⟨le⟩ or ⟨la⟩) for a given noun. Speakers of Modern French can make "mistakes" in this area, and presumably "mistakes" were also made in the selection of inflectional suffixes marking case in Old English times as well.

One must bear in mind the possibility that the choice of these inflectional forms may have been "motivated" at some stage of the language earlier than Old English; that is, nouns sharing a common vowel stem may also have shared the same set of inflectional suffixes. Indeed, there may have been a much larger variety of the latter at this earlier stage. Old English seems to represent what look like a "simplified" version of an originally more complex situation, since there is rarely an instance where a given noun is completely different as regards its inflectional form in every case context from any other. For instance, although the nouns ⟨weg-⟩ and ⟨ʒief-⟩ have different CS rules in some case contexts:

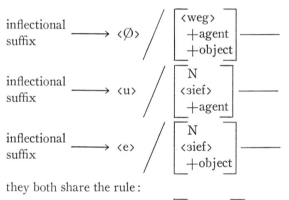

they both share the rule:

inflectional suffix ⟶ ⟨e⟩ / [N ⟨ʒief⟩ ⟨weg⟩ +locative] ———

Perhaps at some earlier stage of the language, the [+locative] context involved a different inflectional selection in each of these nouns, but by the time of Old English there seems to have been a "rule collapse" or deletion brought about, perhaps, because some original underlying motivation for separate suffixation was no longer recoverable in this context by speakers acquiring the language.

In the *Peterborough Chronicle* passage, there is a general tendency for the noun in the singular to have either a ⟨Ø⟩, ⟨e⟩, or ⟨es⟩ inflectional ending, although, in general, ⟨Ø⟩ is more popular than ⟨e⟩ in nonpossessive

N sing.

contexts. For instance, the forms ⟨on . . . gear⟩ (1), ⟨to . . . Frīdǣig⟩ (17), and ⟨to . . . land⟩ (3) would all, in Old English have been found with an ⟨e⟩ inflectional ending: ⟨on geare⟩, ⟨to Frīdæge⟩, and ⟨to lande⟩. Secondly, and of equal importance, the scribe of our extract uses the ⟨e⟩ inflection where in Old English (owing to differences in noun grouping) some other type would have been the rule. For example, one finds ⟨be . . . messe⟩ (19) and ⟨circe⟩ (20), which at an earlier stage of the language would have been ⟨be mæssan⟩ and ⟨cirican⟩. One can explain such examples in terms of the loss of rules in the grammar of English between the Old and early Middle English periods. In Old English, as suggested above, the nonpossessive inflectional forms in the singular for ⟨dæg⟩ and ⟨land⟩ were reached by two different rules:

$$(1) \quad \text{inflectional suffix} \longrightarrow \langle\emptyset\rangle \left/ \begin{bmatrix} \begin{Bmatrix} \langle\text{dæg}\rangle \\ \langle\text{land}\rangle \end{Bmatrix} \\ +\text{agent} \\ +\text{object} \end{bmatrix} \underline{\quad\quad}: \right.$$

$$(2) \quad \text{inflectional suffix} \longrightarrow \langle e\rangle \left/ \begin{bmatrix} \begin{Bmatrix} \langle\text{dæg}\rangle \\ \langle\text{land}\rangle \end{Bmatrix} \\ +\text{locative} \end{bmatrix} \underline{\quad\quad} \right.$$

The evidence provided by the Middle English extract suggests that in some instances at least rule (2) was deleted from the grammar, leaving only one rule to generate acceptable nonpossessive, inflectional suffix forms of nouns in the singular:

$$(3) \quad \text{inflectional suffix} \longrightarrow \langle\emptyset\rangle \left/ \begin{bmatrix} \begin{Bmatrix} \langle\text{dæg}\rangle \\ \langle\text{land}\rangle \end{Bmatrix} \\ -\text{possessive} \end{bmatrix} \underline{\quad\quad} \right.$$

Similarly, in the cases of ⟨mæss-⟩ and ⟨ciric-⟩, one seems to be involved in a rule reduction, since in Old English one would generally require the two rules:

$$(1) \quad \text{inflectional suffix} \longrightarrow \langle e\rangle \left/ \begin{bmatrix} \begin{Bmatrix} \langle\text{ciric-}\rangle \\ \langle\text{mæss-}\rangle \end{Bmatrix} \\ +\text{agent} \end{bmatrix} \underline{\quad\quad} \right.$$

$$(2) \quad \text{inflectional suffix} \longrightarrow \langle an\rangle \left/ \begin{bmatrix} \begin{Bmatrix} \langle\text{ciric-}\rangle \\ \langle\text{mæss-}\rangle \end{Bmatrix} \\ -\text{agent} \end{bmatrix} \underline{\quad\quad} \right.$$

Leaving aside for the moment the question of possessive forms in words of this kind, we can, nevertheless, postulate that in our extract the rule for the locative inflectional form will be the same as that for the agent:

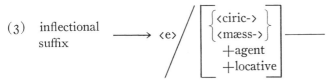

(3) inflectional $\longrightarrow$ ‹e› / $\begin{bmatrix} \begin{Bmatrix} \text{‹ciric-›} \\ \text{‹mæss-›} \end{Bmatrix} \\ +\text{agent} \\ +\text{locative} \end{bmatrix}$ —— suffix

However, one must not assume that wherever the loss of a rule is involved in any language, it is always the same rule; that is, rule deletion need not take place at all times in the same place in the grammar. This point can be illustrated from two examples in the extract. One finds, for example, the form ‹Cristendome› (13) with a [+object] case feature. This is rather unusual when compared with the kinds of rule loss discussed so far, since here there appears to have an extension into [+object] contexts of the inflectional suffix form of the [+locative]. In all the cases so far examined, it has been the rule sensitive to locative contexts that has been deleted in favor of the agent and object types. The opposite is true in the case of ‹Cristendome›. In Old English, words ending in ‹-dom› took inflectional suffixes in the singular in nonpossessive contexts, as for ‹dæg-› and ‹land-› given above. In the extract, however, rather than having a deletion of the rule for the inflectional suffix in the [+locative] context, one seems to find it extended into other contexts, so that there is a (simplified) situation in which one finds:

inflectional $\longrightarrow$ ‹∅› / $\begin{bmatrix} \text{‹-dom-›} \\ +\text{agent} \end{bmatrix}$ —— suffix

inflectional $\longrightarrow$ ‹e› / $\begin{bmatrix} \text{‹-dom-›} \\ +\text{object} \\ +\text{locative} \end{bmatrix}$ —— suffix

Another interesting example is in line 2: ‹æfter Hugo Gerueises sunu›. In Old English, ‹sun-› belongs to the same class as ‹ȝief-› described above; that is, it forms its inflectional suffixes by means of the two rules:

inflectional $\longrightarrow$ ‹u› / $\begin{bmatrix} \begin{Bmatrix} \text{‹ȝief-›} \\ \text{‹sun-›} \end{Bmatrix} \\ +\text{agent} \end{bmatrix}$ —— suffix

inflectional $\longrightarrow$ ‹e› / $\begin{bmatrix} \begin{Bmatrix} \text{‹ȝief-›} \\ \text{‹sun-›} \end{Bmatrix} \\ -\text{agent} \end{bmatrix}$ —— suffix

In our extract, however, it would seem that there is some reason to suppose that for ‹sun-› inflectional forms are generated by means of the single rule:

$$\text{inflectional suffix} \longrightarrow \langle u \rangle \bigg/ \begin{bmatrix} \langle \text{sun-} \rangle \\ -\text{possessive} \end{bmatrix} \underline{\hspace{2cm}}$$

The important feature of the sample is that it shows a considerable simplification in nominal inflection over that which one finds in texts of an earlier date, and for that reason it looks remarkably modern. Nevertheless, two important points must be borne in mind. In the first place, although there were more inflectional types in Old English, it does not follow that with their simplification in early Middle English the latter language was unable to express as clearly as the former certain case relationships. On the contrary, Middle English, as well as Modern English, is capable of manifesting as many such relationships as the more highly inflected forms of English before A.D. 1000—they merely express them in different ways. In other words, there is no difference between the deep-structure case features in Old and Middle English; what has changed is the degree to which, as well as the manner in which, they are reflected at the superficial linguistic level. The second important point is that there could obviously have been no sudden change to a less elaborate from a more elaborate inflectional system. Indeed, the written form of Old English was so conservative that it cannot have reflected some of the actual spoken forms of the language. Consequently, many of the features that have been ascribed to the writer of the *Peterborough Chronicle* may have existed at an earlier date, although they remain absent from the written form of the language.

The rules for superficial case suffixation have been presented in some detail because they provide a good illustration of a common but complex linguistic change. Although speakers of Old and early Middle English automatically assigned correct case suffixes to appropriate noun groupings, as far as is understood, this assignment was of an arbitrary nature. Such may not always have been the case, and there may have been a time in the history of English when the shape of the inflectional suffix was predictable (rather like the shape of the ablaut vowel in the strong verb) from its phonological or syntactical environment. Apparently by the end of the Old English period or at the beginning of the Middle English, children acquiring the language were unable to recover from the data to which they were exposed any underlying motivation for the correlation between certain suffix types and noun groupings. One of the results of this, not unexpectedly, is the complex situation outlined above. The membership of earlier suffix-appropriate noun groups (or *declensions*) either increases or decreases. Nor is it a precondition for this "reshuffling" that certain suffix-forming rules themselves be lost, and the process can happen in several directions at once. In the case of ⟨sunu⟩ and ⟨Cristendome⟩ above, for instance, there are reallocations of declension membership that appear to contradict the major pattern. Indeed, it is possible that speakers even set up partially new declensional groupings based on a different set of underlying principles from the ones to which they were exposed as children, rather than caused all such groupings to have been totally and immediately deleted from the grammar.

Very similar processes can be seen in the changes in inflectional forms in nouns in the plural. In the extract, the majority of plural nouns have as their inflectional ending <es>: <leodbiscopes> (23), <bodlaces> (25), <biscopes> (10), <abbotes> (10), <preostes> (18), and <wifes> (18). Sometimes this form is spelled by the scribe as <as>. Again, this is quite different from the evidence one has from texts of an earlier date. As with the endings of singular nouns, in the plural in Old English several different inflectional endings were used according to the group or declension to which a particular noun belonged. Plural inflectional forms in Old English for subject and object cases alone include as wide a variety as <as>, <u>, <∅>, <a>, <e>, and <an>, as well as a change from the vowel of the singular, as in Modern English <foot/feet>.

In order to see the extent and nature of the changes in plural inflectional forms, one must briefly compare the extract with what is known of earlier English usage. As in the singular, Old English plural nouns show a wide variety of inflectional possibility; these are again governed by two things: (1) the superficial case feature of the noun involved, and (2) the class of nouns (or declension) to which it belongs. Nouns with the same case feature in the plural can have distinct inflections if they belong to different inflectional classes. In a simplified form the rules for the selection of inflectional suffixes in the plural of Old English nouns on the basis of case alone are as follows:

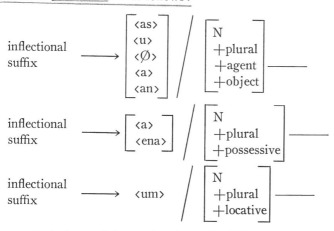

It is impossible to give here the full range of distribution of these forms according to noun declension, but the following is a brief sample of the possibilities:

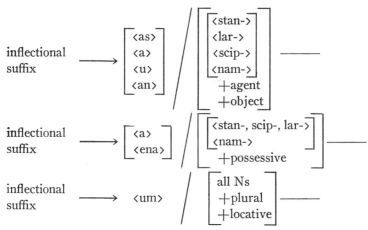

Middle English realizes this system in a much simplified way, and, like the singular, there is a preference for a more limited set of inflections. The extent of the ⟨es⟩ plural inflection in our extract is quite surprising. It is used, for instance, in ⟨wifes⟩ (26), where one would normally expect a ⟨∅⟩ in texts of an earlier date; more especially, it is used in possessive and postprepositional contexts that in Old English would have had quite separate inflectional forms. One has only to compare the *Peterborough Chronicle* possessive plural ⟨earcedæcnes⟩ (18) and ⟨preostes⟩ (18) and the postprepositional ⟨of . . . rihtes⟩ (15) and ⟨of . . . wifes⟩ (18) with their Old English equivalents ⟨-diocena/priosta⟩ (possessive-plural inflection ⟨a⟩) and ⟨rihtum/wifum⟩ (⟨um⟩ inflection after preposition ⟨of⟩) to see how much like our own language early Middle English has become in this respect.

As is true of the singular usage, there are, of course, survivals of earlier forms that are no longer in the language today—the plurals ⟨freond⟩ and ⟨feond⟩ with ⟨∅⟩ plural inflections common in Old English (although even there ⟨as⟩ inflections are used with both nouns on occasion), but these are the exception rather than the rule in our text.

The general tendency in the *Chronicle* extract (and this is quite remarkable for material from such an early date) is for the above rules to be "simplified" into one in which there is deletion of both the case and declensional sensitive contexts:

The Definite Article : realization in OE & eME determined by number, case
                          determinacy, and class (gender) of
Perhaps one of the most puzzling features of any Middle English text,   noun
but especially of those from the early period, is the behavior of the part of

speech traditionally called the *definite article*. The forms of the definite article that one finds in the *Peterborough Chronicle* extract bear hardly any resemblance at all to those used in contemporary English. In the singular, with nouns in the subject position, two forms of the article are found: ⟨se⟩ with ⟨kyng⟩ (1) (24) and ⟨ærcebiscop⟩ (9) and ⟨þet⟩ with ⟨mot⟩ (16). Similarly, postprepositionally the two forms ⟨þone⟩ with ⟨kyng⟩ (4), ⟨eorl⟩ (2) and ⟨þe⟩ with ⟨Fridæig⟩ appear, and there is even a separate form of the article with nouns in the possessive case: ⟨þes kynges⟩ (8) (26). In the plural, ⟨þa⟩ is used with subject and post-prepositional nouns: ⟨þa priores⟩ (11), ⟨þa leodbiscopes⟩ (23), ⟨þa bodlaces⟩ (25), and ⟨on ealle þa cellas⟩ (12). In all there is a system involving no less than six different forms of the article in our text—⟨se⟩, ⟨þet⟩, ⟨þes⟩, ⟨þone⟩, ⟨þe⟩, and ⟨þa⟩—and it is this feature that contributes to its strangeness to the modern reader.

One can, therefore, write a set of rules (in a simplified form) that will generate the correct form of the definite article in our extract:

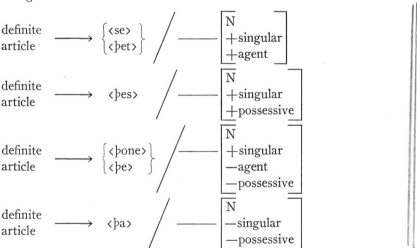

However, these rules are rather general, and it would be interesting if one were able to determine the contexts in which ⟨se⟩ was preferred to ⟨þet⟩ with [+singular, +agent] nouns and in which ⟨þone⟩ rather than ⟨þe⟩ was the rule in nouns with the features [+singular, —possessive, —agent]. If one makes these rules more specific, two facts will be discovered about definite article usage in early Middle English: in the first place, it will be seen that the usage retains characteristics of a much earlier stage of the language, and secondly, that it has undergone, and is undergoing, a great deal of change.

In addition to such features as case and number, nouns also have as an inherent part of their makeup a feature that might be called determinacy;

that is, nouns can be determined or specified in various ways and by various means. One of the ways of specifying nouns in Modern English, for example, is by the addition of a definite or indefinite article before them. In many instances the addition of the former indicates that the N is specified as known or previously mentioned, whereas in the latter case the article can denote a lesser degree of specification. Compare the two sentences:

That was the dog he saw.
That was a dog he saw.

One can, therefore, say that this fact can be accounted for in a (very crude) grammar of Modern English by the two rules:

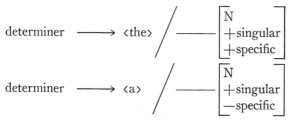

Unlike the form of the definite article in the Middle English rules given above, the form of the article in Modern English is *not* sensitive to the case feature of the noun; nor, indeed, is it on many occasions sensitive to the noun's number feature either—⟨the man⟩, ⟨the men⟩. In other words, as will be seen in more detail below, there has been a deletion from the rules for the selection of the definite article of the case-sensitive restriction. To leave the matter like this would conceal two points: the Middle English forms themselves have undergone a considerable degree of simplification from definite-article usage in earlier texts; the deletion rules that characterize the difference between Modern and Middle English usage in this area of the grammar seem to be already in operation in a limited way in our extract.

In Old, as in early Middle (but not Modern) English, the form of the determiner (including the specific, nonspecific, and other types to be discussed later) was sensitive to the case feature of the noun; that is, given a noun phrase with the features [case, number, determiner] in Old English, selection of the feature determiner would also involve its "copying" from the N the features case and number also. For example, given an Old English noun with the following deep-structure feature makeup:

N [case, number, determiner]

where the determiner is realized in the surface structure as a definite article:

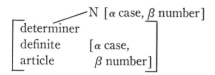

then the selected determiner must "copy" the case and number features of the noun:

$$\underset{\substack{\text{determiner}\\ \text{definite}\ \ [\alpha\ \text{case,}\\ \text{article}\ \ \ \ \beta\ \text{number}]}}{\overbrace{\qquad}} \!\!\!\!\!\!\text{—N } [\alpha\ \text{case, } \beta\ \text{number}]$$

Let us look briefly at the possibilities from which the Old English definite article was selected according to both case and number:

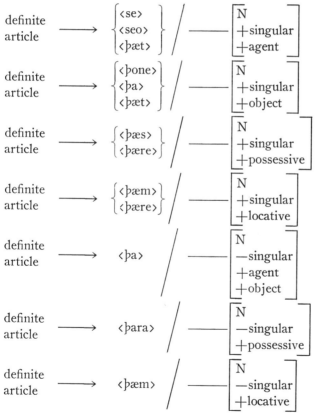

Three comments must be made about these rules: first, in one sense they make the situation look more complex than it perhaps really is. There are many redundant features about such rules that could be eliminated. For example, there is no need to distinguish a plural locative form, since ⟨þæm⟩ can specify both numbers. Relying entirely on the spelling, one can also suggest that the forms ⟨þæt⟩, ⟨þære⟩, and ⟨þa⟩ were ambiguous as markers of case or number. Secondly, the rules are also less complex than they should be, since they do not show the fact that <u>forms such as ⟨þone⟩, ⟨þa⟩, and ⟨þæt⟩ also occur after prepositions denoting locative case relationships.</u>

Thirdly, the most important reservation to be made about these rules is that they are not sufficiently context sensitive, for they allow up to three different forms of the article with any given case in the singular. This is an important limitation, since one has no means of predicting that the agent form ⟨se mann⟩ (⟨the man⟩) would have been regarded as grammatical by an Old English native speaker, while *⟨seo mann⟩ and *⟨þæt mann⟩ (but see below) would not. This brings us to an aspect of the grammars of both Old and (especially much early) Middle English that looks very strange to a speaker of Modern English. It was suggested above that a speaker of Old and Middle English could select different inflectional suffixes for nouns according to case-sensitive rules. However, in addition to this, the speaker had to know what group of nouns the particular item he chose belonged to, since there existed several different surface inflectional forms for any case relationship. He would know, for example, that the noun ⟨mann-⟩, since it belonged to a certain group or declension, would have a possessive suffix in ⟨es⟩, and not in ⟨e⟩ or ⟨an⟩.

A rather similar process had to be activated by a native speaker of Old English to enable him to select the grammatical form of the article with a given case in the singular. In his language there were three large noun groupings (Class I, Class II, and Class III) to which there could correspond up to three types of determiner for a given case relationship. These correspondences are represented in the following sets of rules, using the example of the definite article in the *singular*:

Class = gender

$$
\text{definite article} \longrightarrow \begin{bmatrix} \langle se \rangle \\ \langle \text{þone} \rangle \\ \langle \text{þæs} \rangle \\ \langle \text{þæm} \rangle \end{bmatrix} \Big/ \underline{\quad\quad} \text{N [Class I]} \begin{bmatrix} +\text{agent} \\ +\text{object} \\ +\text{possessive} \\ +\text{locative} \end{bmatrix}
$$

$$
\text{definite article} \longrightarrow \begin{bmatrix} \langle seo \rangle \\ \langle \text{þa} \rangle \\ \langle \text{þære} \rangle \end{bmatrix} \Big/ \underline{\quad\quad} \text{N [Class II]} \begin{bmatrix} +\text{agent} \\ +\text{object} \\ \{ +\text{possessive} \\ +\text{locative} \} \end{bmatrix}
$$

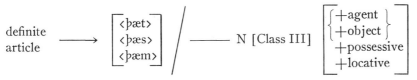

definite article $\longrightarrow$ $\begin{bmatrix} \langle \text{þæt} \rangle \\ \langle \text{þæs} \rangle \\ \langle \text{þæm} \rangle \end{bmatrix}$ / $\underline{\quad\quad}$ N [Class III] $\begin{bmatrix} \begin{Bmatrix} +\text{agent} \\ +\text{object} \end{Bmatrix} \\ +\text{possessive} \\ +\text{locative} \end{bmatrix}$

Class I words include ⟨stan, mann, cniht, ham⟩, Class II ⟨giefu, lar, miltheortnesse⟩, and Class III ⟨hus, wif, mæ3den, wæter⟩.

It is interesting to notice that <u>when one selects the article (or any other determiner) with nouns with the feature [−singular] in Old English, then although it has surface forms sensitive to the noun's case feature, there is no rule that operates to distinguish between different noun classes</u>—a situation rather like that found in both the singular and plural of the definite article in our *Peterborough Chronicle* extract.

Since we shall later be concerned in some detail with the kinds of change undergone by this system in Middle English, it is worth reiterating by means of an example some of the points made above. Let us see how the rules given so far in this chapter will generate the correct Old and early Middle English surface-structure forms of the definite article and inflectional suffix for the noun ⟨3ief-⟩ with the features [+singular, +object, +determiner] :

$\begin{bmatrix} \text{N} \\ +\text{case} \\ +\text{number} \\ +\text{determiner} \end{bmatrix}$

In this instance, we wish to generate for the noun ⟨3ief-⟩ the appropriate definite article and inflectional suffix forms when [case, number] are realized as :

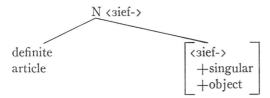

N ⟨3ief-⟩

definite article $\begin{bmatrix} \langle \text{3ief-} \rangle \\ +\text{singular} \\ +\text{object} \end{bmatrix}$

There must now be a rule that copies the features of case and number of the noun onto the definite article; in a simplified form this rule might have the general appearance of :

definite article $\longrightarrow$ $\begin{bmatrix} \alpha\text{case} \\ \beta\text{number} \end{bmatrix}$ / $\underline{\quad}$ N $\begin{bmatrix} \alpha\text{case} \\ \beta\text{number} \end{bmatrix}$

Consequently, one can now have

$$\begin{bmatrix} \text{definite article} \\ +\text{singular} \\ +\text{object} \end{bmatrix} + \begin{bmatrix} \langle \text{ʒief-} \rangle \\ +\text{singular} \\ +\text{object} \end{bmatrix}$$

However, this stage of the derivation of the acceptable form of the definite article is still too general, since it will allow three separate forms to be manifested—⟨þone⟩, ⟨þa⟩, and ⟨þæt⟩. One must, therefore, introduce a further rule; this states that since (and only since) the N has the number feature [+singular], the choice of determiner form depends upon the class of noun to which ⟨ʒief-⟩ belongs, so that

$$\begin{matrix} \text{article} \\ +\text{definite} \end{matrix} \longrightarrow [\gamma\text{class}] \Big/ \underline{\hspace{1.5cm}} \begin{bmatrix} \text{N} \\ -\text{singular} \\ \gamma\text{class} \end{bmatrix}$$

The class feature of the noun ⟨ʒief-⟩ is [II], so that according to the rules given above on page 112, the correct surface form of the article in this case and number context will be ⟨þa⟩.

In order to produce the correct inflectional suffix for ⟨ʒief-⟩ with features [+object, +singular], one has to operate a general rule of the kind:

$$\begin{matrix} \text{inflectional} \\ \text{suffix} \end{matrix} \longrightarrow [\Delta\text{declension}] \Big/ \begin{bmatrix} \text{N} \\ \Delta\text{declension} \end{bmatrix} \underline{\hspace{1cm}}$$

If one applies, therefore, the rules given above on page 105, the acceptable superficial form of the noun ⟨ʒief-⟩ with the given case and number features can be generated:

$$\begin{matrix} \text{inflectional} \\ \text{suffix} \end{matrix} \longrightarrow \langle e \rangle \Big/ \begin{bmatrix} \langle \text{ʒief-} \rangle \\ +\text{singular} \\ +\text{object} \end{bmatrix} \underline{\hspace{1cm}}$$

These rules will ensure that a surface form ⟨þa ʒiefe⟩ is realized and not ungrammatical forms such as *⟨þone ʒiefe⟩, *⟨þæt ʒiefa⟩, *⟨þa ʒiefan⟩, and so on.

It was suggested earlier that noun membership of declensional classes was, at least in Old English, arbitrary and unmotivated and would have to be "learned" by imitation rather than by induction. The same may be true of the class membership of nouns, which is responsible for the selection of the appropriate determiner form. In our treatment of this latter noun grouping, we have referred to the three main types as *classes*. It is worth mentioning here that most books on this subject call these three classes *grammatical genders*. We have avoided the term *gender* because it is so often confused with the notion of sex; that is, there is often the implication that the three genders in Old (and early Middle English)—they are even called the *masculine, feminine,* and *neuter* (corresponding to our Classes I, II, and III respectively)—can be equated in some rather loose way with the extra-linguistic categories of male, female, and inanimate. On the whole, this equation is misleading; and while it may have a very limited adequacy (although there are such startling counterexamples as ⟨þ mæ3den⟩ [⟨the young girl⟩, neuter gender], ⟨se wifmonn⟩ [⟨the woman⟩, masculine gender], and ⟨þ wif⟩ [⟨the woman⟩, neuter gender]), gender terminology is perhaps best put aside.

One is now in a position to account for the forms ⟨þet mot⟩ and ⟨se ærcebiscop⟩ in the *Peterborough Chronicle* extract; although both share the case and number features of [+agent, +singular], they belong to different class groups—⟨mot⟩ to Class III and ⟨ærcebiscop⟩ to Class I. Consequently, in the terms of the class-copying rule given earlier, the definite articles will have a different superficial appearance in each case. The significance of a usage like ⟨to þe Fridæig⟩ (*Pet. Chron.* [17]), where the definite article does not seem to copy the case feature of its noun, will be discussed fully below.

Personal Pronouns

Traditionally, the personal pronoun is said to "stand for" some identical noun to which the speaker may have made an earlier reference or the knowledge of which is shared by his audience. For example, the Modern English sentence

John Smith married Mary Brown because he loved her.

has a deep structure

John Smith married Mary Brown because John Smith
loved Mary Brown.

Let us say that most nouns have a feature [+Pronoun] and that when this feature is selected, one must make sure that many of the other features of the noun are copied in the pronoun. The features of the noun copied by the pronoun are [number, case, and sex], although in Modern English there is not always a one-to-one correspondence between nominal and pronominal feature manifestation. In addition, the personal pronoun at all periods in the English language is marked for person: in Modern English, ⟨I⟩ [I], ⟨you⟩ [II], ⟨he, she, or it⟩ [III]. Although we shall not go into the matter in detail here, it is also worth noting that despite the fact that the pronoun "stands for" and is derived from a deep-structure noun, in the surface structure it behaves very like the article ⟨the⟩ or ⟨a⟩. For instance, unlike nouns, <u>the personal pronoun cannot be preceded by an article,</u> so that sentences like

> *The they don't like a me.
> *An I doesn't like the them.

are clearly ungrammatical. On the other hand, personal pronouns can occur in contexts where articles are also grammatical; compare the following:

> we fine young men
> the fine young men
> our fine young men.

This point in the chapter will be concerned with an examination of a very limited part of the Middle English personal pronoun system; the forms that have some combination of the features [+Pro, ±singular, ±male, −animate, +III]. In the *Peterborough Chronicle* extract one finds the following examples of the personal pronoun:

[+sing] 1 ⟨se eorl com mid him⟩ (6–7)
         2 ⟨se kyng him geaf⟩ (4–5)
         3 ⟨to his agen land⟩ (3)
         4 ⟨buton his castel ane⟩ (5)
         5 ⟨þa hit eall com forð⟩ (17)

[−sing] 6 ⟨swa hi wæron æror feond⟩ (7–8)
         7 ⟨ealle heoldon here wifes⟩ (26)
         8 ⟨se kyng hem geaf⟩ (24)
         9 ⟨hi gisleden hem⟩ (3)
        10 ⟨þet hi scoldon hi forlæten⟩ (19)

The forms in the singular do not appear particularly strange to a speaker of Modern English, even though there is one now-obsolete spelling ⟨hit⟩. In fact, <u>the pronoun with the features [+singular, +male, +III] as it</u> appears at the time of the *Peterborough Chronicle* is <u>identical to its present form,</u> as can be seen from the following rule, which will generate it in both periods:

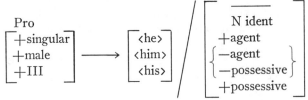

(where *N ident* is the *identical Noun* in the deep structure *Pro* "replaces"). Although it is not fully illustrated in our text, <u>the forms of the pronoun</u>

with the features [+singular, —animate, +III] do not share such a strong resemblance to Modern English forms. The latter can be generated by a rule of the type:

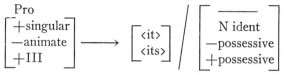

(It is worth mentioning here that there is no real need to specify the features [+singular, +III] in this pronominal form in Modern English, since the only Pro that is unambiguously marked as [—animate] is the one that has these number and person features. As will be seen below, changes in the English personal pronominal system have up to the present time tended to take place in the direction of marking the sex, animateness, or inanimateness of the Pro form.)

For English at the time of the *Peterborough Chronicle,* the Modern English rule for the [—animate] pronoun would generate ungrammatical forms. At this period of Middle English one would require a rule like:

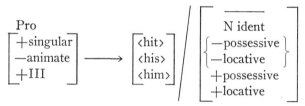

In other words, in early Middle English the [+male] and the [—animate] third-person pronominal form in the singular share in common the locative and possessive forms ⟨him⟩ and ⟨his⟩; in effect, this means that the surface forms of the pronoun in these instances are, at this period, often ambiguous as regards the sex or animateness of the Pro form.

The plural forms of the third-person pronouns in our Middle English extract are in appearance rather unlike their modern "equivalents." The latter can be generated by the rule

Pro
$\begin{bmatrix} -\text{singular} \\ +\text{animate} \\ +\text{III} \end{bmatrix}$ ⟶ $\begin{bmatrix} \langle\text{they}\rangle \\ \langle\text{them}\rangle \\ \langle\text{their}\rangle \end{bmatrix}$ / $\begin{bmatrix} \overline{} \\ \text{N ident} \\ +\text{agent} \\ \begin{Bmatrix} -\text{agent} \\ -\text{possessive} \end{Bmatrix} \\ +\text{possessive} \end{bmatrix}$

In the early Middle English system, however, it is not the equivalent of the modern ⟨them⟩ form that is case ambiguous:

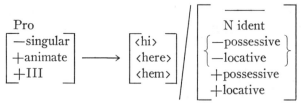

The other difference between the two plural systems is really a non-syntactic one; it is concerned with the origin, distribution, and form of the features of the initial consonantal segment.

II

In the second part of this chapter the same limited set of noun features discussed above will be reexamined in a later sample of Middle English to see what changes, if any, have taken place with respect to them. As far as possible, more stress will be placed upon the nature of these changes and the motivations for their occurrences where these can be recovered.

The following Chaucer extract, for example, is separated in time from the *Peterborough Chronicle* by almost two hundred and fifty years (approximately the same temporal difference between Swift's *Gulliver's Travels* and our own time), and so it would be a mistake to treat it as anything other than almost a different language in its own right and not merely as some slightly changed and developed version of the language of the earlier text. Although there are, obviously, similarities in syntactic features between texts from various periods of Middle English, one must, nevertheless, expect to find as many differences as likenesses and, in general, look at the same time for a complex rather than a simple state of affairs. What is true of one text will not necessarily be true of all texts for a variety of reasons; it even may appear on occasion that an individual scribe or author will be apparently "inconsistent" in his overall usage. Lastly, since our knowledge of the causes and directions of linguistic change is so limited, the answers to the questions raised (and even the questions themselves) can only have a limited value. Bearing these things in mind, one can now look at the second extract, taken this time from *The Parson's Tale,* one of Geoffrey Chaucer's *Canterbury Tales* written about the year 1390 (see *Text II*).

CASE INFLECTION

Nouns

Perhaps the most immediately obvious difference between this and the last extract is that the former superficially resembles Modern English much more closely, one of the most outstanding contributions to this feeling being the form of the nouns and their related features. It was noted above (pp. 99–108) that in Old English and still to a certain extent in the *Peterborough Chronicle* it was important to consider the noun features of declension and gender; that is, for a given case relationship— say, the subject—a given noun had to be assigned a specific inflectional ending from a fairly wide choice of inflectional-suffix types as well as one form (from a choice of two or even three) of definite article, conditioned by the noun's belonging to either Class (or "Gender") I, II, or III. If one considers the nouns in the Chaucer extract, it can be seen that neither declension nor noun (gender) class are as important features in the grammar as they were for Old and early Middle English. In the singular, for example, the great majority of nouns in the passage contain no inflectional ending whatever, regardless of their case relationships. For example, as subject one finds ‹þe serpent› (3), ‹þe womman› (6–7), ‹þe tree› (15): as object ‹good and harm› (14), ‹delit› (23): and many locative types ‹to þe womman› (5), ‹of every tree› (6), ‹of þe fruyt› (7), ‹in Paradys› (8), ‹of deeþ› (12).

Those of the above examples that can be found in Old or early Middle English would form their case-sensitive inflectional suffix forms by the rule

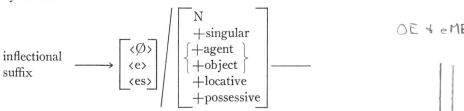

OE ↓ eME

inflectional suffix $\longrightarrow$ $\begin{bmatrix} ⟨\varnothing⟩ \\ ⟨e⟩ \\ ⟨es⟩ \end{bmatrix}$ $\Big/$ $\begin{bmatrix} N \\ +singular \\ \begin{Bmatrix} +agent \\ +object \end{Bmatrix} \\ +locative \\ +possessive \end{bmatrix}$ ——

However, the evidence from the Chaucer extract suggests that this rule has become "simplified"; one of its context-sensitive elements has been deleted from the grammar, so that it now becomes

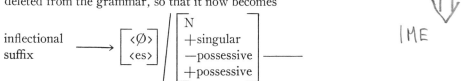

IME

inflectional suffix $\longrightarrow$ $\begin{bmatrix} ⟨\varnothing⟩ \\ ⟨es⟩ \end{bmatrix}$ $\Big/$ $\begin{bmatrix} N \\ +singular \\ -possessive \\ +possessive \end{bmatrix}$ ——

The collapse of the originally distinct rules for agent and locative forms is very clear in the examples

‹(þe serpent) seyde to þe womman› (5)
‹þe womman answerde› (6–7);

in early Middle or Old English one would normally expect the first (locative) occurrence of the noun ‹wifmonn-› or ‹womann-› to have an inflectional suffix in ‹e›. In other words, there has been a further simpli-

TEXT II. THE PARSON'S TALE
from THE CANTERBURY TALES
by GEOFFREY CHAUCER (about 1390)

Looke that in þ'estaat of innocence, whan Adam
and Eve naked weren in Paradys, and noþyng ne hadden
shame of hir nakednesse, how þat þe serpent, þat was
moost wily of alle oþere beestes þat God hadde maked,
seyde to þe womman: "Why comaunded God to yow ye   5
sholde nat eten of every tree in Paradys?" Þe
womman answerde: "Of þe fruyt," quod she, "of þe
trees in Paradys we feden us, but sooþly, of þe fruyt
of þe tree þat is in the myddel of Paradys, God forbad
us for to ete, ne nat touchen it, lest per aventure we   10
sholde dyen." Þe serpent seyde to þe womman: "Nay,
nay, ye shul nat dyen of deeþ; for soþe, God woot
þat what day þat ye eten þerof, youre eyen shul opene,
and ye shul been as goddes, knowynge good and harm." Þe
womman þanne saugh þat þe tree was good to feedyng,   15
and fair to þe eyen, and delitable to the sighte. She
took of þe fruyt of þe tree, and eet it, and yaf to
hire housbonde, and he eet, and anoon þe eyen of hem
boþe openeden. And whan þat þey knewe þat þey were
naked, þey sowed of fige leves a maner of breeches to   20
hiden hire membres. Þere may ye seen þat deedly synne
haþ first suggestion of þe feend, as sheweþ heere by
þe naddre; and afterward, þe delit of þe flessh, as
sheweþ heere by Eve; and after þat, þe consentynge
of resoun, as sheweþ heere by Adam.   25

[See how Adam and Eve in their innocent state were naked without shame in Paradise and how the serpent the most cunning animal in God's creation said to the woman: "Why has God forbidden you to eat from all the trees in Paradise?" She answered saying: "We can feed ourselves from the trees in Paradise, although in truth we are forbidden by God both to eat from and touch the one that is in the center of Paradise lest in so doing we should die." The serpent replied to her: "No, no, you shall not die. On the contrary, God knows that whenever you eat from that tree, you will see things you have never seen before, and you will become gods being able to distinguish good from evil." Then Eve realized that the tree was good to eat from and beautiful to look at. She then took fruit from the tree, ate it, and gave it to her husband. He too ate it and straightway they saw things in a different light, and conscious of their nakedness they made clothes out of fig leaves to hide their limbs. Thus it can be seen that mortal sin is first suggested by Satan as is demonstrated in this instance by the actions of the snake. Secondly, the lust of the body is shown by Eve, and lastly the surrender of reason by Adam.]

simplification of the inflectional markers of declension from the multiple choice possible in Old English and the binary ⟨Ø⟩/⟨e⟩ choice for nonpossessives in the singular in the *Peterborough Chronicle* extract. One can see also, of course, that there are nouns in our extract that end in an ⟨e⟩—at object position ⟨shame⟩ (3), ⟨consentynge⟩ (24), and postprepositionally ⟨to þe sighte⟩ (16), ⟨to hire housbonde⟩ (18), ⟨of hir nakednesse⟩ (3), ⟨by þe naddre⟩ (23). But in these instances the final ⟨e⟩ cannot be regarded as entering into any contrastive system with ⟨Ø⟩ forms in other case relationships, since one would normally expect these words to be spelled with final ⟨e⟩ as part of the stem itself in all case positions in Chaucer's works as a whole.

The form of the noun in the plural is almost identical in the Chaucer extract to that in the earlier piece. In general, the feature of [−singular] is marked by the addition of the ⟨es⟩ inflection, by this date there being no survivals of an ⟨as⟩ spelling form. Examples of this are numerous: ⟨goddes⟩ (14) and ⟨membres⟩ (21) in subject and object position respectively, while after prepositions are found ⟨of alle oþere beestes⟩ (4), ⟨of þe trees⟩ (7–8), and ⟨of fige leves⟩ (20). Again this marks, as noted already (see p. 108) above, a considerable simplification in comparison with the Old and early Middle English usage, where both declension and case could be marked in various different ways in the plural, so that for the example at (7–8) there would be an Old English equivalent ⟨of þæm treowum⟩, where the ⟨um⟩ inflection is used to mark the locative case relationship. However, there is another inflectional signal for the plural in our extract—⟨en⟩: ⟨youre eyen⟩ (13), ⟨eyen of hem⟩ (18), and ⟨to þe eyen⟩ (16) in subject and locative relationships respectively. Modern English, of course, still retains this plural inflectional form in words like ⟨brethren⟩, ⟨oxen⟩, and ⟨children⟩, but it seems that in Chaucer's time not only was the ⟨en⟩ plural inflection more widespread than it is now, but also that it had a different distribution. One finds, for example, in fourteenth-century Middle English such plurals as ⟨foon⟩ (⟨foes⟩) and ⟨toon⟩ (⟨toes⟩), but also ⟨childeris⟩ rather than the Modern English ⟨children⟩.

The above accounts of changes in the English nominal inflectional systems between the earliest recorded texts and Chaucer is, of course, greatly oversimplified. Unfortunately, this fact can mean that at best interesting details are left out, but at worst that one gains a false insight into how the processes of change involved seem to have been working. This last point is important, since if the theory of language acquisition (see above, p. 82) has any validity—that is, if language is acquired by an inductive process, so that in an important sense every new speaker has his own and partly unique set of grammatical rules—one must expect that changes in the system so brought about might not be uniform from speaker to speaker, but (at least as much) haphazard or idiosyncratic. In other words (and this is borne out by a detailed study of the many texts of Middle English), one is likely to find not only tendencies of linguistic change, but also countertendencies as well as apparently "unmotivated" changes at different times and in different dialects.

At the same time, even in the face of apparently general linguistic changes involving, for example, rule deletions, one can still find "remnants" of the predeletion set of rules. A good example of this in Middle English is the already mentioned "survival" in later Middle English (and even in Modern English) of declension-sensitive, inflectional suffix forms in the plural, such as ⟨eyen⟩, ⟨brethren⟩, and so on, even with the existence of what one suggested was a powerful tendency of change to delete declensionally context-sensitive rules of this and other types.

Two points can be made. The first is that language must also be in part learned by imitation, even though a present-day child will on many occasions apply the rule

$$\text{inflectional suffix} \longrightarrow \left\{ \begin{array}{l} \langle es \rangle \\ \langle s \rangle \end{array} \right\} \Big/ \left[\begin{array}{l} N \\ +\text{plural} \end{array} \right] \underline{\quad}$$

where ⟨es⟩ and ⟨s⟩ represent phonetic manifestations such as [ɪz], [s], and [z], so that in addition to generating grammatical forms such as ⟨boats⟩ and ⟨cars⟩, he will also generate what are for language-hearers the "nongrammatical" forms *[mænz] and *[gusɪz]. In the terms of his own grammar, such forms are grammatical, but the child is subject to the pressures of conformity to the rules of the parents' (and other speakers') grammars, and to these he is likely to make some concession. It is misleading to suggest the Middle and Modern English ⟨en⟩ plurals are conscious survivals of earlier grammatical systems. The grammar is apparently made up anew with each speaker who will try to make rules that will account for the language he hears and that will enable him to produce previously unheard, but grammatical, utterances.

As regards ⟨en⟩ plurals, one of the consequences of this process will be that even in Modern English there will exist in the grammar of most speakers something rather like a declensionally context-sensitive rule, so that alongside a "general" rule

$$\text{inflectional suffix} \longrightarrow \left\{ \begin{array}{l} \langle es \rangle \\ \langle s \rangle \end{array} \right\} \Big/ \left[\begin{array}{l} N \\ +\text{plural} \end{array} \right] \underline{\quad} \qquad \| \text{ plurals}$$

there will also be a restriction upon it to the effect that whenever N [+plural] is manifested as ⟨ox⟩, ⟨child⟩, and ⟨brother⟩ (when this word means "a fellow member of a Christian community"), it will then operate as:

$$\text{inflectional suffix} \longrightarrow \langle en \rangle \bigg/ \begin{bmatrix} \text{N} \\ +\text{plural} \\ \langle ox \rangle \\ \langle brother \rangle \\ \langle child \rangle \end{bmatrix} \underline{\quad\quad}$$

That is, items such as ⟨ox⟩, ⟨brother⟩, and ⟨child⟩, are marked as exceptions in the speaker's lexicon. Indeed, the class membership of nouns that form their plurals in an ⟨-n⟩ suffix has, throughout the history of the English language, been subject to a further and further depletion. Presumably, the fewer the members of the group—there being, it seems, no syntactical, phonological, or even semantic motivation at an abstract level for its identity—the more they come to be treated as exceptions. Exceptional features in the grammar are very *marked*—that is, they carry a very high level of information; higher than do other, unmarked, rule-predictable features. There seems to be a characteristic of linguistic change that reduces the number of marked features at every level in the grammar.

It is the case, however, that linguistic changes of all kinds are not "tidy" or necessarily uniform; individuals and groups of individuals will favor particular forms in the grammar—a good example of this is the form ⟨childeris⟩ found in some Northern Middle English dialects where the declensional class-sensitive rule seems to have been deleted, although it has apparently been "reimposed" in Modern English.

The Definite Article

Another feature in which our fourteenth-century extract resembles contemporary English is in its use of the definite article. Unlike Old English and unlike the English of the period two hundred or so years before it, Chaucer's English apparently displays only one form of the definite article both in the singular and in the plural as well as in all case relationships. The necessity to trigger off different forms of the definite article that accord with the "gender" and case features of the noun with which it is in agreement has been, it seems, completely lost. Of course, merely to select two short texts from the beginning and end of the Middle English period is bound to distort to some extent the overall linguistic picture. From our evidence it would seem that the multiple forms of the definite article (selected by the case, "gender," and number features of the noun) found at the beginning of the period simply disappear in favor of a system where these features are no longer "selected" and where the single form ⟨the⟩ with its various spellings is the universal norm. In other words, one might think that somewhere between the time of the *Peterborough Chronicle* and *The Canterbury Tales* there had taken place a simplification in the rules selecting the form of the definite article; that is, the rule for both the Old and early Middle English definite article

$$\text{definite article} \longrightarrow \begin{bmatrix} \alpha\text{case} \\ \beta\text{number} \\ \gamma\text{class} \end{bmatrix} \Big/ \underline{\quad} \begin{bmatrix} N \\ \alpha\text{case} \\ \beta\text{number} \\ \gamma\text{class} \end{bmatrix}$$

[margin: OE ↓ eME ⇓ lME]

had become simplified to

$$\text{definite article} \longrightarrow \langle \text{the} \rangle \Big/ \underline{\quad\quad} N$$

by the time of Chaucer. This display implies that the process of rule loss meant that there was a simultaneous disappearance of all three important environmental features—[case, number, and gender class]. In fact, this is not what appears to have happened at all. The evidence from many early Middle English texts (including the *Peterborough Chronicle*) suggests that the rules assigning a shape to the definite article in case and number environments still existed in the language. At first, only the part of the rule concerned with gender class underwent elimination. In these texts, one finds that the definite article can be produced by a rule that copies only the superficial features of case and number of the appropriate noun:

$$\begin{bmatrix} \text{article} \\ +\text{definite} \end{bmatrix} \longrightarrow \begin{bmatrix} \alpha\text{case} \\ \beta\text{number} \end{bmatrix} \Big/ \underline{\quad} \begin{bmatrix} N \\ \alpha\text{case} \\ \beta\text{number} \end{bmatrix}$$

Two questions must be raised here. In the first place, why does the noun "gender" class rule come to be deleted? It was suggested earlier that the simplification of the rules for case-marking inflectional suffixes also involved some kind of deletion from the grammar of nouns grouped together in (on this occasion, declensional) classes. There seems, in other words, to be some general rule of syntactic change involved in which the apparently unmotivated grouping of nouns into classes is no longer regarded as an important feature of the grammar. It is perhaps the unmotivated nature of the noun groupings (although this would require further investigation) that caused children acquiring English at this period—the change occurs as early as around the middle of the tenth century and seems still to be taking place in certain Middle English dialects in the middle of the thirteenth—to reformulate this aspect of the grammar of their parents.

For example, in the *Peterborough Chronicle* the definite article is generated by the rule immediately above, so that when the noun has the feature [+singular], the following case-sensitive rule is operative:

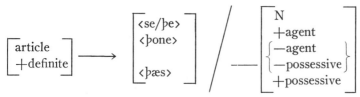

$$\begin{bmatrix} \text{article} \\ +\text{definite} \end{bmatrix} \longrightarrow \begin{bmatrix} \langle \text{se/þe} \rangle \\ \langle \text{þone} \rangle \\ \\ \langle \text{þæs} \rangle \end{bmatrix} \Bigg/ \begin{bmatrix} N \\ +\text{agent} \\ \left\{ \begin{matrix} -\text{agent} \\ -\text{possessive} \end{matrix} \right\} \\ +\text{possessive} \end{bmatrix}$$

The second problem raised by looking at the changes in the definite article in more detail centers around why the change should have taken the form it did. Why are the forms ⟨se/þe⟩, ⟨þone⟩, and· ⟨þæs⟩ selected in the given case contexts rather than say ⟨þæt⟩, ⟨þa⟩, or ⟨þære⟩ (see the rules on p. 109 above)? One (tentative) answer to this question might be that the forms selected are the only unambiguous markers of case features from among the definite-article possibilities: ⟨þæt⟩ can be either [+agent] or [+object], ⟨þa⟩ and ⟨þæm⟩ are ambiguous as regards number, and ⟨þære⟩ can be either [+possessive] or [+locative]. It is not, of course, being suggested that every language-acquirer at this period would produce a grammar of the definite article on the same basis; in different dialectal regions one finds different "solutions," although they all tend to delete the gender-sensitive context. For example, in some Southwest Midland texts (*The Southern Legendary* is one) one finds that definite article forms copy nominal case features; only there are differences in the surface structure choices from those in the *Peterborough Chronicle*:

$$\begin{matrix} \text{article} \\ +\text{definite} \end{matrix} \longrightarrow \begin{bmatrix} \text{þe} \\ \text{þone} \\ \text{þæs} \\ \text{þære} \end{bmatrix} \Bigg/ \begin{bmatrix} N \\ +\text{agent} \\ +\text{object} \\ +\text{possessive} \\ +\text{locative} \end{bmatrix}$$

It could be suggested that in the instance of the definite article, linguistic change in Middle English seems to take the form of some general instruction to the grammar to *collapse all gender-class-distinctive superficial realizations just so long as an unambiguous form reflecting surface nominal case be retained*.

Yet the Chaucer extract shows that this restructuring of the grammar by new speakers was only temporary. Nevertheless, the data suggest that the appearance of the originally [+agent] definite article ⟨þe⟩ in [−agent] contexts was at first restricted to certain syntactical environments, for instance, ⟨to ðe Fridæig⟩ (*Peterborough Chronicle* 17), and that its occurrence was not a random one in texts of this (and even earlier) date. Although not universally true, it seems that one can write for late Old and early Middle English texts the following rule:

$$\begin{matrix} \text{definite} \\ \text{article} \end{matrix} \longrightarrow \quad \langle \text{se/þe} \rangle \; / \; \text{preposition} \underline{\quad} N$$

It may be that in such contexts the case feature of the noun is "sufficiently" marked by the preposition, so that an additional mark by a case-sensitive form of the definite article is "unnecessary." However, this solution still leaves unexplained the fact that all linguistically redundant items are not deleted from grammars (for example, in Modern English the number feature [—singular] is doubly marked in the noun and the verb in sentences like ⟨The boys like chocolates⟩) or why one "nonredundant" solution rather than another should have been selected in the first place.

It is worth mentioning here that a very similar development to that of the definite article can be seen in the *adjective*. The inflectional suffix of the adjective was determined by both the "gender" and the case of the noun in English before and during the early Middle English period. Multiple forms of inflection existed for the adjective in Old English, but even a casual glance at either the *Peterborough Chronicle* or *The Parson's Tale* extract will show that, especially in the singular, the Middle English adjective, like its Modern English equivalent, has no inflectional ending: ⟨to his agen land⟩ (*PC* 5) corresponding to Old English ⟨to his agenum lande⟩, with the ⟨um⟩ inflection used to mark both the case and the "gender" Class III feature of the noun. An Old English "gender" Class II noun would have selected an adjectival ⟨re⟩ inflection, as in ⟨to his agenre cwene⟩ (⟨to his own woman⟩). In both texts the plural form of the adjective is usually marked with the ⟨e⟩ inflection: ⟨of alle oþere beestes⟩ (*PT* 4) and ⟨gode freond⟩ (*PC* 7). The close similarity between the adjective and the definite article in the way they appear to change from Old to Middle English is emphasized by the fact that (like the definite article) the adjective does not undergo some sudden change from multiple inflections dependent upon "gender" and case to a binary ⟨Ø⟩/⟨e⟩ opposition dependent upon number. On the contrary, in much the same way as the definite article, and by and large with the same temporal and dialectal distribution, in early Middle English texts one finds a multiple (if reduced) system of adjectival inflection forms, both in the singular and in the plural, used solely (regardless of any gender-class considerations) to mark the case relationship of the noun with which a given adjective is in concord.

The Personal Pronoun

The interest in this form in the Chaucer extract is centered upon its appearances with the features [+III, +singular, +female] and [+animate, —singular]. The occurrences of the former are as follows:

⟨She took of þe fruyt⟩ (16–17)
⟨yaf to hire housbonde⟩ (17–18)
⟨quod she⟩ (7)

Except for orthographic variation, the Modern English reader finds nothing strange about [+agent] and [+possessive] forms of the third-person female pronoun in the singular in ⟨she⟩ and ⟨hire⟩. In fact, the same rule will generate the <u>third-person female pronoun</u> in both Chaucerian and Modern English.

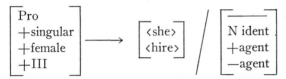

If one compares this rule, however, with that which must be used to generate Old and some earlier Middle English forms of this pronoun, namely,

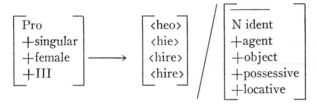

one is faced with two problems. The first is the origin of the form spelled ⟨she⟩ and its relation, if any, to the ⟨heo⟩ form and its orthographic variants. The second—and it will obviously be related to similar problems in the [+singular, +male, +III] and [+singular, −animate] pronoun forms discussed below—has to do with the deletion of the ⟨heo⟩ form in [+object] contexts.

The agent form of the female third-person pronoun appears in many orthographic guises throughout the Middle English period. One finds spellings that suggest variation in the spoken manifestation both of the consonantal and vocalic segments in the words:

⟨hi⟩	⟨she⟩	⟨ȝhe⟩	⟨che⟩
⟨ho⟩	⟨sche⟩	⟨ȝe⟩	⟨xe⟩
⟨heo⟩	⟨scheo⟩	⟨ȝo⟩	⟨xhe⟩
⟨hy⟩	⟨schue⟩	⟨ȝeo⟩	⟨ye⟩
⟨he⟩	⟨schu⟩	⟨ȝheo⟩	
⟨hue⟩	⟨scæ⟩		
⟨hoe⟩	⟨schee⟩		
⟨hoo⟩	⟨ssche⟩		
	⟨scho⟩		
	⟨sho⟩		

Such forms have a fairly regular dialectal distribution and provide one of the best examples of the great range of orthographic variation current in the Middle English period (see "Spellings and Sounds," pp. 45–52).

About the only things known for certain about the ⟨she⟩ type forms of this pronoun are (a) that they are usually to be found most commonly in texts that have an Eastern or Northern dialectal provenance, and (b) the type first appears, spelled ⟨scæ⟩, in the *Peterborough Chronicle*. The introduction (if that is indeed what it was) of this form into the English language appears completely enigmatic, and attempts to derive it from the earlier ⟨h-⟩ forms are all unconvincing. On the basis of a spelling ⟨ʒhe⟩ for this word in the *Ormulum*, it seems that what was once [heow], that is, a combination of [h] + vowel + diphthong, has become [çe], consonant + vowel. By examining the process involved in this tentative approximation, one may also be able to suggest a derivation for the later initial consonantal segment [š]. To explain a change from [heow] to [çe] involves the deletion at one point of one of the segments. This deletion would be possible if some kind of syllabicity shift takes place, caused, perhaps, by a shifting of the stress-assignment rules in this word; that is the segment [e], which in [hĕow] has the feature [+syllable], loses this feature when, owing to a new assignment of stress, it is realized as [hjŏw] (where [1] indicates main stress placement). As the above phonological representation suggests, [e] changes in the process to the front glide [j]. The (simplified) distinctive feature matrices for [hj] are:

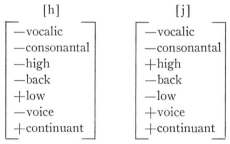

[h]
- —vocalic
- —consonantal
- —high
- —back
- +low
- —voice
- +continuant

[j]
- —vocalic
- —consonantal
- +high
- —back
- —low
- +voice
- +continuant

while the form [ç], represented by Orm as ⟨ʒh-⟩, would have a feature makeup

- —vocalic
- +consonantal
- +high
- —back
- —low
- —voice
- +continuant

although it is difficult to be sure about the nature of the voice feature. What is involved in the change from [hj] ⟶ [ç] is therefore simply an assimilation in height. The sound [h] has taken on the [+high] feature of [j] and a continuant consonant has emerged. This consonant probably also has the feature [+strident] (Chomsky and Halle [1968], p. 329) caused by the narrowing of the passage through which the air has to pass. In the change that realizes the underlying [hj] as [š], with feature composition

$$
\begin{bmatrix}
-\text{vocalic} \\
+\text{consonantal} \\
+\text{high} \\
-\text{back} \\
-\text{voice} \\
+\text{coronal}
\end{bmatrix}
$$

a similar height assimilation has occurred, although in this instance [š], unlike [j] and [ç], is [+coronal] and not [−coronal]. This feature, not introduced before, refers to the height of the *blade* of the tongue (its front part), whereas [±high] refers to tongue *body* height. In other words, the assimilation of [h] to [j] entails a generally greater articulatory gesture of heightening to produce [š] rather than [ç]. The tentative nature of this "explanation" cannot be overemphasized, and one may even be wrong in assuming that the ⟨sh-⟩ types are "derived" from those with initial ⟨h-⟩ or ⟨3h-⟩. As we have said, all the theories that have been put forward to date to explain this phenomenon are unsatisfactory, although some more so than others. Among the least convincing is the one that suggests the initial ⟨sh-⟩ forms to be derived by means of a sandhi construction in such contexts as ⟨was heo⟩ or ⟨comes heo⟩. It is doubtful whether an apparently new syntactical item could possibly be formed in this way; at the same time, there is no attempt to show that this *verb* + *agent* ordering was a typical feature of the texts in which it occurs—indeed, even a cursory statistical count shows that such constructions are far from being the most frequent.

Another common, but unconvincing, "derivation" of the ⟨sh-⟩ types is that which suggests the analogy (whatever this word means in linguistic theory [King (1968), pp. 127 ff.]) with the definite-article Gender II (the "feminine" gender) form ⟨seo⟩. This theory will be convincing only if and when evidence is produced that will show some nontrivial correspondence between the three gender classes and some system (which is hardly likely to be tripartite) of sex representation in language.

Perhaps the most obvious question one might now want to ask is why forms in ⟨sh-⟩ should ever have appeared in the grammar at all. The answer to this question is tied up with the reasons for the particular form of the changes in the third-person singular pronoun in general. This form undergoes considerable alteration in surface manifestation (not unlike the changes in the definite article) in texts written after approximately the year 1000. In essence, the change means that one less case-sensitive shape of this pronominal form was generated by the rules of the grammar. The following branching diagram displays the relationship between surface case contexts and the realization of the male third-person pronominal form in the singular for most Old English and some early Middle English texts:

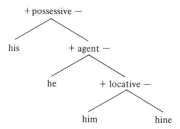

Speakers exposed to this data, even by the date of the *Peterborough Chronicle,* and certainly by Chaucer's time, seem to have restructured it by means of deleting the [—locative] realization, to:

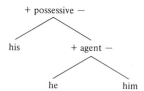

A very similar process seems to be taking place in the changes to the third-person inanimate singular pronominal form between Old and Middle English. An early system

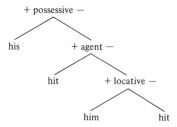

became restructured to:

In like manner, <u>the female equivalent of these pronouns,</u> before the introduction of the ⟨sh-⟩ forms, undergoes a restructuring of

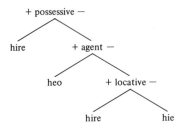

to some system like:

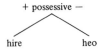

although, in many texts, the [—possessive] form was orthographically
realized as ⟨he⟩. As with the definite article, <u>it might be possible to ex-</u>
<u>plain the direction of these pronominal changes in terms of a general in-</u>
<u>struction to the grammar to the effect that</u> *superficial case-marking forms*
may be deleted just so long as distinctions involving sex and animateness are
not impaired. The result of these changes is that, with the exception of the
[+possessive, —animate] ⟨his⟩, there is now no sex-ambiguous, case-
sensitive singular pronominal form of the third person. <u>Perhaps the spell-</u>
<u>ings in ⟨sh-⟩ came to be part of the grammar just to carry the above in-</u>
<u>struction to the grammar one stage further, since the ⟨he⟩ spellings for the</u>
<u>female forms suggest the possibility of homophony with the corresponding</u>
[+agent] male form. It is interesting to notice that the one further change
that has taken place in this system since Middle English is also within the
terms of the general instruction, since the [—animate, +possessive] comes
to be realized as ⟨its⟩, thus removing the final sex-ambiguous surface
pronominal form.

   Another interesting pronominal development in the Chaucer extract
is to be seen when the form has the features [—singular, +III]. The
following rules will generate the surface pronominal forms with these
features in case sensitive environments:

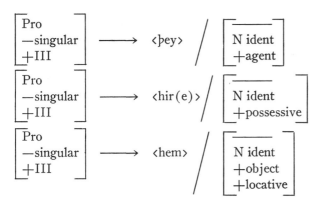

Here too one can postulate a restructuring in this part of the grammar involving the deletion of the surface [—locative] feature, so that an earlier

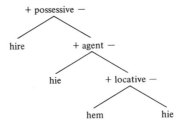

appears by Chaucer as

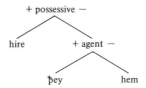

Another important aspect of this later system lies in the appearance of the [+agent] surface form ⟨þey⟩; the forms of this pronoun "remaining" with initial ⟨h-⟩ in all other case contexts. Third-person plural pronouns spelled with initial ⟨þ-⟩ are most frequent in texts with a Northern dialectal provenance; and even in texts of an early date written in these areas, one can find ⟨þ-⟩ initial forms in all case contexts, very much like modern usage: ⟨þei⟩, ⟨þeir⟩ and ⟨þem⟩ with, of course, orthographic variation in the vocalic segment.

The fact that the ⟨þ-⟩ forms are found in Northern geographical regions has led to the belief that they originate from the contemporary Norse third-person, male, plural pronominal form ⟨þeir⟩, since there is said to have been some bilingualism in these areas, owing to earlier Viking invasions. It is also argued that the forms in ⟨þ-⟩ were introduced into the language for "functional" reasons; that is, since there was probably some kind of homophonic clash between pronouns with the features [+ and —singular]—compare the plural spellings ⟨he⟩, ⟨hire⟩, and ⟨hem⟩—the forms in ⟨þ-⟩ were a useful innovation, for they kept this important distinction marked in the surface structure. However attractive and "logical" theories of this kind may appear, they can have only a limited value, since, among other things, one would probably be mistaken to think that linguistic change necessarily worked in such a systematic way. As with the rules given above for the singular third-person pronominal "behavior," such explanations are essentially ideal rather than true. There is always a considerably more complex situation presented by the data, and for this the theory of change is as yet too inadequate to give anything but a very general picture. For example, how on the basis of a "functional" theory can one account for the fact that ⟨þ-⟩ forms appear to be used only in [+agent] contexts; Chaucer's other case forms are ambiguous as regards number superficially, so why were the ⟨h-⟩ types kept in these contexts? It is only rather late in the fifteenth century (and then not entirely) that the ⟨þ-⟩ forms in the plural generally supplanted those in ⟨h-⟩ in non-Northern dialect texts.

The second-person pronoun in the singular and plural appears in Chaucer, not unlike the way it does in Modern English. To generate the forms in the extract one needs the following rule:

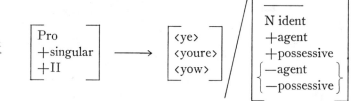

In Modern English there is only a possessive/nonpossessive surface distinction between ⟨your⟩ and ⟨you⟩, and there is some evidence to suggest that this was also the case in some texts of the late Middle English period. However, there still exist (and they were more common in Middle English) forms of this pronoun spelled ⟨thou⟩. The history of these forms is interesting, since at one stage in English (notably in Old English) they were used to mark the singular number in contrast to forms with initial glide segment (spelled ⟨ȝ⟩ and ⟨e⟩ in Old English and ⟨y⟩ and ⟨i⟩— among others—in Middle English). The rules needed to generate the forms of the second-person pronoun in Old English were:

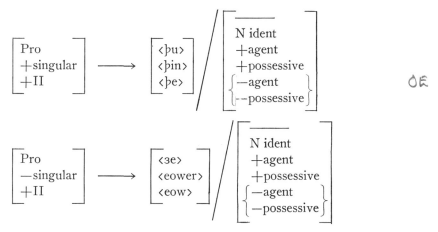

One seems to be witnessing a very strange kind of syntactic change when one compares the Old and Middle English rules for this item, because the latter has apparently deleted the singular forms, whereas the surface forms "originally" unambiguous for number are now unmarked for this feature.

However, the situation is even more complex than this, a fact that can be seen from a consideration of the Modern English usage. Here, the ⟨thou⟩ form, although it is rare, has not been completely lost, but is rather confined in its use to certain sociolinguistic contexts. In other words, the form of this pronoun, together with many other syntactical and phonological features, will depend upon the variety of language (appropriate to a given nonlinguistic or linguistic situation) one happens to be using. The ⟨thou⟩ forms, for example, are restricted to such varieties as deliberately "archaic" English (in some plays), religious English, and some literary contexts.

The evidence suggests that, as in Modern English, a speaker, say in the fourteenth century, was not at liberty to select ⟨thou⟩ and ⟨ye⟩ forms at will; rather there were certain contexts in which one form rather than the other was conventionally regarded as more "appropriate." One of the nonlinguistic situations that seems to have determined the selection of these forms was the status relationship that existed between the speaker and the hearer. When one addressed persons of a higher social rank, it appears to have been a fourteenth-century linguistic custom to use the pronoun ⟨ye⟩, whereas those of a lower rank than the speaker could expect to be addressed by the form ⟨thou⟩. This is, of course, an oversimplification of the restrictions on the use of the second-person pronominal forms, but it points to the need to include in our grammar rules of the type that will allow for <u>situational as well as syntactic and phonological context sensitivity</u>:

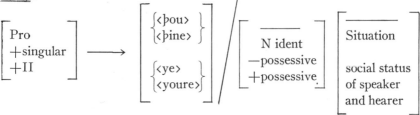

The Relative Pronoun

An examination of the use of the relative pronoun in Middle English quickly reveals two things: the variety and complexity of the surface appearances of the form make predictive rules difficult to draw up; secondly, a multiplicity of linguistic criteria (situational as well as syntactic) will have to be drawn upon if the rules are to have any adequacy.

Like the personal pronoun, the <u>relative "stands for" an identical noun in the deep structure, and varieties in its surface appearance will be due to attempts to "copy" features of the identical noun.</u> In Modern English, the <u>features copied include case, animateness, and the degree to which the identical noun is specified or determined, as well as situational features.</u> There are <u>three surface forms</u>: ⟨wh-⟩, ⟨that⟩, and ⟨Ø⟩; for example, ⟨the man whom I knew⟩, ⟨the man that I knew⟩, and ⟨the man I knew⟩, all of which can occur in the singular or plural, although they do not exist in free variation with each other, <u>surface forms being selected by rules sensitive to the kind of syntactic and situational contexts suggested above.</u>

In the Middle English extracts in this chapter, however, not only do <u>the ⟨wh-⟩ and ⟨Ø⟩ relative types not occur, but surface forms are also to be found that are no longer current in Modern English.</u> Instances of the last include ⟨<u>se þe⟩</u> in ⟨se þe þet ne wolden done forgede his circe⟩ (*Peterborough Chronicle*, 20) as well as ⟨<u>þa⟩</u>, especially in the context of plural noun "antecedents" as in ⟨canonias þa wæron on ealle þe cellas⟩ (*Peterborough Chronicle*, 11–12). On the other hand, in the Chaucer extract, one does not find any ⟨se þe⟩ or ⟨þa⟩ forms at all, the surface form of the relative (after singular as well as plural noun "antecedents") being everywhere ⟨<u>þat⟩</u>: ⟨þe tree þat is in þe myddel⟩ (9) and ⟨alle oþere beestes þat God hadde maked⟩ (4).

Because the use of the different forms of the relative pronoun in Middle English is so complex, we shall only be able to set up rules that are limited in their temporal and dialectal application; even the use of an individual scribe in a given manuscript can apparently vary to a considerable

MₙE

ME

eME

lME

extent. One can begin by mentioning what appear to be a few universal tendencies of the form in Middle English. The first of these is that early Middle English usage is very different from that found in texts written later in the period. The second is that the later the date of composition of the text, the more likely one is to find the surface relative as ⟨þat⟩ and even ⟨wh-⟩; hence, perhaps, the high frequency of ⟨þat⟩ types in the Chaucer extract. Thirdly, it seems that (even in early Middle English) if the text is written in a Northern dialect, there is a high likelihood that ⟨þat⟩ rather than any other relative form will appear.

Perhaps the most difficult problem lies in the attempt to formulate adequate rules for the selection of the surface relative form in early Middle English texts of a non-Northern origin. In singular contexts, two surface forms of the relative ⟨þe⟩ and ⟨þat⟩ exist side by side in these texts, and it is often hard to see the "motivation" for the use of one against the other. Rules that can be set up for one text will apparently not work for another. For example, in some parts of the *Peterborough Chronicle,* the surface relative form seems to be selected according to the + or —animate feature of the identical noun "antecedent," so that one can write a rule

$$\text{relative pronoun} \atop [+\text{singular}] \longrightarrow \begin{bmatrix} \langle þe \rangle \\ \langle þat \rangle \end{bmatrix} \Bigg/ \begin{bmatrix} \text{N ident} \\ +\text{animate} \\ -\text{animate} \end{bmatrix} \text{———}$$

and so account for the examples ⟨ic Saxulf þe wæs first abbot 7 nu eam biscop⟩ (*Peterborough Chronicle,* annal 675) and ⟨in an ceste þat was scort 7 nareu 7 undep⟩ (*Peterborough Chronicle,* annal 1137). This rule, however, has only a limited generality even for the *Peterborough Chronicle* and is very often inadequate for the usage in other texts of similar date; compare the examples ⟨þu singest þe salm þat is cleped pater noster⟩, ⟨þu singest þe salm þe me clepeð crede⟩, and ⟨alse he þat is recheles⟩ from the text known as the *Trinity Homilies.*

It may be, therefore, that in some texts the selection of surface relative form is completely arbitrary; but before committing oneself to this position, one might want to ask whether there is any significance in the fact that the early Middle English relative pronouns share a surface appearance common to some definite-article forms. Consider the following examples from the *Lambeth Homilies:*

(1) ⟨þe mon þe þus fest crist him geueð swilcne mete⟩
     (⟨Christ will give this kind of food to the man [that is, any man] who will fast in this way⟩)

(2) ⟨þe mon þe heleð his sunne aðisse liue ne siht he nefre almihtin drihten⟩

(‹The man who hides his sins in this life will never see Almighty God›)

(3) ‹ah þenne þe preost hine hat aȝefen þa ehte þon monne þet hit er ahte›

(‹But when the priest bids him give back the goods to the man who formerly owned them›)

(4) ‹on sume stude þer hit beoð wel bitoȝen for cristes luue 7 for þene mon þet hit er ahte›

(‹[The priest will order him to distribute the property] in some place where it will be used in a good way for Christ's love, and for [the good of] the man who previously owned it›)

At first sight it would appear that a quite contradictory usage is involved in these examples. In all four cases the "identical" noun antecedent is ‹mon›, yet in the first two examples the surface relative is ‹þe›, whereas in the second two it is ‹þet›.

However, although they apparently share the same surface-structure form, the deep structure of the "identical" noun in the first two examples is different from that in the second two. In the former, one is dealing with a deep-structure noun of the type *any man* (that is, some person to whom no previous mention has been made, and about whom there is no shared knowledge between the speaker and the hearer), and here the ‹þe› relative appears. In the latter, however, the underlying noun form is *some man* (about whom something is known or who has been mentioned earlier), and the ‹þet› relative is used. In the first two instances it is the relative clause itself that, as it were, specifies the *any man,* so that, in effect the *any* + N + relative clause is "equivalent" to the surface-structure ‹mon› (without relative clause) in the last two examples. Or it can be said that underlying the *some man* level of structure is a more abstract *any* + *man* + identifying relative clause.

One is now faced with a very difficult problem. If it is true, as has been (tentatively) suggested, that in some Middle English texts the ‹þe› relative form is selected after antecedents whose underlying structure is *any* + N, whereas those with a deep-structure *some* + N will trigger off ‹þet›, how can one account for such a system in terms of the few remarks made earlier about language acquisition? There seems to be hardly any evidence for suggesting that the form ‹þet› was used as a relative at all in Old English. How then does it come to appear in this context in Middle English and in such numbers?

Unlike many other of the linguistic changes so far discussed, the use of *that* seems to represent an innovation in the grammar rather than a deletion. However, it is only an innovation in a rather restricted sense, since, as has been seen, the language already had a surface form ⟨þet⟩ for the definite article in certain case and "gender" class-sensitive contexts. According to the rules given above for the definite article (see pp. 109–115), it would seem that with the deletion of "gender" sensitive contexts from English in the late Old English period, the form ⟨þet⟩ could no longer be expected to be found. However, things are more complex than this, and the ⟨þet⟩ form survived as an article (as it still does), but with a special function. Consider, for example, the Modern English sentence: ⟨He saw the man walking down the street and then that man disappeared⟩. In this kind of context, at least one of the functions of ⟨that⟩ (and it can have many others in Modern English) is to mark some feature of identity between the second ⟨man⟩ and the first, or indicate that the second ⟨man⟩ is now known. This identifying function of the article ⟨that⟩ is difficult to demonstrate in Old English because of the restrictions put upon articles by the gender class-copying rules. Nevertheless, there are some clear cases of something very like the modern usage in such an early text as the Old English gloss to the *Lindisfarne Gospels*.

One can see this from the following example from that gloss:

7   ðidder   ic   geonga   gie uutton   7   ðone uoeg   gie uuton
ET   QUO   EGO   UADO   SCITIS   ET   UIAM   SCITIS·
cuoeð   him   ðomas   drihten   nuutwe   huidder   7   huu
DICIT   EI   THOMAS   DOMINE   NESCIMUS   QUO UADIS   ET   QUOMODO
mago ué   þ uég   gewuta
POSSUMUS   UIAM   SCIRE

In both its occurrences the noun ⟨u(o)eg⟩ has the case feature [+object] and the gender class feature [I] (the so-called masculine) under "normal" circumstances in Old English. How then does it in this text have a gender class [I] feature (copied in the definite article as ⟨þone⟩) in one line, while a few words later it appears with a definite article form that "normally" occurs only with nouns that belong to gender class [III]?

The answer must be that even by this date definite-article gender-copying rules could be deleted from the language and that in this example one is dealing with ⟨þ⟩ as a marker of identity with some previously mentioned N.

It would seem, therefore, that the function of identification of the ⟨þ⟩ definite article is shared by its identical surface relative form, and this is hardly surprising as an innovation, since both the definite article and the relative clause, although they appear quite different in the surface structure of English, in fact can be two different superficial appearances of the same underlying or deep-structure feature of nouns—*specification*.

One must not think, of course, that the above will satisfactorily account for all occurrences of the ⟨þe⟩ and ⟨þet⟩ relative forms in early Middle English. There seem, in fact, to be several other selectional restrictions on the use of these forms; one rather interesting one is in the *Peterborough Chronicle* with relative clauses of the type corresponding to Modern English *who/which is called*. In Middle English as a whole, this construction has two surface appearances: relative word + ⟨man cleopeð⟩ and relative word + ⟨is/wæs + gehaten⟩. In the *Peterborough Chronicle* in the first of these types, the relative word is almost without exception ⟨þet⟩, but in the second it is ⟨þe⟩ :

> ⟨æt þone stede þet man cleopeð Heatfelde⟩
> ⟨se biscop of Lundone, þe was Wina gehaten⟩

Yet another selectional restriction on the use of ⟨þe⟩ and ⟨þet⟩ appears in the *Lambeth Homilies*. Throughout this text there is much alternation between the two relative forms, but in the homilies that are Middle English renderings of the *Credo* and the *Pater Noster,* the ⟨þet⟩ relative is almost completely dominant. It may be that the selectional restriction in this instance involves language variety; that is, in the context of a formal prayer, the ⟨þet⟩ relative is conventionally felt to be the more appropriate one to use. It is interesting that restrictions of this type are very important for the selection of the ⟨wh-⟩ relative, which is not found commonly until well after Chaucer's time. Certainly by the sixteenth and seventeenth centuries the ⟨wh-⟩ form seems to have been restricted almost entirely to formal written contexts, whereas ⟨that⟩ was apparently regarded as the spoken, conversational (and even "vulgar") relative variety; this probably accounts for its scarcity in nearly all the written texts of the period. In Steele's "Humble Petition of *Who* and *Which*" in the *Spectator* (No. 78), the ⟨that⟩ relative form is condemned as "Jack Spratt *That.*" Even in Modern English there is a tendency to use ⟨wh-⟩ relative forms more frequently than ⟨that⟩ or ⟨∅⟩ in contexts such as formal letter writing or formal speaking.

BIBLIOGRAPHY

GENERAL DISCUSSIONS OF THE NOUN AND RELATED MATTERS

BENNETT, J. A. W., and G. V. SMITHERS (1966), "Introduction," pp. xviii–lviii.

BRUNNER, K. (1948), pp. 48 ff.

CLARK, C. (1958), "Introduction," pp. xxx ff.

JACOBS, R. A., and P. S. ROSENBAUM (1968), pp. 10–30, 44–51, 81–99, 217–223.

KING, R. (1969), chapters 4 and 6.

LYONS, J. (1968), chapters 6–8.

MOSSÉ, F. (1952), pp. 44 ff.

MUSTANOJA, T. F. (1960), pp. 43 ff., 55 ff., 67 ff., 120 ff., 126 ff.

WARDALE, E. E. (1949), pp. 72 ff., 86 ff.

WEINSTOCK, H. (1968), pp. 133 ff.

WRIGHT, J. (1957), pp. 103–149, 150–158, 159–174.

BOOKS AND ARTICLES OF A MORE DETAILED NATURE

ANDREW, S. O., *Syntax and Style in Old English,* Cambridge, 1940.

BACQUET, P., *La structure de la phrase verbale à l'époque alfrédienne,* Paris, 1962.

BARRETT, C. R., *Studies in the Word Order of Ælfric's Catholic Homilies and Lives of Saints,* Cambridge, 1953.

BERKO, J., "The Child's Learning of English Morphology," in *Psycholinguistics: A Book of Readings,* edited by S. Saporta, New York, 1961.

BLAKE, N. F., "Caxton's Language," *Neuphilologische Mitteilungen,* LXVII (1966).

BLAKELEY, L., "Accusative-Dative Syncretism in the *Lindisfarne Gospels,*" *English and Germanic Studies,* I (1947–1948).

BRAINE, M. D., "The Ontogeny of English Phrase Structure," *Language,* 39 (1963).

BROWN, R., and U. BELLUGI, "Three Processes in the Child's Acquisition of Syntax," *Harvard Educational Review,* 34 (1964).

BROWN, R., and C. FRASER, "The Acquisition of Syntax," in *Verbal Behaviour and Learning,* edited by C. N. Cofer and B. Musgrave, New York, (1963).

BRYAN, W. F., "The Midland Present Plural Indicative Ending -e(n)," *Modern Philology,* XVIII (1921).

CHOMSKY, N. (1965), pp. 170–184.

CLARK, C., "Gender in the *Peterborough Chronicle,*" *English Studies,* XXXV (1957).

DIEHN, O., "Die Pronomina im Frümittelenglischen," *Kieler Studien zur englischen Philologie,* Heidelberg, 1901.

DIETH, E., "Hips: A Geographical Contribution to the 'She' Puzzle," *English Studies,* XXXVI (1955).

EVANS, W. W., "Dramatic Use of the Second Person Singular Pronoun in *Sir Gawain and the Green Knight,*" *Studia Neophilologica,* 39 (1967).

FLOM, G. T., "The Origin of the Pronoun 'She,'" *JEGP,* VII (1908).

FRENCH, R. D., *A Chaucer Handbook,* New York, 1947.

GLAHN, N. V., "Zur Geschichte des Grammatischen Geschlechts," *Anglistische Forschungen,* LIII (1918).

GREENBERG, J. H., C. E. OSGOOD, and S. SAPORTA, "Language Change" in *Psycholinguistics: A Survey of Theory and Research Problems,* edited by C. E. Osgood and T. A. Sebeok, Cambridge, Mass., 1965.

GUMPERZ, J. J., "On the Ethnology of Linguistic Change," in *Sociolinguistics,* edited by W. Bright, The Hague, 1966.

HALLBECK, E. S., *The Language of the Middle English Bestiary,* Christianstad, 1905.

HARRIS, D. P., "The Development of Word-Order Patterns in Twelfth-Century English," in *Studies in Language and Linguistics in Honour of C. C. Fries,* edited by A. H. Marckwardt, Michigan, 1964.

HORSTMANN, C., *The Early South English Legendary,* Early English Text Society, O.S. 87, 1887.

JONES, C., "The Functional Motivation of Linguistic Change," *English Studies,* XLVIII (1967).

————, "The Grammatical Category of Gender in Early Middle English," *English Studies,* XLVIII (1967).

————, "Some Features of Determiner Usage in the Late Old English Glosses to the *Lindisfarne Gospels* and *Durham Ritual,*" *Indogermanische Forschungen,* 1971.

KARPF, F., "Studien zur Syntax in dem Werken Geoffrey Chaucers," *Wiener Beiträge zur englischen Philologie,* LV (1930), Wien und Leipzig.

KELLER, W., "Skandinavischer Einfluss in der englischer Flexion," in *Probleme der englischen Sprache und Kultur, Festschrift, Johannes Hoops,* Heidelberg, 1925.

KENNEDY, A. G., *The Pronouns of Address in English Literature of the Thirteenth Century,* Stanford, 1915.

KIVIMAA, K., "*Þe* and *Þat* as Clause Connectives in Early Middle English with Especial Consideration of the Pleonastic *Þat,*" *Societas Scientiarum Fennica. Commentationes Humanarum Litterarum,* 39 (1966), Helsinki.

KOZIOL, H., "Grundzüge der Syntax der Mittelenglischen Stabreimdichtungen," *Wiener Beiträge zur englischen Philologie,* LVIII (1932), Wien und Leipzig.

LEHNERT, M., "Sprachform und Sprachfunktion im *Ormulum,*" *Wissenschaft Zeitschrift der Humboldt Universität zu Berlin,* II (1952–1953).

LINDHEIM, B. VON, "Studien zur Sprache des Manuscriptes Cotton Gallia E ix," *Wiener Beiträge zur englischen Philologie,* LIX (1937), Wien und Leipzig.

LINDKVIST, H., "On the Origin and History of the English Pronoun *She,*" *Anglia,* XLV (1921).

MCINTOSH, A., "The Relative Pronouns þe and þat in Early Middle English," *English and Germanic Studies,* I (1947–1948).

MACLEISH, M., *The Middle English Subject-Verb Cluster,* The Hague, 1969.

MARCHAND, H., "The Syntactical Change from Inflexional to Word Order Systems," *Anglia,* LXX (1951).

MARTINET, A., *A Functional View of Language,* Oxford, 1962.

MENNER, R. J., "The Conflicts of Homonyms in English," *Language,* XII (1936).

MITCHELL, B., "Syntax and Word Order in the *Peterborough Chronicle, 1122–1154,*" *Neuphilologische Mitteilungen,* 65 (1964).

MOORE, S., "Grammatical and Natural Gender in Middle English," *PMLA,* XXXVI (1921).

———, *Historical Outlines of English Phonology and Morphology,* Ann Arbor, 1925.

———, "Earliest Morphological Changes in Middle English," *Language,* IV (1928).

———, "Loss of Final -*n* in Inflectional Syllables of Middle English," *Language,* III (1927).

MORRIS, R., *Historical Outlines of English Accidence,* London, 1895.

———, *Old English Homilies,* EETS, O.S. 34, 1868.

MORSBACH, L., *Grammatisches und Psychologisches Geschlecht im Englischen,* Berlin, 1926.

NATHAN, N., "Pronouns of Address in the *Friar's Tale,*" *MLQ,* XVII (1956).

NIDA, E., *Morphology: The Descriptive Analysis of Words,* Ann Arbor, 1949.

PASCHKE, E., *Der Gebrauch des bestimmten Artikels in der spätmittelenglischen Prosa, 1380–1500,* Emsdetten, 1934.

PETERS, G., *Der syntaktische Gebrauch des unbestimmten Artikels im zentat und spätmittelenglischen,* Göttingen, 1937.

RENNHARD, S., *Das Demonstrativum im Mittelenglischen 1200–1500,* Winterhus, 1962.

ROBERTS, J., "Traces of Unhistorical Gender Congruence in a Late Old English Manuscript," *English Studies,* 51 (1970).

ROSS, A. S. C., "Studies in the Accidence of the *Lindisfarne Gospels,*" *Leeds School of English Language Monographs,* II (1937), Leeds.

———, "Sex and Gender in the *Lindisfarne Gospels,*" *JEGP,* XXXV (1936).

RUND, M. B., "A Conjecture Concerning the Origin of Modern English *She,*" *MLN,* XXV (1920).

———, "*She* Once More," *RES,* II (1926).

SARRAZIN, G., "Der Ursprung von NE 'She,'" *Englische Studien,* XX (1895–1896).

SENFF, H., "Die Nominalflexion im *Ayenbite of Inwyt,*" *Forschungen zur englischen Philologie,* Jena, 1937.

SMITH, A. H., "Some Place Names and the Etymology of *She,*" *RES,* II (1926).

STIDSTON, R. O., *The Use of Ye in the Function of Thou in Middle English Literature from Manuscript Auchinleck to Manuscript Vernon: A Study of Grammar and Social Intercourse in Fourteenth-Century England,* Stanford, 1917.

ŚWIECZKOWSKI, W., *Word Order Patterning in Middle English,* The Hague, 1962.

TRNKA, B., *Chaucers Sprache und Verskunst,* Leipzig, 1920.

————, "Analysis and Synthesis in English," *English Studies,* X (1928).

WALCUTT, C. C., "The Pronouns of Address in *Troilus and Criseyde,*" *Philological Quarterly,* XIV (1935).

WELLS, J. E., "Accidence in the *Owl and the Nightingale,*" *Anglia,* XXXIII (1910).

ZENGEL, M. S., "Literacy as a Factor in Language Change," in *Readings in the Sociology of Language,* edited by J. A. Fishman, The Hague, 1968.

ERB MORPHOLOGY
AND SYNTAX /FIVE

I

In this chapter we shall isolate for discussion three very important functions of verbs in utterances. The first, and perhaps the most difficult, will be the role played by verbs (especially auxiliary verbs) in marking the kind of action denoted by the utterance; the second will be the ways in which the verb in particular can indicate whether the utterance has reference to *past* or *nonpast* time; the third (closely related to the second) will denote whether the past or nonpast action is one that has started, is still going on, or has been completed. Traditionally, these three verbal functions are called *modality, tense,* and *aspect.* It will, of course, be impossible to examine the operation of these functions in great detail, nor will one be able to write "everywhere" rules for their appearance in Middle English; one will, therefore, following the practice in Chapter Four, be content to select aspects of these three important features of the grammar and to restrict descriptions wherever practical to limited selections of the total data.

Some traditional grammars of Modern English treat all the following sentences as *statements:* ⟨I command you to sing⟩, ⟨I promise I will sing⟩, ⟨I guarantee he will sing⟩, ⟨I bet you he will sing⟩, ⟨He is singing⟩. But this kind of interpretation conceals some very important features of utterances; for example, to say ⟨I bet you he will sing⟩ is not to make a statement or a report about something one believes to be true or otherwise; it is *to perform an act of betting.* Similarly, in ⟨I promise he will sing⟩, the speaker is performing an act of *promising;* and in ⟨I command him to sing⟩, he is performing the act of *command.* In the sentence ⟨He is singing⟩, neither of these speech acts is being performed; rather the act or performative is *statement:* ⟨I state he is singing⟩. Underlying every utterance is a performative, or marker of the nature of the speech act. All sentences have an "illocutionary force" or an "illocutionary potential" (Austin, J. L. [1962]).

Every utterance is, therefore, some kind of *speech act* and contains an underlying performative that may or may not be realized in the surface structure of the sentence. The truth value of speech acts cannot be questioned. For example, one cannot ask whether it is true or false to say ⟨I bet he will sing⟩, since whoever utters the sentence is actually performing the speech act. If, however, he were to use the past tense and say ⟨I bet he would sing⟩ or ⟨I was betting he would sing when—⟩ or ⟨He bet he would sing⟩, then the truth or otherwise of the utterance would be open to question, since some kind of report is involved and not the speech act of betting itself. One can, therefore, say that _performatives_ must be in the present tense and have subjects of the first person. The action they refer to must not be continuing —that is, the performative verb must be nonprogressive in aspect—nor must it be habitual. Lastly, the sentences in which performatives occur must have an illocutionary potential other than statement. Of the following sentences, for instance, only the first contains a performative (*command*); all the others are statements:

I order you to you.
I ordered you to go.
He orders you to go.
I am ordering you to go.
I always ordered you to go.

Our examination of Middle English performatives will concentrate upon the following three ways in which they can be manifested: (1) where there is a "modal" verb [V + modal]; (2) where there is no surface realization ⟨Don't go home⟩, ⟨go home⟩: negative command and command performatives respectively; and (3) where the performative has a surface realization as a full lexical verb: ⟨christen, name, acquit, order⟩.

The second part of the chapter will be taken up with a discussion of *tense* and *aspect* in Middle English. By _tense_ is meant whether an utterance has reference to past or nonpast tense (the reasons for not including "future" time will be given below). *Tense* and *time* tend not to exist in any one-to-one correspondence in natural languages. *Time* is a continuum, whereas *tense* is a grammatical category marking only some of the points on that continuum. In Modern English, *tense* can be realized morphologically in the superficial structure (for example, in the case of [+past] by inflectional extension or vowel variation in the verb "stem") as well as by adverbs; for example, ⟨He looked at it yesterday⟩, ⟨He looked at it yesterday evening at 7:30 P.M.⟩, ⟨John saw Bill today⟩, and so on.

Aspect on the other hand refers to the state of completion or continuousness of the verbal action (actions still in progress are *durative;* those over and done with, *completive*). *Aspect* in Modern English is often marked by auxiliary [Aux] verbs, such as ⟨have⟩, ⟨be⟩ as well as by adverbial words, such as ⟨still⟩, ⟨yet⟩, ⟨completely⟩; examples of the types suggested might be: ⟨John is still eating his dinner⟩, ⟨John had eaten his dinner by seven o'clock⟩.

II

THE PERFORMATIVE

Negative Sentences

Declarative statements may have the performative feature [+Negation]. For example, in Modern English one can say ⟨John likes Mary⟩ and derive from it its negated form: [+Negation] ⟨John likes Mary⟩, that is, ⟨John does not like Mary⟩. In the syntactic *transformation* (Jacobs and Rosenbaum [1968], Chapters 4 and 5) from the nonnegative to negative utterances, a number of operations are involved. The most obvious of these is the addition of the surface realization of [+Negative] ⟨not⟩ or ⟨n't⟩, for example:

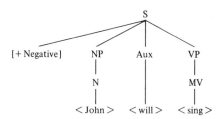

The above display is a much simplified version of the underlying syntactic structure of the sentence ⟨John will sing⟩, since many essential features of N, such as [+proper, +male], have not been included; and the modal ⟨will⟩ has been entered without an indication that it is a superficial realization of a performative *to predict* and not a mark of the "future" tense.

Sentences of this type—NP + Aux + MV—in Modern English are made negative by what we shall call the *negative-placement transformational rule* (Jacobs and Rosenbaum [1968], pp. 20–21) that realizes:

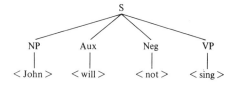

However, this rule, which inserts ⟨not⟩ after the modal auxiliary, will only apply when the Aux element is realized on the superficial structure of the sentence. The following structure will generate ⟨John sings⟩ or ⟨John sang⟩ according to whether we select [+tense] ⟶ [±past] ; the reason for relating [+tense] to the Aux and not the MV will become clear below. Whenever the modal Aux is unrealized in Modern English, the operation of the *negative-placement transformation* involves the introduction of what we will call *do-support.*

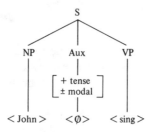

In sentences such as ⟨John sings⟩ the Aux is [—modal] and is not realized in the superficial structure, the circumstances where it is deleted in the superficial structure being whenever it comes immediately before the MV, thus

Aux [—modal]   ⟶   ∅ / —— MV

This rule is overly simple, since one would have to allow aspectual auxiliaries such as ⟨be⟩ and ⟨have⟩ to be manifested in this context—for example, ⟨John has sung⟩. However, if some other feature (say X) occurs between the nonmodal auxiliary and the MV, then the former is realized as *do:*

Aux [—modal, —aspect]   ⟶   ⟨do⟩ / —— XMV

Therefore, the negation transformation of sentences such as ⟨John sings⟩ involves:

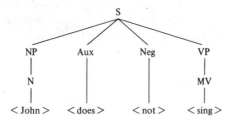

It is here that one can see the importance of inserting the feature [+tense] with the auxiliary, since it enables one to generate ⟨John did not sing⟩ as

well as ⟨John does not sing⟩, where [+tense] is realized as [+past] and [−past] respectively.

This *do-support rule* has been entered into in some detail because Middle English is, in this respect, very different in its treatment of negative sentences from the grammar of contemporary English. One can find, for instance, in *Text III,* an excerpt from the *Ancrene Wisse* (Tolkien [1962]), an early thirteenth-century book of instruction for nuns, many examples of this fact. Consider the negative sentence ⟨wepmen ne seoð ow⟩ (1) and what would presumably be its positive counterpart ⟨wepmen seoð ow⟩. It is clear, therefore, that in such an instance, Middle English does not seem to illustrate the presence in its grammar of either of the above transformational rules, *negative-placement* and *do-support,* in the way postulated for them for negative sentences in Modern English. Rather one might represent the Middle English transformation in the following display:

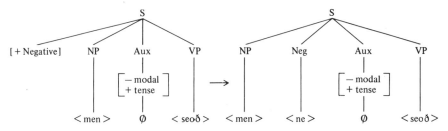

In other words, although the [−modal] Aux is not realized at the surface, there is no *do-support* rule; there is, however, *neg placement,* but it is different from Modern English in coming before the Aux element and having a different phonological realization spelled ⟨ne⟩.

Although there are no examples in the passage (except where an imperative modal is involved), Middle English could also employ an additional surface negative signal: ⟨ʒef he ne spekeð nawt⟩ (*AW* 34/11–12) (references marked *AW* refer to Tolkien [1962] page and line), ⟨ʒet ne seið hit nawt þet ha biheolð wepmen⟩ (*AW* 32/19). Then:

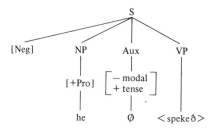

TEXT III. ANCRENE WISSE, MS. CORPUS CHRISTI COLLEGE, CAMBRIDGE 402

FOR þi þ wepmen ne seoð ow neȝe ham wel mei don of
ower cla beo hit hwit beo hit blac bute hit beo
unorne. warm 7 wel iwraht. felles wel itawet. 7
habbeð ase monie as ow to neodeð to bedde 7 to rugge.
Nest flesch ne schal nan werien linnene cla bute hit   5
beo of hearde 7 of greate heorden. Stamín habbe hwa
se wule hwa se wule beo buten. ȝe schulen in an
hetter ant igurd liggen. swa leoðeliche þah þ ȝe mahen
honden putten þer under. Nest lich nan ne gurde hire
wið na cunne gurdles bute þurh schriftes leaue. ne   10
beore nan irn ne hére. ne ilespiles felles. ne ne
beate hire þer wið ne wið scurge i leadet. wið holín
ne wið breres. ne biblodgi hire seolf wið ute schriftes
leaue. nohwer ne binetli hire. ne ne beate bi-
uoren. ne na keoruunge ne keorue. ne ne neome ed eanes   15
to luðere disceplines. temptatiuns forte acwenchen.
ne for na bote aȝein cundeliche secnesses. nan
uncundelich lechecreft ne leue ȝe ne ne fondín. wið
uteɪɪ ower meistres read leste ow stonde wurse.
Ower schon i winter beon meoke. greate 7 warme.   20
I sumer ȝe habbeð leaue bearuot gan 7 sitten 7 lihte
scheos werien. Hosen wið ute vampez ligge ín
hwa se likeð. Ischeoed ne slepe ȝe nawt. ne nohwer bute i bedde. Sum wummon inohreaðe wereð þe
brech of hére ful wel icnottet. þe streapeles dun   25
to þe vet ilacet ful feaste. ah eauer is best þe
swete 7 te swote heorte.

[Since men do not see you nor you them, it makes no differences whether your garment is white or black as long as it is not ornamented. Let it be warm and well-made, its skins well-finished, and you can have as many of them as you need for blankets and for wearing. Nobody is allowed to wear linen clothes next to her skin unless they are of a rough and coarse finish. Anyone who wants one can wear an undergarment; anyone who doesn't need not. You must sleep in a garment which is tied at the waist but loosely enough for you to put your hand through. It is forbidden to tie anything round the body other than by the permission of your confessor. The wearing of iron and penitential haircloth garments is also forbidden as also are hedgehog skins. No one is allowed to beat herself with a lead scourge, holly, or thorns or to draw blood from herself unless her confessor gives her permission to do so. Let no one chastize herself with nettles, scourge herself in front, cut herself, nor take too severe disciplines all at once in order to drive away temptation. Do not trust or experiment with any unnatural remedies for natural diseases before asking the advice of your superior lest you harm yourself. In the winter let your shoes be large and warm. In summer you are permitted to walk or sit barefoot or to wear light footwear. Whoever so desires can sleep in stockings without feet, but do not sleep in shoes and do not sleep anywhere but in a bed. Sometimes women take to wearing breeches made of hair tied tightly around them with close lacing of the leggings down to their feet. Nevertheless the soft and gentle heart is always the best thing to have.]

is superficially realized as:

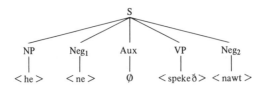

In the *Ancrene Wisse* this "double negative" construction is not numerically so frequent as those with ⟨ne⟩ alone, and indeed it may exist as a free variant of the other construction. Compare—⟨ʒet ʒe ne mahen eauer halde þe time⟩ (*AW* 15/4–5), ⟨moni ne mei nawt (þolien)⟩ (*AW* 7/8). It may be that there are CS rules (perhaps only of a superficial kind—although some scholars suggest the ⟨nawt⟩ denotes *emphasis,* that is, "definitely not")—but they are too complex to go into here; one can suggest, however, that the "double negative" is most frequently to be found with verbs that have at least a surface auxiliary (modal and nonmodal) appearance (see pp. 153–154 below), notably, ⟨mahe⟩ (⟨to be able⟩), ⟨wulle⟩ (⟨wish⟩), ⟨habben⟩ (⟨to have⟩); compare ⟨þah nulle ich nawt⟩ (*AW* 9/18), ⟨Ah alle ne mahe nawt halden a riwle⟩ (*AW* 7/29), ⟨þa naueð nawt hire leor forbearnd þe sunne⟩ (*AW* 33/8–9), where ⟨naueð⟩ is a contraction of ⟨ne + haueð⟩, the latter being [+perfective aspect] auxiliary. It is very rare to find [+Negation] marked solely by ⟨nawt⟩ at least in the *Ancrene Wisse:* ⟨þ tis uuel of dyna com nawt of þ ha seh sichen emores sune⟩.

However, we shall have to be more precise in our definition of different types of negation in Modern English if our description is not to be overly simple. There are at least two types—*sentence negation* and *constituent negation.* Consider the sentence ⟨I want somebody to see you⟩. This can have several negative manifestations, including: (a) ⟨I don't want anybody to see you⟩, (b) ⟨I want nobody to see you⟩, and even (c) ⟨I don't want nobody to see you⟩. In *sentence negation,* it is the case that if one is given a proposition X is Y, this whole proposition can be denied: ⟨It is not true that X is Y⟩; so that if one makes the proposition ⟨I want somebody to see you⟩, one can deny it by ⟨It is not true that I want somebody to see you⟩. One can, however, alternatively (or simultaneously) negate not the whole proposition, but only a part of it—*constituent negation.* In this instance, one can negate the subject pronoun in the subordinate sentence—⟨somebody sees you⟩—thus ⟨I want [Neg] [somebody sees you]⟩, that is, ⟨I want nobody to see you⟩. In other words, there is a difference in the *scope* of the negative feature in each case:

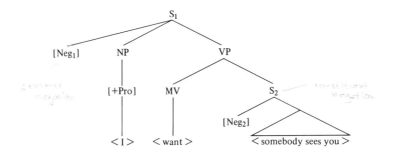

Application of [Neg₁], or *sentence negation,* will produce ‹I don't want [S]›, whereas [Neg₂] will have its scope limited to a negative realization of the subject pronoun in the subordinate sentence, realizing ‹I want nobody to see you› (see Jackendoff [1969], Klima [1964]). One must then have a *negative-placement rule* to produce the appropriate superficial structure. In the case of sentence negation, [Neg₁] ‹I want› ⟶ ‹I don't want› (do-support also applied), whereas with constituent or [Neg₂] instances, there will, in addition to *negative placement,* be a later rule of *negative incorporation* realizing the underlying ‹somebody› as ‹nobody›. Notice that ‹noht› is itself the output of the two last-mentioned rules, since it can be derived from ‹ne a wiht›, ‹not anything›.

Although a great deal of detail has been omitted, this area of this syntax has been treated in some depth, since the rules that give a surface appearance to its underlying shape are rather different in Middle English from their Modern English counterparts. Consider the example from *AW* 33/24–26 ‹Nulle ich þet nan iseo ow›, where ‹nulle› is a contracted form of ‹ne wille›. Is this sentence to be translated as equivalent to the Modern English (c) above ‹I don't want nobody to see you›, with both sentence and constituent negation realized superficially? Or is it to be treated as equivalent to (a) or (b) or both? The most unlikely is (c), since it appears that in Middle English the scope of the negation feature was more extensively realized at the surface level of the grammar than now. Thus, if [Neg₁] was operative, its scope extended to any surface position where both itself and [Neg₂] could be realized, without involving, apparently, any of the semantics of constituent negation in the process. There are instances, however, where only sentential negation is possible, and others where both negation types seem to mean the same thing. For instance, [Neg] ‹Something makes her angry› ⟶ ‹Nothing makes her angry›, where negative-placement and incorporation rules affect only the subject indefinite quantifier ‹something›. The grammar of Modern English blocks sentences like *⟨Something does not make her happy⟩ and *⟨Nothing does not make her happy⟩, at least for the writer. In the grammar of Middle English, however, the larger scope of the negative rules will allow superficial elements of negation to appear both at NP and VP, thus ⟨nawt ne makeð hire woh⟩ (*AW* 7/24).

The fewer restrictions of application of both negative-placement and negative-incorporation rules in the grammar of Middle English can be seen when one considers how they affect adverbials. For example, if there is sentential negation in the sentence ⟨He will always change his home⟩, one can then expect to find either ⟨He will not change his home ever⟩ or ⟨He will never change his home⟩, with negative placement at either VP or with the adverbial element. In Middle English, on the other hand, the scope of the negation will include not either but both these spots, as well as any other pronominal indefinite quantifier that may be present. The result is that a sentence like ⟨He ne schal þ stude neauer mare changin⟩ will be the Middle English output, with negative placement at two positions, as well as negative incorporation to realize [Neg] ⟨eauer⟩ as ⟨neauer⟩. There are even instances of negative placement at three places in a sentence, as in *Text I*, the *Peterborough Chronicle:* ⟨neframa nan clepunge þærto na hafde mare⟩ (21–22), underlying which is ⟨[Neg] euerma [Neg] an clepunge þærto [Neg] hafde mare⟩ (⟨[he would] have no further claim [to his properties] at any other time⟩).

Unfortunately, the situation in Middle English is rather more complex, although its workings are not fully understood. One negative manifestation of the Modern English sentence ⟨John always likes Mary⟩ is ⟨John never likes Mary⟩. Yet there is also the possibility of ⟨John doesn't always like Mary⟩, where the meaning of ⟨not always⟩ is not ⟨on no occasion⟩ but ⟨on some occasion not⟩. At least in some instances one finds that in Middle English sentences of the latter variety, there is a restricted scope of the negative-placement rule, for example, ⟨ʒef ʒe ne mahen eauer halde þe time⟩ (⟨if you cannot always keep to the right time [for saying your prayers]⟩) (*AW* 15/4–5). In this case, it seems that *sometimes* is implied, and such a sentence would presumably contrast with one like ⟨ʒef ʒe ne mahen neauer holde þe time⟩, where the negated adverb would be equivalent to ⟨on no occasion⟩.

The Imperative

In Modern English, utterances that have the illocutionary force of, or that contain a performative denoting, *command* are in part characterized by the following features: in sentences like ⟨Go!⟩, ⟨Stop!⟩, and ⟨Shut up!⟩, the subject of the verb does not appear in the surface structure. Yet many linguists in the past have suggested that the subject is "understood," since one can find such alternatives as ‹You, go!›, ‹Shut up, you!›, and so on. In fact, this ‹you› is not a *subject* at all, but represents the person addressed by the command; the grammatical term given to this ‹you› is the *vocative*. Although we cannot go into the point in detail (see Thorne, J. P. [1966]), sentences with an [Imp] (imperative) performative have the following underlying structure:

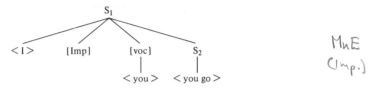

Transformational rules then operate that will delete the subject [+Pro] in S₂ and the vocative on occasion. In general, the Middle English imperative construction has the same surface appearance as Modern English, for example, ‹habbeð as monie as ow to neodeð› (*Text III* [4]), although sometimes the underlying vocative is realized where it would be deleted now, especially when the utterance has a negative illocutionary potential as well as command: ‹Ischoed ne slepe 3e nawt› (*Text III* [23]) or at other places in the manuscript ‹Ne speoke 3e wið namon› (*AW* 37/4) and ‹Ne halde 3e tale wið namon› (*AW* 37/18–19). This realization of the underlying [voc]ative may exist simply in free variation with the following instances where it is deleted: ‹Ne wene 3e ðer neauer god ah leueð him þe leasse› (‹Don't think any good of it, but trust him less›) (*AW* 33/22–24), although there may be CS rules that will dictate a preference for one superficial manifestation rather than another.

When it is found in sentences with the feature [+Negative], the Middle English imperative, unlike its Modern English counterpart, does not have the *do-support* rule. For example, in Modern English, the following represents a possible underlying structure for negative imperative sentences:

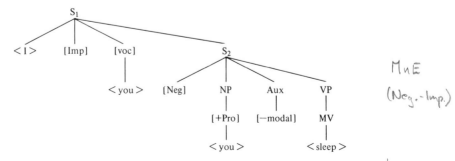

To produce an acceptable surface form three things must happen: (a) the NP subject ⟨you⟩ must be deleted, (b) the Aux [—modal] *do* must be selected and given initial position, and (c) negative placement must be made before the MV of S_2, thus:

MnE

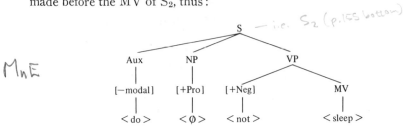

The [voc] ⟨you⟩ may of course be deleted also, although it can be realized as ⟨You, don't sleep⟩ and ⟨Don't sleep, you⟩.

In the example ⟨ne slepe ȝe nawt⟩ (*Text III* [24]), rule (b)—the *do-support* rule—is not required, and the [voc] element is also retained in the superficial structure:

ME

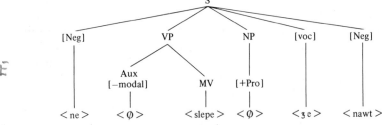

Unlike Modern English, Middle English requires a further set of morphological (inflectional suffix) rules to obtain the grammatical surface form of the MV. These rules depend upon the [±singular] feature of the [voc] and NP elements: the inflectional extension spelled ⟨e⟩ is found in [+singular] contexts as above, but in [—singular] contexts ⟨eð⟩ is selected (at least in texts of the same date and dialect as the *Ancrene Wisse;* see Chapter Six, p. 208.

Since there is such a difference in the grammars of Middle and Modern English concerning *do-support* rules, it is perhaps worthwhile to discuss the little that is known about the historical "development" of the verb ⟨do⟩ itself. It is only in modern times (from the seventeenth century onward) that its use as a meaningless (or dummy) verb in such contexts as [+Neg] and [+Imp+Neg] is to be found with any degree of statistical frequency. Before this time it is hardly used in such contexts, although it can be found with other functions. One of the most common of these is as a causative— that is, ⟨I cause something to be done⟩: ⟨I do þe lete blod ounder þe brest⟩ —⟨I will have you bled⟩ (*Fox and Wolf* [51]; Bennett and Smithers

[1966], p. 68); ⟨do⟩ can also be used as a substitute for another verb (a
Pro-verb) (it may be this usage that underlies the modern "dummy" form)
—⟨þu tuengest þarmid so doþ a tonge⟩—⟨You pinch with (your claws)
like a tong⟩ (*The Owl and the Nightingale* [112]; Bennett and Smithers
[1966], p. 6). Thirdly, ⟨do⟩ could be used as a marker of perfective aspect
⟨Ac nou of me idon hit hiis⟩ (⟨It's all up with me⟩) (*Fox and Wolf*
[106]; Bennett and Smithers [1966], p. 70). Nevertheless, there is no
really satisfactory answer as to how the Modern English usage developed,
but for some interesting suggestions, see Samuels (1965).

It is worth noting too that in [Imp] as well as [Neg] sentences, there
is a considerably greater scope of negative incorporation than in Modern
English: ⟨nohwer ne binetli hire⟩ (*Text III* [14]), ⟨Nest lich nan ne
gurde hire wið na cunne gurdles⟩ (*Text III* [9–10]).

Interrogative or question sentences are rather like commands, of which
they form a subset. Questions, in other words, are really demands for some
kind of action or information—they are commands to reply, and they can
be said to have an underlying structure like:

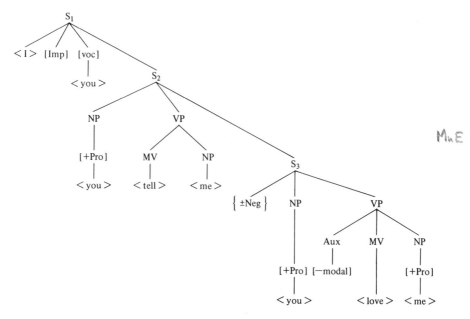

In other words this (simplified) display suggests a deep structure ⟨I ask
you to tell me either you love me or you do not love me⟩ for interrogatives
such as ⟨Do you love me?⟩. This type of question suggests a ⟨yes⟩ or ⟨no⟩
reply and like the other main type in Modern English ⟨What do you love?⟩,
⟨Why do you love?⟩, where an introductory "interrogative word" is used,
involves both the introduction of *do-support* rules and the realization of the

[—modal] auxiliary in the lower sentence. As might be expected, the grammar of Middle English has no such rule in this context, and one finds superficial interrogative structures such as the yes/no type: ⟨Luuest tu me?⟩ (*AW* 194/30). The surface-structure rule in Middle English (with no *do-support*) that generates such subtypes of imperatives from statements simply involves the reversal of order of the NP subject and its verb. Presumably also there was some difference in intonational pattern, but there are no clues to its nature. In addition, it is possible to find what are apparently questions with statement superficial structures, again presumably (as in Modern English ⟨You like milk?⟩) distinguished intonationally. Yes/no questions involving a modal auxiliary like ⟨will⟩ or ⟨shall⟩ or ⟨must⟩ are formed, as in Modern English ⟨Must I drink milk?⟩, with the modal auxiliary transposed to sentence-initial position. However, when a [+Negative] feature is involved, there are some differences, for example, ⟨Nult tu as ofte smiten?⟩ (*AW* 167/26), where in addition to the modal transposition rule there is negative incorporation in the modal. But in Modern English this incorporation takes place in a different way: ⟨Will you not drink your milk?⟩, ⟨Won't you drink your milk?⟩; and compare in *be + complement* constructions: ⟨Nis he mare þæn amead?⟩ (*AW* 766/24) and ⟨Nis nawt good qð ha se grimm as ȝe him fori makieð? Na he seið dauið⟩ (*AW* 171/18–19) with Modern English ⟨Is he not⟩ and ⟨Is God not⟩ with different negative placement.

Rather similar differences in the grammars of Middle and Modern English are found when the question is not of the yes/no type, but involves some introductory "interrogative word." In Middle English such words as ⟨hwi⟩ and ⟨hwæt⟩ were used without *do-support* rules and with noun/verb inversion in such sentences as ⟨Hwi luuedest tu þe mon?⟩ (*AW* 207/19–20), ⟨Hwet þolieð men?⟩ (⟨What do men suffer?⟩) (*AW* 194/34). However, in sentences involving the modal auxiliary or *be + complement* construction, the rule for the generation of interrogatives is much the same in Middle English as in Modern English—⟨Hweðer is wisre of þes twa? Hweðer is betere his ahne freond? Hweðer luıeð himseolf mare? Ant hwa nis sec of sunne?⟩ (*AW* 186/15–17); ⟨Hu schall him stonde þenne?⟩ (*AW* 157/20).

III

For some other features of the surface manifestation of the illocutionary potential of utterances, we shall consider the forms of the modal auxiliaries in Middle English with especial reference to the following passage from *BM MS Royal 18 B xxiii Sermon No. 27*, written between 1378 and 1417 (W. O. Ross [1940]). See *Text IV*.

[+*Prediction*]

In Modern English the modal auxiliaries ⟨will⟩ and ⟨shall⟩ can be used to mark the fact that a speaker makes a prediction—for example, ⟨John will go to Edinburgh tomorrow⟩ is not a statement, but represents ⟨I predict John goes to Edinburgh tomorrow⟩. Predictions, or forecasts, have a different status and illocutionary force from statements, so that in consequence we shall recognize only [±past] tense and not the future, treating the latter rather as a predictive speech act. Such predictive utterances in this extract include: ⟨is goostely fadur will enioyne hym⟩ (26–27), that is, ⟨I predict his priest commands him⟩. Both ⟨will⟩ and ⟨shall⟩ are to be found in Middle English as marks of predictive speech acts, but there is no sign of the Modern English habit of using ⟨shall⟩ with first-person pronouns and ⟨will⟩ with third-person pronouns. The Middle English use of ⟨shall⟩ and ⟨will⟩ presents a considerable surface distinction from Old English, where predictive speech acts could be superficially unmarked, for instance, ⟨Ga ȝe on minne winȝeard and ic selle eow þæt riht bið⟩ (⟨Go into my vineyard and I shall give you what is just⟩), ⟨will⟩ and ⟨shall⟩ more commonly marking volition and obligation respectively.

ME

Examples of this usage are still to be found in the above Middle English extract, for instance, ⟨All þo þat will amende hem to God⟩ (*Text IV* [29]), where ⟨will⟩ does not show a nonstatement illocutionary potential, but represents the full lexical nonauxiliary verb ⟨to wish⟩ or ⟨desire⟩. Another example from a different part of the same manuscript (Ross [1940], p. 147, ll. 22–23) is: ⟨Deff we been when þat we myght here Goddes word 7 will not, ne will not be a-knowen of our synnes⟩.

Both ⟨will⟩ and ⟨shall⟩ can be used both in Middle and Modern English (much more commonly than in Old English) to manifest a guaranteed or promised prediction:

Compare ⟨And if þou will luf Jhesu verraly, þow sal noght only lufe hym stalwortly and wysely, bot also devowtly and swetely⟩ (*English Writings of Richard Rolle,* edited by H. E. Allen [1931], p. 113, ll. 171–173) with the modals ⟨will⟩ and ⟨sal⟩ marking what appear to be [prediction] and [guaranteed prediction] or [promise] respectively.

[+*Obligation*]

Underlying sentences with this form of illocutionary potential is some form

TEXT IV. MIDDLE ENGLISH SERMON, MS ROYAL 18 B xxiii

Good men, þe tyme of Lenten entred, þe wiche tyme
we must clense vs of all oure mysdedis þat we haue done
before. And þis holytyme we shuld absteyne vs more
from synne and wrechednes þan an-oþur tyme of þe
ȝere. And so holywritt techeþ vs. seying, "Emendemus   5
in melius." In þis tyme seyþ God in holywritt þat we
shuld liff vertewesly and turne oure . . . in-to þe amende-
ment of oure lyvynge, þat we haue trespassed all þe
ȝere be-fore þorow necligens. Now shall we strenght
vs to faste, to come to þe churche, and to serue God   10
in holy preyours, and to shryve vs of oure mysdedis.
   ȝe shall vndirstond þat iij þinges makeþ a man
acceptable to þe mercy of God. Þe first is for-þenkyng
in herte, þat a man shuld repente hym for is synnes þat
he haþ don aȝeyns God and is soule. The ij is shrifte   15
of mouthe; for as sone as a man repenteþ hym in is
herte for is foule synnes, þan he shall com to
holychurche to is goostely fadur and mekely knele
afore hym, and tell is synne and crye God mercy. And
tell how and on what maner of vise þat þou hast synned,   20
and exscuse not þi-selfe to sey þat þou myȝthe no
noþur veys don. For as verely as þou will hope to
haue þe mercy of God, so verely and oponly knalage
þou trespasse. The iij is penaunce. And þat is
fastynge, wakyng, bedynge, and amesdede doyinge,   25
and all oþur þinges þat is goostely fadur will
enioyne hym in þe stede of penaunce. Þese iij
þinges, penaunce, shryft, and repentaunce ben
nedefull to all þo þat will amende hem to God.
And be þise iij þinges shall you make you redie þis   30
holy tyme of Lenten, þat ȝe may worthely on Esturday resceyve youre Saviour.

   knalage: to acknowledge.   *enioyne:* to prescribe, to impose.
bedynge: praying, earnestly requesting.

of imperative or command. The imperative may be a direct one, that is, ⟨I command you, you do something⟩, or it may involve a statement by someone or something about a command to do something, that is ⟨I state someone or something commands you, you do something⟩.

Examples of the first type can be expressed by the use of a modal verb ⟨shall⟩ in Middle English, thus ⟨3e shall vndirstond þat⟩ (*Text IV* [12]) and ⟨þise iij þinges shall you make you redie⟩ (*Text IV* [30]), manifested in Modern English by ⟨must⟩ and ⟨have to⟩:

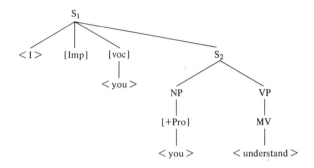

This type is also shown, it seems, although in the context of "indirect speech," as ⟨shuld⟩: ⟨seyþ God in holywritt þat we shuld liff vertewesly⟩ (*Text IV* [6–7]). Sentences are also found where there are statements about external commands to do something, often signaled in Modern English by ⟨should⟩ or ⟨ought to⟩, and in Middle English by ⟨shall⟩ or ⟨must⟩: ⟨Now shall we strenght vs to faste⟩ (*Text IV* [9–10]), ⟨þan he shall com to holychurche⟩ (*Text IV* [17–18]), and ⟨we must clense vs⟩ (*Text IV* [2]). Underlying sentences of this type might have a structure (Thorne and Boyde [1969]):

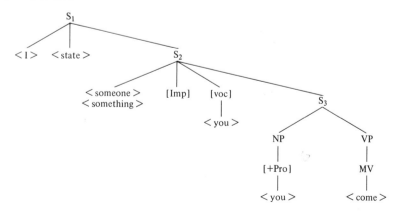

It will be obvious to the reader on the basis of the above interpretations that the recovery of the historical illocutionary potential of utterances is an area where one suffers greatly from the lack of native informants.

In Middle as in Modern English ⟨may⟩ is ambiguous. It can represent a full lexical verb meaning ⟨to be able⟩, as in ⟨þou myȝthe no noþur veys don⟩ (*Text IV* [21–22])—where ⟨myȝthe⟩ is the past form of ⟨may⟩—and also ⟨Behold now how sone a man may amend hym for all mane[r] of trespasse⟩ (Ross [1940], p. 199, ll. 25–26). On the other hand, ⟨may⟩ can be used to mark utterances with an illocutionary force of [permit] that possibly underlies a sentence like: ⟨þat ȝe may worthely on Esturday resceyve youre Saviour⟩, that is, ⟨so that nothing will stand in the way of your receiving . . . ⟩ (*Text IV* [31–32]). Although common throughout the period, the nonperformative ⟨may⟩, meaning ⟨to be able⟩, appears to become less and less frequent, and its use as a realization of utterances with the force of [permit] increases.

In Modern English such sentences can also have a surface form involving the modal auxiliary ⟨can⟩, as in ⟨He can go⟩, although (like those with ⟨may⟩) such sentences are ambiguous, since ⟨can⟩—among other things—also represents the full lexical verb ⟨to be able⟩. In Middle English, however, ⟨can⟩ is usual only as a full verb and not as a modal: ⟨He knowe no more þe[r]-of þan can þe howle of musik⟩ (⟨He knows no more about it that does the owl how to sing⟩) (Ross [1940], p. 194, l. 14).

IV

TENSE

The following discussion will look at the manifestation in selected areas of the grammar of Middle English of the tenses past and nonpast; only these two seem to be treated as tenses, since the so-called future is better thought of as signifying utterances that have a predictive illocutionary power. We shall in the first place examine the various surface manifestations of present time as they are grammatically realized by the [—past] in *Text V: Vices and Virtues: Of Forsceawnesse,* written around 1200 in the Southeast dialect. From this we shall go on to consider the two main types of [+past] realization, and this will lead us in turn to a further detailed discussion of the phenomenon of verbal *ablaut,* which was briefly mentioned in "Spellings and Sounds" (see above pp. 77–86).

Looking first of all at the forms of the [—past] in the singular with pronouns of the second and third persons—⟨ðe þencþ⟩ (2), ⟨Mihtest tu⟩ (11), ⟨ðu . . . forlatst⟩ (15–16), ⟨he ðe haueð⟩ (27)—one can set up rules enabling one to generate the appropriate number, person, and tense-sensitive inflectional suffix or extension:

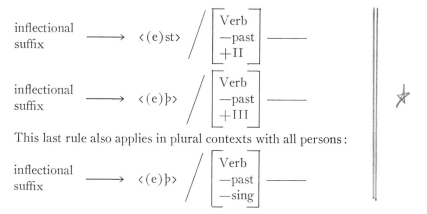

This last rule also applies in plural contexts with all persons:

In other parts of this text there are, however, some rather interesting forms of the inflectional suffix in the person III [+sing] context—compare ⟨ðu finst⟩ (45/27) with ⟨he fint⟩ (95/8), ⟨ðu behatst⟩ (9/29) with ⟨he behat⟩ (87/25), ⟨ðu forlatst⟩ (65/28) with ⟨he forlat⟩ (71/22) (references are to page and line of Holthausen [1888, Part I]). In these instances the ⟨eþ⟩ graphemes turn up as ⟨t⟩. This is not a random phenomenon, since it occurs only when the verb stem ends in the [−continuant] [+obstruent] [d] or [t]. It seems that the ⟨eþ⟩ inflectional suffix has at some stage undergone contraction to ⟨þ⟩, the [+voc] segment having been deleted, so that possibly forms such as *[⟨behatθ⟩] occurred; in such contexts, assimilation of the [continuant] feature takes place in the two final [+consonant] segments by the following rule:

$$\begin{bmatrix} +\text{cons} \\ +\text{obst} \\ +\text{ant} \end{bmatrix} \longrightarrow [\alpha\ \text{cont}]\ /\ \begin{bmatrix} +\text{cons} \\ +\text{obst} \\ +\text{ant} \\ \alpha\ \text{cont} \end{bmatrix} \underline{\qquad}$$

At the same time, if one compares [+III, −past, +sing] forms such as ⟨fast⟩ (5/27) (infinitive ⟨fasten⟩) with ⟨fint⟩ (95/8) (infinitive ⟨finden⟩), one sees also that in the process of the assimilation the voice feature of the inflectional suffix [+cons] is mapped onto the stem final consonant, such that [d] ⟶ [t]; thus one might have operating before the above rule one that will allow for voicing assimilation of the stem final with the continuancy assimilating inflectional consonantal segment:

$$\begin{bmatrix} +\text{cons} \\ +\text{obst} \\ +\text{ant} \end{bmatrix} \longrightarrow [\alpha\ \text{voice}]\ /\ \underline{\qquad}\ \begin{bmatrix} +\text{cons} \\ +\text{obst} \\ +\text{ant} \\ \alpha\ \text{voice} \end{bmatrix}$$

TEXT V. VICES AND VIRTUES: OF FORSCEAWNESSE (about 1200)

PROUIDENTIA, þat is, forsceawnesse, is an oðer
hali mihte, ðe þencþ and lokeð alle þing beforen (ar
ðanne hie comen). For ði ne rewð hire after
hire dædes. To-foren ðare burh of Ierusalem is an
muchel dune, ðe hatte Syon, þat is tokned "Sceawinge." 5
Þærupen weren ðe sceaweres ðe lokeden ðe hali burh,
and warneden fram alle here unwines. Al swo doð ðies
mihte upe ða dune of muchel embeðanke. Hie sceaweð
and lokeð ferrene to, and ðus seið: "VVelle, ðu
earme saule, ðe, ic segge, ðe none ȝieme ne nemst 10
of ðe seluen! Mihtest tu isien alle ðine unwines
ðe bieð abuten þe, also alse i do, sari woldest tu
bien, ȝierne woldestu clepien to gode þat he ðe aredde!
Ic ðe warni te-foren. Ne biest ðu naht hier lange
wuniȝende; forlat ðine sennen! ȝif ðou hier he ne 15
forlatst, ær ðanne ðu fare of ðare woreld, full ȝewiss
ne forlateð hie ðe næure, ær ðanne hie ðe bringen to
here eldren. Ðat bið ðo werewede gostes ðe waitið ðo
soules hier buuen on ðe wolkne. Þo þe hie findeþ upe
ðe of here werkes, ne mai þe helpen non angel ðat tu 20
ne scalt in to pine, and ðar abeggen. Quia nullum
malum inpunitum. 'Ne scall non euel bien unpined,
oðer hier oðer ðar.' Of ðare gode saule hie ȝesieð
and inherð merigne song: Veni, sponsa Christi, accipe
cŏronam, "Cum, ðu Cristes awen bried, and underfoh 25
ðe michele wurðscipe and ðe michele merhþe of heuene
riche, þe he ðe haueð iȝarked æurema to habben for
ðare gode trewðe ðe ðu him bere!'"

"The Nature of Foresight"

[Providentia, that is to say Foresight, is another holy virtue which thinks about and looks at everything (before it actually happens). Therefore it does not repent its actions. Outside the city of Jerusalem there is a large hill, called Zion, which signifies "Sight." On it used to be the watchmen who guarded the holy city and protected it against all its enemies. In like manner does this virtue upon the great hill of Consideration. It looks and watches into the distance and says thus: "Well, you wretched soul, you, I say, who takes no heed of yourself! If you could see all the enemies who are surrounding you as I can, how miserable you would be and eagerly would you call out to God to defend you! I give you advance warning. You will not be living here (in this world) for ever; give up your sins! If you do not abandon them before you leave this world, they will certainly never leave you before they will have brought you to their parents. They are those wretched spirits who wait for souls here above the clouds. If they find any of their works about you, then no angel can help you from going into suffering and there paying the penalty. Quia nullum malum inpunitum. 'No evil shall go unpunished either here or there.' It sees and hears a joyful song about the good soul: Veni, sponsa Christi, accipe coronam, 'Come, you who are Christ's own bride, and receive the great worship and great joy of Heaven, which He has prepared for you to have ever after for the good faith which you have borne Him!' "]

and in fact this may represent a constraint on the phonology in general in that <u>any two consonants in a consonantal cluster must agree in voice (if they form part of the same syllable)</u>.

This last rule is very clearly shown by a comparison between the spellings ⟨bringð⟩ (129/10) and ⟨brinkgð⟩ (83/1). If our rule holds, then (129/10) is a "morphophonemic" spelling representation—that is, the scribe represents the underlying stem-final-consonantal segment as ⟨g⟩ even though the voicing assimilation rule is probably in ·operation (see Chapter Six, pp. 205–207). The spelling of (83/1) seems on the other hand to be of the "autonomous phonemic" type, the symbol ⟨k⟩ being added as some kind of diacritic to represent the superficial phonological variation, although even here the underlying [g] is "represented" as well.

It must be added that these are not "everywhere" rules for two reasons: (1) they are minor because one finds ⟨fandeð⟩ (3/18) and ⟨hateð⟩ (37/28) (although there may be special reasons for these forms); and (2) this assimilation rule is, in *Vices and Virtues* at any rate, restricted to the syntactic context of [+sing], since in [−sing] contexts are found ⟨fundeð⟩ (13/4), ⟨biзeteð⟩ (79/27). One can argue that the assimilation does not take place in plural contexts for "functional" reasons, but it is perhaps more satisfactory to suggest that for some reason the underlying vowel of the singular inflectional suffix—[i]—tended to be deleted historically sooner (and thus create the conditions necessary for assimilation) than the underlying vowel—[a]—of the plural inflection ⟨eð⟩.

A characteristic of the grammar of *Vices and Virtues* is that it seems in some syntactical contexts to have deleted the <u>vowel-height-assimilation rule</u>:

$$\begin{bmatrix} +\text{voc} \\ -\text{cons} \\ -\text{low} \end{bmatrix} \longrightarrow [\alpha \text{ high}] \; / \; \underline{\quad} \; C_2^2 \begin{bmatrix} +\text{voc} \\ -\text{cons} \\ \alpha \text{ high} \end{bmatrix}$$

mentioned above in Chapter Three, "Spellings and Sounds." This rule states that <u>if there are up to two consonantal segments intervening between the radical vowel and the inflectional vocalic segment, there will then be a tendency for the former to come into height harmony with the latter</u>, for example, the person II and III [+sing, −past] forms of the verb ⟨to bear⟩ in some early Middle and many Old English dialects are ⟨birest⟩ and ⟨bireþ⟩; underlying these are the forms *[berist] and *[beriþ], whereas the [+sing, −past, +I] form ⟨bere⟩ has an underlying *[bere] form with the inflectional vocalic segment [−high, −low]. In *Vices and Virtues* are spellings such as ⟨berest⟩ (33/31) and ⟨berð⟩ (39/14), where such a height-harmony rule appears to have been deleted from the grammar.

Spellings such as ⟨nimþ⟩ (5/1), ⟨nemð⟩ (129/6) and ⟨nimst⟩ (77/

21), ⟨nemst⟩ (103/17) are found for the [+singular, —past, +III/+II] of the verb ⟨nimen⟩ ⟨to take⟩. Even in the [—past] plural there are ⟨nimeð⟩ (5/33) and ⟨nemeð⟩ (27/22). The radical vowel might be expected at least to be [+high] in the singular because of the vowel-height-assimilation rule; doubly so because the ⟨nasal-raising rule⟩ should also be operative. One solution would be to treat both rules as minor in *Vices and Virtues,* not applying on all occasions when the contexts indicated they could. The apparent arbitrariness of the application of these two rules might also suggest that the spelling is unreliable as an indicator of the surface phonetic features—in other words it is possibly morphophonemic. The scribe would not hesitate to use the ⟨e⟩ symbol, for although it did not represent the superficial shape of the vowel, it did bring out its underlying representation.

The rule that generates the appropriate inflectional extension for the verb with features [+sing, —past, +I] is:

$$\text{inflectional suffix} \longrightarrow \langle e\rangle \ / \ \begin{bmatrix} \text{Verb} \\ +\text{sing} \\ -\text{past} \\ +\text{I} \end{bmatrix} \underline{\qquad}$$

Examples are ⟨ic segge⟩ (*Text V* [10]), ⟨ic bidde⟩ (7/21), and ⟨ic bringe⟩ (33/20). There are, however, some exceptions to this, prominent among which are those forms that show an inflectional suffix in ⟨ie⟩ or ⟨i⟩, for example, ⟨ic warni⟩ (*Text V* [14]), ⟨ic hatie⟩ (67/1). These are restricted to verbs of a special type, that is, those with a stem-final-glide segment [j]—compare Old English ⟨luffian⟩, ⟨bodian⟩, ⟨lecgan⟩ (compare Old Saxon ⟨leggian⟩), ⟨settan⟩ (Old Saxon ⟨settian⟩). Such verbs, which we shall look at in more detail below, are traditionally referred to as "weak" or thematic verbs.

All the above inflectional suffix rules do not, of course, apply to the morphology of the Middle English present tense as a whole. They apply with any degree of rigor only to texts that belong to the regional and temporal dialects of the *Vices and Virtues.* Consequently, one must expect different spellings of the inflectional suffix in texts in the Midland and Northern regions and in texts written at different periods. Some of the more important discrepancies (and their distribution is usually very complex) are that in northern texts, even in late Old English times, one finds an inflectional suffix ⟨(e)s⟩ in the [+singular, +III, —past] context, thus ⟨he findes⟩ (this ⟨es/eð⟩ isogloss in the first half of the fourteenth century is rather similar in its geographical distribution to that of ⟨ch/k⟩ in Map I in Chapter Six). In late Middle English texts in the London area, for instance, ⟨es/eð⟩ forms exist side by side in the same texts, although their distribution may not be random. In *The Reeve's Tale,* Chaucer apparently uses the ⟨es⟩ suffix in this context to characterize the speech of Aleyn, who was born ⟨fer in the north⟩—⟨How fares thy faire doghter and thy wyf?⟩. Preliminary studies of the same phenomenon in Elizabethan English have shown some principles for the selection of the two forms: assimilation of the stem-final consonant with some of the features of the inflectional consonant may result in [s] ; ⟨eth⟩ may be more popular in "formal" sociolinguistic contexts, a situation that still prevails ; ⟨eth⟩ provides an extra syllable, often required for rhythmical reasons, for instance, ⟨who wanteth food and will not say he wants it⟩ (Shakespeare's *Pericles*) ; one form may be more common with verbs that are monosyllabic.

Other regional and temporal dissimilarities between the nonpast inflectional suffix rules are that in Midland manuscripts one finds ⟨e(n)⟩ in [—singular] environments, but ⟨∅⟩ in the same contexts in works written by northern scribes. Modern English has derived its inflectional suffix forms from those dialects that (unlike *Vices and Virtues*) have [+singular, +III, —past] ⟨s⟩ forms and [—singular, —past] ⟨∅⟩ forms.

Before we leave nonpast morphological features, it is worth commenting upon the inflectional suffixes found in the *Vices and Virtues* that contradict the above rules : ⟨ar ðanne hie comen⟩ (2–3), ⟨ær ðanne ðu fare of ðare woreld⟩ (16), ⟨ær ðanne hie ðe bringen⟩ (17), ⟨þat he ðe aredde⟩ (13), and ⟨ðe ðu him bere⟩ (28). Traditionally, verbs with the above set of inflectional forms are said to be in the *subjunctive mood:*

$$\left. \begin{array}{l} \text{inflectional} \\ \text{suffix} \end{array} \right\| \longrightarrow \quad ⟨e⟩ \quad \Bigg/ \quad \left[\begin{array}{l} \text{Verb} \\ \text{+subjunctive} \\ \text{+singular} \end{array} \right] \text{———}$$

$$\left. \begin{array}{l} \text{inflectional} \\ \text{suffix} \end{array} \right\| \longrightarrow \quad ⟨en⟩ \quad \Bigg/ \quad \left[\begin{array}{l} \text{Verb} \\ \text{+subjunctive} \\ \text{—singular} \end{array} \right] \text{———}$$

It is difficult to discover what traditional grammarians understand by the subjunctive mood and to equate it with any of the aspects of modality or the illocutionary potential of utterances. It may be that historically verbs with "nonindicative" inflections were used in contexts that could be shown to be related to some underlying phenomenon (be it modality or something else), but in English texts of the earliest dates this does not seem obviously to be the case, and one can only conclude that the "subjunctive" is a superficial set of inflectional suffixes that (it appears in an *ad hoc* way) are selected in certain syntactic contexts. In the above examples, these include certain "subordinate" or embedded clauses : those introduced by the temporal adverb ⟨ær ðanne⟩, "clauses of result," and "relative clauses." Although "subjunctive" inflectional suffixes are consistently used in the context of ⟨ær (ðanne)⟩ clauses, their appearance in relative clauses is only a minor feature in *Vices and Virtues* as a whole. Indeed, the superficial, syntactically context-sensitive rules that select such inflections are deleted from more and more of the grammars of Middle English, especially in its later manifestations.

[+*Past*]

English is traditionally said to form its past tense in two ways: (1) by the addition to the verb stem of an inflectional suffix or extension, and (2) by apparently regular alternations in the quality and quantity of the radical or stem vowel. In Modern English one can class among the first (and now commonest) type, verbs such as ⟨I judge⟩—⟨I judged⟩; ⟨I look⟩—⟨I looked⟩, while among the second are ⟨I see⟩—⟨I saw⟩; ⟨I meet⟩—⟨I met⟩; and ⟨I take⟩—⟨I took⟩. These two types are given a variety of names, most commonly *weak* and *strong, thematic* and *athematic,* or *consonantal* and *nonconsonantal.*

[+*Thematic*] *i. e. wk*

Both weak and strong verbs existed in Middle English, although the latter in greater numbers than now. It seems possible that at least originally the division of verbs into these two classes was not as apparently "unmotivated" as it seems to be now—that is, the speaker did not simply have to learn in an *ad hoc* way which verb belonged to which type. Rather it appears that the *thematic* type was that used in the formation of verbs from other "parts of speech," that is, from prepositions, nouns, and even athematic verbs—for example, in Old and Middle English one finds ⟨fremman⟩ apparently derived from the preposition ⟨fram⟩, ⟨deman⟩ from the noun ⟨dom⟩. Also there is in Old English the noun ⟨cwealm⟩ (Modern English ⟨qualm⟩) meaning ⟨death⟩, ⟨slaughter⟩, together with the athematic verb ⟨cwelan⟩; from these it appears that the verb ⟨to cause to die⟩, ⟨to bring death on⟩, or ⟨to kill⟩—⟨cwellan⟩—thematic with $Pret_1$ ⟨cwealde⟩ was derived. Thematic verbs are characterized in Old and Middle English by a number of

OE & ME

morphological features. Perhaps the two most obvious are: ① the infinitive inflectional suffix has an initial glide segment, for instance, ⟨warnien⟩, ⟨folʒien⟩, sometimes superficially manifested by consonantal gemination, as in [cwellan] from underlying [cwaljan] and [fremman] from underlying [framjan]; ② the past tense is superficially marked by the addition to the verb stem of a "dental suffix," which has various phonological shapes. The origins of this dental extension are too complex to discuss here (but see Prokosch [1960], pp. 194 ff.), and we shall restrict ourselves to the statement that <u>at an abstract level past tense in *thematic* verbs is formed by a rule of the following type</u>:

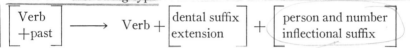

$$\begin{bmatrix} \text{Verb} \\ +\text{past} \end{bmatrix} \longrightarrow \text{Verb} + \begin{bmatrix} \text{dental suffix} \\ \text{extension} \end{bmatrix} + \begin{bmatrix} \text{person and number} \\ \text{inflectional suffix} \end{bmatrix}$$

The rules for the generation of the forms marking number and person of the postextension inflectional suffix are rather similar to those given above for the [—past] tense, the only difference being the conflation of the [+sing, person III and I] forms:

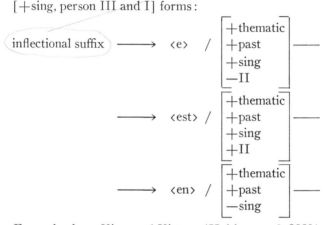

$$\text{inflectional suffix} \longrightarrow \langle e\rangle \quad / \quad \begin{bmatrix} +\text{thematic} \\ +\text{past} \\ +\text{sing} \\ -\text{II} \end{bmatrix} \underline{\qquad}$$

$$\longrightarrow \langle est\rangle \quad / \quad \begin{bmatrix} +\text{thematic} \\ +\text{past} \\ +\text{sing} \\ +\text{II} \end{bmatrix} \underline{\qquad}$$

$$\longrightarrow \langle en\rangle \quad / \quad \begin{bmatrix} +\text{thematic} \\ +\text{past} \\ -\text{sing} \end{bmatrix} \underline{\qquad}$$

Examples from *Vices and Virtues* (Holthausen [1888]) include ⟨ic folȝede⟩ (13/27), ⟨þu folȝedest⟩ (23/11), ⟨he folȝede⟩ (83/11), ⟨alle ðe modi ðe . . . ðe dieule folȝeden⟩ (⟨all the proud who followed the devil⟩) (57/5), also *Text V* (6 and 7). <u>In Middle (as well as Old) English it is very common to find the deletion or syncope of the initial vocalic segment of the number/person inflectional suffix in this tense context as well as in the</u> [—past]: hence ⟨astrehte⟩ (113/32), ⟨ararde⟩ (91/10), ⟨aliesde⟩ (119/ 26); and as the example from (113/32) shows, <u>when this syncope occurs, the nature of the consonantal dental extension can be affected.</u> In *Vices and Virtues,* for example, the dental extension is normally (as in Middle English in general) spelled ⟨d⟩ or ⟨t⟩, and if (on the basis of Modern English practice, if for no other reason) one assumes that this represents a [±voice] distinction between anterior obstruents, one can formulate the following voicing-assimilation rule, which should predict the acceptable surface phonological form of the dental extension:

$$\begin{bmatrix} -\text{voc} \\ +\text{cons} \\ +\text{obst} \\ +\text{ant} \end{bmatrix} \longrightarrow [\alpha\ \text{voice}] \quad / \quad \begin{bmatrix} -\text{voc} \\ +\text{cons} \\ \alpha\ \text{voice} \end{bmatrix} \underline{\qquad}$$

This rule states that the dental extension will be voiced or unvoiced according to the nature of the corresponding feature in the immediately preceding consonant (providing there is no vocalic segment intervening): hence, ⟨awerhtest⟩ (21/26), ⟨besohte⟩ (143/30) as against ⟨fastede⟩ (137/13) (without syncope) and ⟨ararde⟩ (91/10), ⟨aliesde⟩ (119/26) in voiced environments.

[*—Thematic*] *i.e.* stv.

We have already made a brief comment on the nature of [—thematic] verbs in the chapter on "Spellings and Sounds." However, the phenomenon of verbal ablaut—specifically the vocalic variation apparently conditioned by tense and number contexts of the [—thematic] verb—is so important as to warrant a further, though far from exhaustive, treatment. Traditional scholarship has noted that although variation of the vocalic segment of verb radicals exists, it is far from being unsystematic; and on the basis of surface-structure phonological forms, seven major types or classes have been recognized, five of which will be dealt with in some detail here. Consider the following examples of vocalic segment variation arranged according to these five major classes of the *athematic* verb as they might appear in a hypothetical dialect of early Middle English:

	Pres	*Pret₁*	*Pret₂*	*Part*
Class 1	drīve	drāve	driven	driven
	bīde	bād	biden	biden
Class 2	beode	bead	biden	biden
	forleose	forleas	forluren	forloren
Class 3	helpe	healp	hulpen	holpen
	binde	band	bunden	ibunde
Class 4	bēre	bār	bāren	boren
Class 5	ēte	ēt	ēten	eten
	drēpe	drāp	drāpen	drepen

The main point to be made here (again following Anderson [1971]) is that despite the apparent variety of superficial vocalic radical segments, there is, underlying each surface manifestation, an *unspecified* vocalic segment whose features (for example, of backness, height, or length) are determined by (and can be predicted from) the phonological contexts in which it occurs. Traditionally, two main kinds of difference in the radical vowel have been observed: the first is a difference of quality (usually said to be between the segments [e] and [o]) or *qualitative ablaut* (*Abtonung*); the other, a difference in the quantity (usually the length or duration) of the radical vocalic segment—hence *quantitative ablaut* (*Abstufung*). Some attempt has already been made in this book (see above pp. 77–86) to simplify these views by showing general rules, including nasal-raising and vowel-height assimilation, for the realization of a limited set of ablaut vowel surface shapes from a single underlying segment. The remainder of this chapter will expand this idea to include some of the more complex cases so far left untreated, as well as to include *Abstufung* differences within the same general framework.

Qualitative ablaut

Let us consider first of all a relatively simple case from the examples given above. Only in the Classes 4 and 5 do the $Pret_2$ radical vocalic segments have the feature [+long] (marked by superscripted $^-$). One could, presumably, write a rule that would explain the lengthening in a *syntactic* context, thus:

$$\begin{bmatrix} +voc \\ -cons \end{bmatrix} \longrightarrow [+long] \bigg/ \begin{bmatrix} \overline{} \\ Pret_2 \\ +athematic \end{bmatrix}$$

However, this misses the important generalization that at this slot only Classes 4 and 5 share a similar *phonological* context, that is, where one finds the sequence *radical* V + C + V. In other words, one can predict this [+long] feature of the vocalic root segment by a *phonological* rule:

$$\begin{bmatrix} +voc \\ -cons \end{bmatrix} \longrightarrow [+long] \bigg/ \underline{} C_1^1 V$$

that is, vowels are lengthening when they occur before one (and only one) consonantal segment followed by another vowel (see lengthening-in-open-syllables rule above, pp. 74–75). In other words, an apparently superficial phonological difference can be accounted for by reference to a common underlying form modified by a stated phonological environment.

This process is even more revealing when one considers what appear to be such unrelated forms (to each other as well as to the other classes) as the *Pres* and $Pret_1$ forms of Classes 1 and 2 ⟨drīve/drāve⟩ and ⟨beode/bead⟩. These superficial forms (as all others so far examined) are the result of a phonological context on an underlying unspecified vocalic segment. In these cases, Class 1 and 2 verbs have a radical vocalic segment followed by a nonsyllabic vowel that appears as [i] in Class 1 and [u] in Class 2, the radical deleted in $Pret_2$ and *Part* contexts. These vowels appear to be superficially represented in Gothic—compare ⟨beidan/baiþ⟩ and ⟨biudan/bauþ⟩. Assume for the moment that the first vocalic element in *Pres* and $Pret_1$ is [e] and [a] respectively, as in their Class 4 and 5 counterparts. How is it therefore possible to arrive at superficial forms such as [eo] (⟨beode⟩) and [ea] (⟨bead⟩), and [ii] (⟨drīve⟩), and [aa] (⟨drāve⟩)?

Let us consider first of all the Class 2 forms [eo] and [ea]. It is traditionally assumed (and probably correctly) that the latter is a diphthong, the initial segment of which is a low (not a mid) front vowel, and the second a low back vowel, thus [æa]. If this is the case, one has to suggest a reason why the underlying representations [eu] ⟶ [eo], and [au] ⟶ [æa].

There is, in fact, little difficulty in this if one suggests that a process of height assimilation takes place between the second (nonsyllabic) element of the diphthong and the first, that is, [eu] ⟶ [eo], where the second [+high] segment ⟶ [−high, −low] assimilating to the highness feature of [e]. In the same way, [u] ⟶ [+low] ⟶ [a]. This *vowel-height-assimilation* rule can be formulated as follows:

$$\begin{bmatrix} +\text{voc} \\ -\text{cons} \end{bmatrix} \longrightarrow \begin{bmatrix} \alpha \text{ high} \\ \beta \text{ low} \end{bmatrix} \Big/ \begin{bmatrix} +\text{voc} \\ -\text{cons} \\ \alpha \text{ high} \\ \beta \text{ low} \end{bmatrix} \underline{\quad\quad}$$

It states height assimilation between the first and second segments of the divocalic cluster. This rule will, of course, similarly account for the *Pret₁* Class I ⟨bād⟩ from its underlying ⟨baid⟩, the second [i] element having height assimilation with the first to become [+low], so that [ai] ⟶ [aa], although this represents a considerable simplification since other "sound changes" are also involved.

The *Pres* of Class I types seems rather exceptional in its behavior, since an underlying [ei] is realized as [ii], when by the above rule one might expect [ee]. This indicates a lack of adequacy in the rule, which will only operate on those divocalic segments that *contrast in backness,* which is not the case with [ei], so it must be reformulated as:

$$\begin{bmatrix} +\text{voc} \\ -\text{cons} \\ \gamma \text{ back} \end{bmatrix} \longrightarrow \begin{bmatrix} \alpha \text{ high} \\ \beta \text{ low} \end{bmatrix} \Big/ \begin{bmatrix} +\text{voc} \\ -\text{cons} \\ \alpha \text{ high} \\ \beta \text{ low} \\ -\gamma \text{ back} \end{bmatrix} \underline{\quad\quad}$$

This rule will be known as the *diphthong-height-harmony* rule. When its conditions for operation are not fulfilled, there is height assimilation in which the first vocalic segment, provided it is not [+low], takes on the height value of the second, if zero or two segments intervene:

$$\begin{bmatrix} +\text{voc} \\ -\text{cons} \\ -\text{low} \end{bmatrix} \longrightarrow [\alpha \text{ high}] \Big/ \underline{\quad\quad} C_0^2 \begin{bmatrix} +\text{voc} \\ -\text{cons} \\ \alpha \text{ high} \end{bmatrix}$$

thus [ei] → [ii]. Note how similar this rule is to the one given in Chapter Three (p. 8) for the production of the root vowels in *Pret₂* and *Part* forms—the vowel-height-assimilation rule. The derivations, in a much simplified and rather speculative form, of the *Pres* and *Pret₁* forms of Classes 1 and 2 can be represented as:

	Pres	*Pret₁*	*Pres*	*Pret₁*
Input	[drViv-]	[drViv]	[cVus-]	[cVus]
1. Present-tense rule	ei	inoperative	eu	inoperative
2. Past-tense rule	inoperative	ai	inoperative	au
3. Diphthong-height-harmony rule	inoperative	aæ	eo	inoperative
4. Fronting rule	inoperative	æeæ	inoperative	æu
5. Diphthong-height-harmony rule	inoperative	inoperative	inoperative	æa
6. Vowel-height-assimilation rule	ii	inoperative	inoperative	inoperative
Output	[driiv-]	[drææv]	[ceos-]	[cæas]

Rules 1 and 2 (which apply simultaneously) supply [e] and [a] for the unspecified vowel [V] in *Pres* and *Pret₁* environments respectively. Rule 3 brings those vowels that are different in frontness into height harmony, thus not applying to [ei] or [au]. Rule 4, one not so far detailed, traditionally called *fronting*, moves low back vowels to a low front position. The application of this rule now allows rule 3 to operate again, this time to [æu], since a frontness discrepancy has been created. Lastly, height harmony converts [ei] to [ii]. A later rule will alter the backness feature of [ææ] to [aa].

A more sophisticated approach could probably keep all rules involving syntactic information to a minimum. For instance, the rules so far given show that the underlying *Pres* root vowel is always realized as [—back, —low], whereas in *Pret₁* it is [+low]. This information can be captured by the rule:

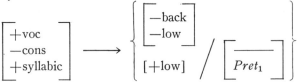

$$
\begin{bmatrix} +voc \\ -cons \\ +syllabic \end{bmatrix} \longrightarrow \left\{ \begin{bmatrix} -back \\ -low \end{bmatrix} \\ [+low] \right\} \Big/ \left[\underline{\qquad} Pret_1 \right]
$$

We can, however, even remove the necessity to include this remaining syntactic information by saying that the [+low] vowel is found only in inflectionless forms of the paradigm (which is *Pret₁*) so:

$$\begin{bmatrix} +\text{voc} \\ -\text{cons} \\ +\text{syllabic} \end{bmatrix} \longrightarrow \left\{ \begin{matrix} \begin{bmatrix} -\text{back} \\ -\text{low} \end{bmatrix} \\ [+\text{low}] \; / \; \underline{\quad} \; (\text{S}) \; \text{C}\# \end{matrix} \right\}$$

that is, the syllabic root vowel will be [—back, and —low] in all contexts except those where it precedes (one other consonantal or vocalic segment may intervene) a consonantal segment in word final position (#).

Quantitative ablaut variation (that is, in *Pret₂* and *Part,* where the underlying vowels undergo changes in their length rather than quality) can be explained by suggesting that reduction takes place only under conditions of lack of stress accent, whereas quantitative gain occurs where the syllable in question takes the main stress accent: for example, all vowels in (*Pret₂* and *Part*) are short unless accented:

$$V \longrightarrow \left\{ \begin{matrix} [-\text{long}] \\ [+\text{long}] \; / \; \begin{bmatrix} \underline{\quad} \\ +\text{accent} \end{bmatrix} \end{matrix} \right\}$$

In other words, in those areas where quantitative differences are involved in the ablaut series, that is, the *Pret₂* and *Part,* all vowels that do not carry the main stress accent are [—long] (and when a divocalic segment is involved, as in Classes 1 and 2, the first [syllabic] element is deleted:

$V \longrightarrow \emptyset \; / \; \underline{\quad} \; [\overset{V}{\quad}\text{accent}]$, so [drV̆ivun] [*Pret₂*] $\longrightarrow$ [drØivun]),

while the feature [+long] is added under conditions of main stress accent. The position of this main stress accent itself need not be described in syntactical terms, but is "conditioned" by the phonological context, thus:

$$V \longrightarrow \left\{ \begin{matrix} [-\text{accent}] \\ [+\text{accent}] \; / \; \underline{\quad} \; \text{C}^1_1 \; V \; (\text{C})\# \end{matrix} \right\}$$

that is, whenever quantitative ablaut is involved (as in *Pret₂* and *Part*), the syllabic vowel will carry the main stress accent wherever it occurs before one, and one only, consonantal segment + one vocalic segment (optionally + one consonantal segment) and word boundary. Hence one finds [bāren] $\underline{\quad} V + C^1_1 + V + C\#$, but [hŭlpon] $\underline{\quad} V + C^2 + V + C\#$ and [drĭven] $\underline{\quad} V + i + C^1 + V + C\#$.

The changes in the ablaut system that appear in later Middle English are very complicated and have never been fully examined (but see Rettger [1934]). It was seen in Chapter Three (pp. 83–85) that some superficial differences, notably the "analogical spread" of *Pret₂* root vowels into *Part,* and vice versa, could be accounted for by the deletion from the grammar of the vowel-height-assimilation rule. Yet the picture presented by the orthographic dialectal and temporal manifestations is most often very puzzling. Compare the following (incomplete) selection of the forms of the verb <to choose> in Middle English after 1200:

Pres	Pret₁	Pret₂	Part
cēse	chēs	chosen	chosen
cheose	ceas	curen	ʒecoren
chiese	cheas	cusen	ʒecuren
cheys	chǣs		icore
chōse	chōse		icorn
chūse	chāse		ichosen
	chesede		
	chused		

In the above display, there is not meant to be any horizontal dialectal correspondence between forms. Underlying this multiplicity of superficial forms are sets of rules (often dialect specific) of a rather complex kind. An interesting fact in connection with the above verb is that its contemporary form <choose> seems to be derived from the second vowel of the Middle English <cheose> and not, as one might expect, the first. To account for this, one would have to postulate some kind of syllabicity shift (see above, p. 129) such that the first element in the diphthong, [e], becomes [—syllabic]; and the second, [o], [+syllabic]. Thus [eo] ———→ [e̥o] (where ̥ represents syllable placement). The nonsyllabic vowel of the pair then undergoes assimilation with certain of the distinctive features of its neighbor (see Chapter Six for a more explicit statement of the rules involved), so that [e̥o] ———→ [e̥e], and [e̥o] ———→ [o̥o]. The [oo] then acts as input to the *vowel-raising rule* to make [uu], as in <chūse>. Such derivations are, of course, highly speculative, and it may be the case that in later Middle English verbal ablaut rules were coming to be nonproductive; that is, speakers exposed to data based upon the ablaut rules given in this chapter and Chapter Three might not be able, on the basis of what they heard, to recover the underlying system suggested. Consequently, they may have selected the vowel alternatives according to some other set of rules, or even on a completely *ad hoc* basis. Compare some of the late Middle English dialect realizations of the Class 1 <bīden>:

Pres	Pret₁	Pret₂	Part
bīden	bōd	bēden	beden
		bōden	
		bāden	

The *Pret₂* form ‹bēden› seems to indicate a restructuring in the ablaut process, so that the unspecified root vowel is seen as coming before a true consonant, like Class 5 types (see p. 172 above), suggesting that speakers were unable to recover from the data they heard that an underlying V + i was involved.

In some extreme instances, the ablaut system may have been completely unproductive, and the rules for the selection of radical segments come to be rather like *declensional* rules; that is, the speaker has to learn what appears to be the rather *ad hoc* rule that long, low, back vowels are characteristic of the *Pret₂* of ‹bāden› in his dialect, much in the same way that in some dialects of early Middle English speakers would have to know in an apparently similar arbitrary fashion that the N ‹dæȝ› belonged to Gender Class I and therefore demanded a particular set of surface-structure, definite-determiner forms. It is probably an oversimplification to say that in all later Middle English dialects the ablaut variants in athematic verbs are characterized by rules based upon syntactical and not phonological information—there may indeed be a considerable remnant of the latter type of rule.

Yet is it worth bearing in mind that from the later Middle English period onward there has been a tendency to form verbs which were "originally" athematic as thematic; this tendency is, in fact, much later than most traditional accounts would have one believe, but since one can find late Middle English forms such as *Pret₂* and *Part* ‹helped›, ‹drivede(n)›, ‹drepede›, ‹forleosede(n)› (where [+past] tense is marked by the addition of the dental extension and not the "historical" alteration in radical vowel quality or quantity), it is perhaps reasonable to suggest that the very *ad hoc* declension nature of the ablaut rules in later Middle English meant that such verbs tended more and more to be grouped in the *thematic* "declensional" class. This is far from being an "unnatural" process (as far as "naturalness" in grammars is understood), since, as we have suggested, the thematic verb class was historically used as a means of forming verbs from other "parts of speech" (including athematic verbs). The popularity of the rule for past tense formation

$$\left[\begin{array}{c} \text{Verb} \\ +\text{past} \end{array}\right] \longrightarrow \Big/ \text{V} + [\text{dental suffix extension}]$$

is evidenced by the fact that verbal lexical "borrowings" from French, Latin, and Scandinavian languages into Middle English are almost all, without exception, entered in the grammar as [+thematic].

[*Aspect*]

Unlike tense, aspect is a grammatical category used to describe, not when in the present or nonpresent actions take place, but wherever these actions are continuing or completed. Traditionally, these two actions are referred to as *progressive* and *perfective* aspect. Perhaps the most significant feature of verbal aspect in Middle English is the extent to which it relies upon auxiliary (or periphrastic) verb forms in superficial structure; Middle English, compared with earlier stages in the language, is characterized by the number and frequency of these auxiliary verbs.

[*+Progressive*]

In Old English, as well as in Middle English, progressive or durative aspect could be expressed without recourse to an auxiliary verb, but with increasing frequency in Middle English the auxiliary becomes a feature of this syntactic context: ⟨Eft he cwæð se þe mid him *sprecende wæs*⟩ (Sweet [1954], p. 43, l. 35). In the *Vices and Virtues* extract, for example, one finds ⟨Ne biest ðu naht hier lange wuniȝende⟩ (14–15), where durative aspect is marked by *be + Pres Part* construction; the *Pres Part* being distinguished by its inflectional suffix ⟨ende⟩. One of the notable surface changes in Middle English, for which no satisfactory explanation has as yet been proposed, is the substitution (especially in non-Southern dialects) of an inflectional suffix ⟨ing⟩ or ⟨ung⟩ for the "original" ⟨ende⟩; and it is this *be + V + ing* surface form that is to be found in Modern English grammar: note that in the Southeast dialect of the *Vices and Virtues* (also because of its early date) one finds the ⟨ende⟩ *Pres Part* inflectional suffix. Perhaps the most likely explanation for this change in the grammar lies in the close similarity between the deep structure of [+progressive] aspect and that of the "verbal noun" or gerund, the latter generally having an inflectional suffix in ⟨vowel + ng(e)⟩ in Middle English: ⟨For ðessere swete clepienge cumeð baðe gode and euele⟩ (*Vices and Virtues*, 71/32–33).

[*+Perfect*]

A common surface realization of this aspectual feature in Modern English is *have + Part:* ⟨John has gone home⟩. Old and Middle English both employ this construction, but to a considerably smaller extent. It is common in these languages to find the [+perfect] unmarked in the superficial structure by any auxiliary verb form, the [+past] tense alone being used. The *have + Part* construction has, however, existed in English from the earliest recorded data (although it has been suggested that it is an imitation of similar constructions in Latin); for example, compare the Old English ⟨he ofslog þone aldormon þe him lengest wunode⟩ (⟨he killed the earl who had been with him the longest⟩) (*Cynewulf and Cyneheard* [Sweet

(1954), I, l. 4]), where the perfective aspect is unrealized by an auxiliary verb, alongside, in the same text ‹hie alle on þone cyning wærun feohtende oþ þæt hie hine ofslæзenne hæfdon› (‹They were all fighting around the king until they had killed him›) (ll. 17–18), showing auxiliary marked progressive and perfect aspectual features. Note that in Old English and in some early Middle English texts, the *Part* could often be found with an inflectional suffix copying features of number and perhaps sex of the noun subject.

The *have + Part* construction becomes increasingly common in Middle English: ‹þe he ðe haueð iзarked› (*Text* V [27]); also ‹ic me hadde maked unwurð› (*Vices and Virtues,* 55/12), and ‹ðe hali words ðe ic habbe iwriten› (*Vices and Virtues,* 55/23). Old and Middle English, however, have also a surface realization of the perfect that utilizes the auxiliary ‹be› rather than ‹have›, for instance, ‹All he зeald ðane harm ðe was зecumen ðurh Adam› (‹He paid for all the harm that had come through Adam›) (*Vices and Virtues,* 117/33) and ‹Nu we alles bieð зecumen› (‹Now we have all come›) (*Vices and Virtues,* 141/17) and perhaps ‹(he) ne hafð god зedon on ða time ðe he naure mo eft nacoureð, 7 is forð зegan› (‹He has not done good in the time he will never recover and which has gone by›) (*Vices and Virtues,* 121/24–26). It is sometimes suggested that the *be + Part* is limited more frequently to *mutative* verbs—that is, verbs denoting change, whereas *have + Part* is customarily found with nonmutatives. At any rate the *have + Part* construction is found with increasing frequency throughout the later Middle English period (even in "mutative" contexts as early as *Vices and Virtues*—‹he mid muchels iswinke hadde iwant to Criste› [27/20] [‹(all those whom) he had turned with great effort toward Christ›])—and the Aux ———→ ‹be› comes to be deleted from the grammar in the [+perfective] aspectual context.

Nevertheless, auxiliary aspect markers are as a whole infrequent in the grammar of Middle English at all periods, and what (for Modern English) are relatively "simple" realizations of the [+perfect] and [+progressive] aspects by two auxiliaries, as in ‹He has been going there for years›, are almost never found.

BIBLIOGRAPHY

GENERAL TREATMENTS OF THE MIDDLE ENGLISH VERB

BENNETT, J. A. W., and G. V. SMITHERS (1966), pp. 74 ff.

BRUNNER, K. (1948), pp. 74 ff.

MOSSÉ, F. (1952), pp. 67 ff.

MUSTANOJA, T. F. (1960), pp. 429 ff.
WARDALE, E. E. (1949), pp. 101 ff.
WEINSTOCK, H. (1968), pp. 159 ff.
WRIGHT, J. (1957), pp. 174–204.

WORKS OF A MORE DETAILED NATURE DEALING WITH
THE VERB PHRASE IN MIDDLE AND MODERN ENGLISH

ANDERSON, J. M., " 'Ablaut' in the Synchronic Phonology of the Old
    English Strong Verb," *Indogermanische Forschungen,* 1971.
AUSTIN, J. L., *How To Do Things With Words,* Oxford, 1952.
BAKER, C. L., "Notes on the Description of English Questions," *Founda-
    tions of Language,* 6 (1970).
BLACKBURN, F. A., *The English Future: Its Origin and Development,*
    Leipzig, 1892.
BLOCH, B., "English Verb Inflection," *Language,* XXIII (1947).
BRADLEY, C. B., "*Shall* and *Will:* An Historical Study," *Transactions of
    the American Philological Association,* XLII (1911).
CARO, G., "Das englische Perfectum und Praeteritum in ihrem Verhältnis
    zu einander historisch Untersucht," *Anglia,* XXI (1899).
CLARK, C., (1958), "Introduction," pp. xxx ff.
CURME, G. O., "Has English a Future Tense?," *JEGP,* 1913.
EHRMAN, M., *The Meaning of Modals in Present Day American English,*
    The Hague, 1966.
ELLEGARD, A., "The Auxiliary 'Do,' " *Gothenberg Studies in English,* II
    (1953), Stockholm.
ENGBLOM, V., "On the Origin and Early Development of the Auxiliary
    'Do,' " *Lund Studies in English,* VI (1938), Lund.
FORSTRÖM, G., "The Verb 'To Be' in Middle English," *Lund Studies in
    English,* XV (1948), Lund.
FRIDÉN, G., "On the Use of Auxiliaries to Form the Perfect and the Plu-
    perfect in Late Middle English," *Studia Linguistica,* XI (1957).
————, *Studies on the Tenses of the English Verb from Chaucer to
    Shakespeare,* Uppsala, 1948.
FÜLLER, L., *Das Verbum in der Ancrene Riwle,* Jena, 1937.
GRAEF, A., *Das Futurum und die Entwicklung von Schal und Wil zu
    futurischen Tempusbildnern bei Chaucer,* Flensburg, 1893.
————, *Das Perfectum bei Chaucer,* Keil, 1888.
————, "Die präsentischen Tempora bei Chaucer," *Anglia,* XII (1889).
HAÜSERMANN, H. W., "Studien zu den Aktionsarten im Frühmittelengli-
    schen," *Wiener Beiträge zur englischen Philologie,* LIV (1930),
    Wien und Leipzig.

JACKENDOFF, R. S., "An Interpretive Theory of Negation," *Foundations of Language,* 5 (1969).

JESPERSEN, O., *A Modern English Grammar on Historical Principles,* iv; *Syntax,* 3: "Time and Tense," Heidelberg, 1931.

KENYON, J. S., *The Syntax of the Infinitive in Chaucer,* London, 1909.

KLIMA, E. S., "Negation in English," in *The Structure of Language,* edited by J. J. Katz and J. Fodor, Englewood Cliffs, 1964.

LEVIN, S. R., "Negative Contraction: An Old and Middle English Dialect Criterion," *JEGP,* LVII (1958).

LONG, M. M., *The English Strong Verb from Chaucer to Caxton,* Menasha, 1944.

LYONS, J. (1968), pp. 304 ff.

MARCHAND, H., "Syntaktische Homonymie; das umschreibende *do,*" *Englische Studien,* LXXIII (1938–1939).

MARQUARDT, P., *Die starke Participien Praeteriti im Mittelenglischen,* Berlin, 1920.

MITCHELL, B., "Some Problems of Mood and Tense in Old English," *Neophilologus,* 1965.

MOORE, S., *Historical Outlines of English Phonology and Morphology,* Ann Arbor, 1925.

———, "Robert Mannyng's Use of *Do* as Auxiliary," *MLN,* XXXIII, 1918.

ÖFVERBERG, W., *The Verbal Inflection of the East Midland Dialects in Early Middle English,* Lund, 1924.

ORTMANN, F. J., *Formen und Syntax des Verbs bei Wycliffe und Purvey,* Berlin, 1902.

PROKOSCH, E., *A Comparative Germanic Grammar,* Yale, 1960, pp. 120 ff.

RETTGER, J. F., "The Development of Ablaut in the Strong Verbs of the East Midland Dialects of Middle English," *Language Dissertations, Linguistic Society of America,* XVIII (1934), Philadelphia.

ROYSTER, J. F., "The *Do* Auxiliary, 1400–1450," *Modern Philology,* 12 (1915).

———, "A Note on Lydgate's Use of the *Do* Auxiliary," *Studies in Philology,* XIII (1916).

SAMUELS, M. L., "The Role of Functional Selection in the History of English," *Transactions of the Philological Society* (1965).

THORNE, J. P., "English Imperative Sentences," *Journal of Linguistics,* II (1966).

———, and J. BOYD, "The Deep Grammar of Modal Verbs," *Journal of Linguistics,* V (1969).

VOGEL, E., *Zur Flexion des englischen Verbum im XI und XII Jhdts,* Jena, 1902; Berlin, 1903.

WELLS, J. E., "Accidence in *The Owl and the Nightingale*," *Anglia,* XXXIII (1910).

ZENKE, W., "Synthesis und Analysis des Verbum im *Ormulum*," *Studien zur englischen Philologie,* XL (1910).

EDITIONS

ALLEN, H. E., *The English Writings of Richard Rolle,* Oxford, 1931.

HOLTHAUSEN, F., *Vices and Virtues, I and II, EETS,* O.S. 89 (1888), 159 (1920).

ROSS, W. O., *Middle English Sermons, EETS,* O.S. 209, 1940.

SWEET, H., *Anglo-Saxon Reader,* Oxford, 1954.

MIDDLE ENGLISH DIALECTS /SIX

I

It was seen in the chapter on "Spellings and Sounds" that one of the most important consequences of the fact that English did not employ a nationally current orthographic system between the eleventh and mid-fifteenth centuries was that linguistic variation between different geographical areas tended to be highlighted. Not only does this nonnational spelling standard enable one to see in some detail how the language was developing and changing from period to period, but the wealth of data is also such that it is possible (at least in some areas of the grammar) to make quite explicit statements relating to both geographical and temporal phenomena. Nevertheless, for the most part, the most crucial question has only been touched upon. Indeed, as suggested above in Chapter Three, the problem of what scribes meant by what they wrote, or what, in general, orthographic systems represent, is an area of linguistic study about which little is known at present.

This has particularly drastic consequences, of course, for any attempted reconstruction of a historical phonology, although it is probably magnified even further when one is faced with manuscripts of a given text all written at approximately the same point in time, but composed or copied in different parts of the country. This situation in Middle English produces many differences in the syntax, morphology, and (it would seem from the orthography) the phonology, yet, especially in the last area, one has continually to beg the question of interpretation.

How is one to interpret, for instance, the relationship between the following orthographic representations (taken from some of the manuscript versions of the *Cursor Mundi*—a text to be discussed in more detail later) and some posited phonological reconstruction?

⟨Bath þi drems are als an⟩   (*Cotton MS,* l. 4605)
⟨Baþ þer dremes ar als ane⟩   (*Fairfax MS*)

⟨For bath þir dremes er als on⟩ (*Göttingen MS*)
⟨For boþe þe dremes ben as oon⟩ (*Trinity MS*)

This chapter will have to take up again some of the problems already raised in the earlier discussions on phonology. As suggested there, the difficulty is many-sided: one must try not only to reconstruct from the written symbols or graphemes some sound system that they may be trying to represent, but also to decide upon the status of the graphemes themselves to determine whether they can, on all occasions, be used as evidence for spoken features at all. It would seem, for example, quite possible that such spelling contrasts as ⟨an⟩ and ⟨on⟩, ⟨Baþ⟩ and ⟨boþe⟩ reflect some spoken distinction either in the frontness or the height of the root vocalic segment in each case. Or it might be that the scribes are in each instance concerned with representing different levels of phonological abstraction. Even if their spellings do manifest superficial differences, it is most unlikely that one is likely to make any phonetic statement concerning these with any degree of reliability.

The matter is further complicated by such alternatives as ⟨an/ane⟩ and ⟨on/oon⟩. What is the precise nature of the vocalic difference, if any, in the radical segment? Does the geminate graph imply length, and does the addition of a word-final ⟨e⟩ suggest a device to keep distinct in the orthography what would otherwise be identical entities, since they had a contrastive root vocalic segment in nonwritten contexts? One may even conclude that orthographic features such as these have no status whatever in the written "manifestation" of spoken sounds. Certainly, this would seem very clear in the orthographic contrasts ⟨Bath⟩/⟨Baþ⟩, where the ⟨th⟩/⟨þ⟩ "opposition" can hardly be supposed to denote some phonetic difference like the presence or absence of a feature [+voice]. One might conclude that situations such as the last do not deserve the attention of the historical phonologist or dialectologist, since they provide no information. But such a conclusion would be quite wrong because the *graphemic* contrast of ⟨th⟩ and ⟨þ⟩ (quite apart from any phonetic considerations) can be an important clue to a text's geographical provenance, since scribes living and writing in various parts of the country did not necessarily use the two forms in free and random variation to each other, but one form could be favored more than the other in the orthographic system of a scribe living or trained in a certain geographical area.

In more general terms, the problems raised by dialectal linguistic variation at a synchronic level are very similar to those of diachronic change. It would seem likely, for example, that languages are heterogeneous dialectally and historically for the same kinds of reasons: somehow in the acquisition process and later when other innovations are added to speakers' grammars, there arise discrepancies between the internalized system of rules of individuals. There is every reason to believe that such rule differences existed between speakers of English living in distinct geographical areas as much in 1400 as today, but one must add that very often in the past descriptions of such dialectal contrasts have suffered from the same kinds of inadequacies as those to be found in general theories of linguistic change. Since to a large extent workers in the fields of temporal and geographical change have generally concentrated their efforts upon matters phonological, many of their findings in both areas have been suspect because of the limitations of the theoretical framework within which they were working. Not only did they in general ignore purely graphemic contrasts (graphemes with no "corresponding" sound being treated as irrelevant, and the spoken word somehow regarded as more important than the written even though the latter can be shown to be as "structured"), but they also concentrated all their efforts on what we have called the language user's *performance* rather than his *competence*.

This has led to the idea that since even individual speakers are subject to differences in the size and shape of their vocal apparatus, any attempt to reproduce a given sound, say [k], will lead to a sometimes considerable discrepancy in performance. Owing to such physical variety, it is argued, no speaker will be able to have an identical performance of the consonantal segment [k] on any occasion or with any other speaker. The result of this will be some random and gradual shift around some "local frequency maximum," so that one should not be surprised to find [k] eventually turning up in another dialect as [g]. The speaker is unable, as it were, to hit the target exactly on each occasion, so that individuals can only approximate to some ideal pronunciation. In theories concerned with any resultant gradual movement away from this ideal, only variables in the speaker's performance are involved; his competence, that is, the implicit knowledge he has of his language, the internalized system of rules that constitute his grammar, is ignored. It is the failure to take into account this very feature of the speaker's competence that makes such theories unattractive, and many linguists now believe that the level of performance is not the primary consideration in the differences between geographical and temporal "dialects."

What distinguishes one geographical dialect from another is not discrepancy in performance, but competence; that is, the speaker of dialect A may have *x* number of rules more or less than a speaker of dialect B. This will almost certainly result in differences at the superficial levels of performance in each case, but it would be mistaken to think that these differences were the result of some random inability to "copy" the speech of others and so set in motion some gradual shift from one phonological or syntactical system to another. In the process of acquisition, a child, as has been seen, may add or subtract rules in relation to the grammars to which he is exposed, with the result that his grammar (the internalized series of rules that generate all the correct sentences of the language) may be unique to him and almost certainly rather different from that of another speaker living in a different geographical area. In other words, rather than talk about sound change or dialectal change, one should be concerned with *grammar change*. If, for example, dialect X has the sound [k] and dialect Y manifests this in the same contexts as [g], rather than postulate a random and gradual sound change from [k] to [g], one might suggest that there has been a rule added to dialect Y to the effect that:

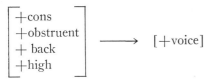

$$\begin{bmatrix} +\text{cons} \\ +\text{obstruent} \\ +\text{ back} \\ +\text{high} \end{bmatrix} \longrightarrow [+\text{voice}]$$

In fact, <u>there is hardly any evidence for linguistic variation being caused by gradual shifts</u>; and it is difficult to see, for instance, what is gradual in the changes in the personal pronoun system in Middle English, where one finds ⟨heo⟩ ⟶ ⟨hire⟩ or ⟨hie⟩ ⟶ ⟨þei⟩ (see above, pp. 116 and 131). Equally, it is not probable that theories concerned with "failure to hit the correct articulatory target" will satisfactorialy account for such temporal and dialectal variations as ⟨to þæm wife⟩ and ⟨to þe wif⟩ in Middle English. It is surely the speaker's competence that has changed, so that for the last example one can posit a simplification in the internalized system of morphological rules such that those assigning case and number (and gender) surface realizations to nouns and articles are deleted in certain environments.

Such remarks are, of course, equally true and relevant for comments made about dialectal as well as temporal changes (Weinreich [1968] and [1961]). The fact that speakers living in different geographical areas have sometimes divergent linguistic performances or outputs means that they have to a greater or lesser extent a different set of internalized grammatical rules—one speaker may have one rule more or less at a given point in the grammar than another speaker from a different geographical area. One must assume this to be true for all languages, and there is no doubt that it is so for Middle no less than Modern English.

In the western Midland and northwest Midland counties of England in the middle of the fourteenth century, there are many recorded orthographic variants of the pronoun with the features [+female, +III person, +singular]. Our concern here is with those varieties with initial segment spelled ⟨h-⟩: ⟨heo⟩, ⟨hoo⟩, ⟨hoe⟩, ⟨ho⟩, and ⟨he⟩, among others. On the surface, the evidence might persuade us to accept the idea that there has taken place some gradual and imperceptible shift in pronunciation from some "original" Old English form ⟨heo⟩ and that the variety of the Middle English forms is a clear indication of the inability of the speakers to hit the right phonetic "target" with obvious random results. However, it is equally likely, and we claim more plausible, to suggest that the results are less haphazard than they appear and that it is possible to explain some of the spelling varieties in terms of competence differentials rather than gradual sound changes. Compare such spellings as ⟨heo⟩ and ⟨hoo⟩. If the latter is "derived" from the former, one might suggest that the first element of the diphthong [eo] has come to show features of the second, so that:

$$\begin{bmatrix} +\text{voc} \\ -\text{cons} \\ -\text{high} \\ -\text{low} \end{bmatrix} \longrightarrow [+\text{round}] \Bigg/ \underline{\hspace{2cm}} \begin{bmatrix} +\text{voc} \\ -\text{cons} \\ +\text{round} \\ -\text{syllabic} \end{bmatrix}$$

This rule states that before the second element of a diphthong (that is nonsyllabic) having the feature [+round], in other words having lip-rounding, the first element of the diphthong will undergo lip-rounding assimilation, so that [eo] ⟶ [oo]. Such an interpretation assumes that long vowels and diphthongs are both to be treated as [VV] in the grammar; in other words, where the vowel has the feature [+long], the V's are identical (see Anderson and Lass [forthcoming]), whereas in the case of diphthongs, the second element is different from the first (perhaps in height or blackness), in both instances the second element being nonsyllabic, hence the *syllabicity-assignment* rule:

$$[V] \longrightarrow [+\text{syllabic}] \Big/ \underline{\hspace{2cm}} [\overset{.}{V}]$$

On the other hand, such a *rounding-assimilation* rule as the one above does not seem to appear in the grammar of those dialects with spellings such as ⟨he⟩. Such spellings suggest the existence of what might be called a *backness-identity* rule, as follows:

$$\begin{bmatrix} +\text{voc} \\ -\text{cons} \\ -\text{high} \\ -\text{low} \end{bmatrix} \longrightarrow [-\text{back}] \Bigg/ \begin{bmatrix} +\text{voc} \\ -\text{cons} \\ -\text{back} \end{bmatrix} \underline{\hspace{2cm}}$$

This rule states there is assimilation between the features of frontness and backness in the nonsyllabic second element to those same features in the first vocalic segment, so that [eo] ⟶ [ee], resulting in the development of a long vowel. To explain why the first element of the diphthong assimilates to features of the second, and vice versa, it might be necessary to allow for a *syllabicity-shift* rule of the type mentioned above on page 176, such that [eo̥] ⟶ [e̥o]. A simplified derivation of these divocalic segments in two dialects might be:

	Dialect A	Dialect B
Input	[eo]	[eo]
1. Syllabicity-assignment rule	e̥o	e̥o
2. Syllabicity-shift rule	inoperative	eo̥
3. Roundness-assimilation rule	inoperative	oo̥
4. Backness-identity rule	e̥e	inoperative
Output	[he̥e]	[ho̥o]
Orthographic representation	⟨he⟩	⟨hoo⟩ ⟨ho⟩

Note that rule 1 will have to be applied again, under this interpretation, to the output of dialect B's rule 3. Speakers of dialect A appear not to have either rules 2 or 3 in their grammars, whereas those of dialect B do not have rule 4, but do have rules 2 and 3. Speakers with an output [heo] have neither rules 2, 3, or 4. Thus the phonological implications of such spellings can be accounted for in terms of rule additions to grammars rather than within the framework of a theory of gradual sound change.

Matters are, however, often more involved than this, since it can be shown that according to one interpretation of the orthographic evidence, there exist phonological discrepancies even within the confines of one geographical dialect. These discrepancies can also be dealt with in terms of the presence or absence of rules in respective grammars. In the fourteenth-century alliterative poem *Sir Gawain and the Green Knight,* which is written in the Northwest Midland dialect (see below, pp. 214–217), are found pairs such as ⟨bront/brond⟩ (⟨a sword⟩), ⟨blende/blent⟩ (⟨mixed together⟩), ⟨bult/bulde⟩ past tense (⟨to build⟩), ⟨gylt⟩/⟨gyld⟩ (⟨gilded⟩), ⟨policed⟩/⟨polyst⟩ (⟨polished⟩), ⟨slypped⟩/⟨slypte⟩ (⟨slipped⟩), ⟨ȝonge⟩/⟨ȝonke⟩ (⟨youthful⟩), as well as ⟨lenkþe⟩ (⟨length⟩) and ⟨rink⟩, ⟨rynkande⟩ (⟨ring⟩, ⟨ringing⟩) corresponding to ⟨lengþe⟩ and ⟨ryngange⟩ in other Northwest Midland dialects. One interpretation of this evidence might be to suggest that there is some kind of partial rule in this dialect involving the devoicing of obstruents mainly (but not always) in final word position:

$$\begin{bmatrix} -\text{voc} \\ +\text{cons} \\ +\text{obstruent} \end{bmatrix} \longrightarrow [-\text{voice}] \;/\; \underline{\qquad} \; \#$$

where # represents the word final position. Assuming for the moment that
the orthographic ⟨d⟩/⟨t⟩ and ⟨g⟩/⟨k⟩ forms represent some phonetic difference, how is one to account for the apparent inconsistency of the rule
application within the one grammar? A number of points can be made.
Firstly, one can assume that a rule of this kind could be more or less powerful in individual grammars; it may have been extensive in some and rarer
in others, so that any "dialectal" statement about the distribution of its
phonetic values would have to be very detailed indeed. Certainly, a general
statement that the rule is to be found in one dialect, but not in another,
would be rather trivial. Secondly, the addition of a rule to the grammars of
some speakers of a given dialect need not imply that that rule will occur
on every occasion; one must be prepared to accept the notion of major and
minor rules in grammars. The rule for final devoicing in the Northwest
Midland dialect of *Sir Gawain and the Green Knight* would, therefore,
qualify as a minor rule. In other words, the rule extends its areas or domain
of applicability only to a rather limited area of the lexicon—"exceptions" to
it being shown in spellings such as ⟨bynde⟩, ⟨bidde⟩, ⟨gyld⟩, ⟨spend⟩,
⟨bryng⟩, and many others. These are the contexts in which the rule does
not (as yet) apply in this dialect, and they are not purely phonetic contexts. One can say, consequently, that the final devoicing rule is not "highly
valued" in this dialect (although it may be in others), since one has to
explain its limitations by introducing nonphonetic specifications such as
that it occurs only with a given set of items in the lexicon and not with
others.

   Dialects, in fact, may differ from one another, not because one has a
rule A, while the other has not, but because in one rule A may be only
a minor rule, while in the other it is a major one always occurring in a
specified context. A good example of this lies in the usage of the pronoun
with the features [—singular, +animate, +III]. As seen above (p. 133)
in what can for the moment broadly be called Northern Middle English
dialects in the fourteenth century, the initial consonantal segment of this
form was represented orthographically as ⟨þ⟩ ([ð]) in all case relationships—⟨þei⟩ [+agent], ⟨þem⟩ [—agent, —possessive], and ⟨þer⟩ [+pos-
sessive]. However, in the contemporary London dialect of Chaucer, it was
seen that it was only in the [+agent] case contexts that forms with this
initial consonantal segment appear, ⟨h-⟩ types (⟨here⟩ and ⟨hem⟩) being
the rule elsewhere. It might, therefore, be concluded that the rule introducing the innovation of the initial ⟨þ-⟩ in the third-person pronoun in the
plural was a minor one in Chaucer's dialect, but a major one in some contemporary northern texts.

   As will be argued further below, it is perhaps best not to place too
much emphasis on the idea of a geographical dialect with some homogene-

ous set of syntactical and phonological features, since it will not be sufficiently adequate to account for the wide variety and complexity of the
data. In the long run, one may be forced to recognize only individual
grammars, which themselves may not always show a very wide symmetry
in their manifestations.

Yet the recognition of major and minor rules in historical grammars
depends, again, on the kind of interpretation given to what the scribe has
written. It cannot be too strongly emphasized that the criteria for distinguishing underlying = (morphophonemic) and superficial = (autonomous
phonemic) orthographic representation are in their infancy. Some cases
are clearer than others. In Modern English, for instance, ⟨profound⟩ and
⟨profundity⟩ show a different symbol for the vowel in the second syllable,
even though, as the following (simplified) derivations show, a common
underlying vowel is involved. In this instance, Modern English utilizes
an autonomous phonemic orthographic representation:

Input	[profund]	[profundɪtɪ]
1. Tensing rule	ū	inoperative
2. Lengthening rule	ūu	inoperative
3. Glide-addition rule	ūw	inoperative
4. Vowel-lowering rule	ōw	inoperative
5. Not given	inoperative	ʌ
Output	[profōwnd]	[profʌndɪtɪ]
Orthographic representation	⟨profound⟩	⟨profundity⟩

(For the failure of the *tensing rule* in contexts such as ——— C^2V, see
Chomsky and Halle [1968], p. 52; and for the rule that manifests the
underlying lax [u] as [ʌ], see the same book, p. 203.)

The ⟨f⟩ symbol in Orm's spellings ⟨hafe⟩ and ⟨forr⟩ is unlikely to be
a realization of superficial phonological identity, but seems rather to represent a more abstract level of the sound system. The scribe seems to be
indicating that the two different surface pronunciations of this symbol derive from a single, common underlying consonantal segment:

Input	[hafe]	[forr]
Intervocalic-voicing rule	v	inoperative
Output	[v]	[f]
Orthographic representation	⟨f⟩	⟨f⟩

In fact, Orm's spellings of these words (unlike another Middle English spelling such as ⟨haue⟩) is very close to their lexical shapes (Chomsky and Halle [1968], p. 44).

There has never been any systematic attempt to work out the systems or combinations of systems involved in the spelling conventions of Middle English scriptoria. Although anything more than an approximation to such systems is not likely to be discovered, much of the evidence of spelling habits provided by the McIntosh/Samuels Middle English dialect survey (see below, pp. 211–217) will prove invaluable in the attempt.

No one orthographic system will probably turn out to be consistently either morphophonemic or autonomous phonemic, and both systems will in all certainty exist side by side. The problem for the historical phonologist lies in the setting up of a theory that will enable him to predict when one or the other is being used.

An often advocated third level of orthographic representation has never been (and probably could never be) found in any alphabetical system. This is the so-called purely *phonetic* type, where every different articulatory manifestation is accorded a unique symbol, so that there is no ambiguity in the superficial realization of sound and symbol. There are many arguments against this suggestion that cannot be gone into here, but since the range of speech performance is infinitely variable (see the "target-missing" theories discussed earlier), the number of symbols and diacritics would also presumably be open-ended and therefore impossible to learn, if nothing else. Is it "necessary" in English to have two different ⟨p⟩ symbols in words like ⟨speak⟩ and ⟨peak⟩ since there is a clear articulatory difference in performance (the latter having a much greater degree of aspiration than the former)?

As already suggested, one might perhaps even go as far as to say that the notion of a geographical dialect, although it is a convenient one, may be of little use in a general theory of language. Although most people would intuitively agree that they think there are large homogeneous linguistic usages in geographical areas other than their own, they rarely realize the complexity and variation that exist within dialects, nor do they give much credence to the idea of the individual internalized grammar. Certainly, in the Middle Ages there is evidence of popular notions about distinct regional grammars; Trevisa's translation of Higden's *Polychronicon* shows such a consciousness intermingled with some value judgments, which are, unfortunately, still all too current today:

Also Englyschmen, þey3 hy hadde fram þe bygynnyng þre maner speche, Souþeron, Norþeron, and Myddel speche in þe myddel of þe

lond, as hy come of þre maner people of Germania, noþeles by com-
myxstion and mellyng, furst wiþ Danes and afterward wiþ Normans,
in menye þe contray longage ys apeyred, and som vseþ strange wlaf-
fyng, chyteryng, harryng, and garryng grisbittyng.

[In the same way the English, even though they originally had three
kinds of language, Southern, Northern and Midland (in the central
regions), coming as they did from three distinct German nations,
nevertheless through intermingling and mixing, first of all with Danes
and afterward with Normans, their language has been impaired in
many parts of the country, some people using an odd stammering and
chattering, a snarling and grating and gnashing of teeth.]

Even many twentieth-century scholars have talked about "five main
dialects" that constitute Middle English: the *Northern* (all counties north
of a line drawn between Morecambe Bay in Lancashire to the Humber),
the *West Midland* (those English counties, as well as parts of the Welsh
ones, between Morecambe Bay and the Bristol Channel, extending as far
east as the middle of the counties of Staffordshire, Warwickshire, and
Gloucestershire), the *East Midland* (from the Humber south to the northern Thames estuary extending as far west as mid-Oxfordshire and Derbyshire and including the southern part of the West Riding of Yorkshire),
the *Southeastern* (the counties of Sussex, Surrey, and Kent and the east
part of Hampshire), and the *Southwestern* (all counties south and west of
a line running from north Gloucestershire to the Isle of Wight). But such
divisions tend to be both misleading and confusing. They conceal the fact
that within and across their boundaries other groupings can be made, they
are clearly too great an oversimplification to be of much value, and they
seem by definition to imply that within their boundaries there existed some
homogeneous set of grammars (although one is rarely ever given more
than a very few of their characteristics), an idea that we have suggested
might not be altogether acceptable. However, the most telling argument
against such neat groupings is their very low descriptive adequacy. This
can be illustrated simply by taking an individual feature in which Middle
English dialects are known to vary. Map I shows the distribution (after
McIntosh and Samuels) of the orthographic representations of the words
⟨kirk⟩ and ⟨church⟩ in Middle English in the first half of the fifteenth
century. Many scholars have suggested that the ⟨kirk⟩ form, said to be
"borrowed" from Scandinavian languages, is a characteristic of the Northern dialect in Middle English, whereas forms with initial ⟨ch-⟩ are confined to the Midlands and the South. Map I certainly belies such statements, since the ⟨kirk⟩ form at this date can be seen to be much further

south than any line drawn between Lancashire and the Humber. But perhaps the most important information given by this map (if one accepts for the moment that many, if not all, of the orthographic variants it shows represent phonetic differences of some kind) is that it immediately shows how complex any meaningful statement must be. This is especially true when one realizes both that the map contains only approximately 75 percent of the data for these two words collected by McIntosh and Samuels and that much of the evidence for ⟨k-⟩ and ⟨ch-⟩ forms in the Norfolk region has not been included. Such evidence suggests that the isogloss line may come down as far as the Norfolk/Suffolk border. One can see, for example, that there are forms, such as ⟨cherche⟩, which cut well across the traditional Middle English dialect boundaries, but that others, such as some ⟨k-⟩ types, appear in the middle of areas where one would not "normally" expect them, for example, the ⟨k-⟩ forms around Gloucester. Others, such as ⟨churche⟩ and ⟨chirche⟩ types, appear in large numbers alongside each other in similar geographical areas, so that it is difficult to draw boundary lines between them with any degree of certainty; and this may provide a very revealing picture of the complexity of the phonetic data in these regions at this period.

As suggested over and over again, such complexity should not be a matter for surprise, but should indeed be expected; it is not difficult to imagine how much more complex the picture would become if one was to add to the map even a few more of the syntactical and phonological differences found in geographical regions within the very narrow temporal confines of the thirty or so years represented in Map I. Failure to represent this elaborate (but it seems highly ordered) picture has led in the past to oversimplified statements and conclusions about the nature and extent of the dialects of Middle English.

It is, consequently, impossible in this short space to give a list of the "characterizing features" of Middle English dialects. Such an undertaking, if it is possible at all, would take up many volumes. As so often before, we shall again have to confine ourselves to an examination of a very small part of the data and be content to show the difficulties rather than universally applicable "facts."

II

Such is the wealth of material surviving from the Middle English period that there are many instances where literary and other written products exist in many contemporary versions copied into various regional orthographic systems. There are, for example, over one hundred surviving manuscripts of Chaucer's *Canterbury Tales* (in varying degrees of completeness) from the century following Chaucer's death; many of these survive in regional spelling standards. Even more varied, both in the number of surviving manuscripts and in the diversity of the geographical regions in which it was copied, is the *Ayenbyte of Inwyt,* originally composed at Canterbury in 1340 by Michael of Northgate: it has over two hundred surviving manuscript versions. This situation is not unusual in the material left to us and, depending upon how one interprets it, it can provide much valuable information of a "dialectal" kind.

In the pages that follow we shall take a very brief look at an important text that survives in several manuscript sources. There are five principal extant versions (all composed in the late fourteenth or early fifteenth centuries) of the *Cursor Mundi* or *þe Cours of þe Werlde* or *The Cursur o the World,* a lengthy (in the region of thirty thousand lines) religious text: these are *Cotton Vespasian A iii* in the British Museum; *Fairfax MS 14* in the Bodleian Library, Oxford; the *Göttingen MS theol. 107;* *Trinity College, Cambridge MS R 3.8;* and the *Additional MS 36983* (what we shall call the *Bedford MS*) in the British Museum. There is much controversy about the location of the source manuscript from which these five derive either by direct or secondary copying; part of the *Fairfax MS* seems almost certainly to be copied from an original composed in the region of south Lincolnshire around the Wash. *Fairfax 14* seems also to have been commissioned in Lancaster, and many scholars believe that the *Göttingen* and *Cotton* are to be located in this area too although perhaps further to the north. The *Trinity MS* seems almost certainly to have been produced in or near Lichfield in southeast Staffordshire, while there is also internal evidence to suggest an area of composition in Bedfordshire for the British Museum *Additional 36983*. One has, consequently, a reasonably good geographical "spread" in the manuscripts of this text; and one should, therefore, expect to find at least a considerable amount of similarity between the "Northern" group, which will in turn contrast with features in the "West Midland" and "Central Midland" texts.

CURSOR.MUNDI

Cotton Vespasian A. iii, British Museum

Bitid þan in a litel quile
Iacob yode walcand be þe nile
He sagh apon þe watur reme
Caf flettand dunward þe strem
O þᵗ sight wex he ful blith   5
And til his suns he tald it suith
Childir he said yee list and lete
I sagh caf on þe wat[er] flete
Queþen it com i can not rede
Bot dunward flette it wel god spede   10
If it be commen fra fer land
Lok quilk of us sal tak on hand
For vs alle do þis trauail
Þar of es god we ta consail
Again þe flum to folu þe sloth   15
Corn þan sal we find to folu for soththe
Ruben said þan his resun
Lo me i am redi bun
Our aller nedes vnd[er] ta
Giue me mi graith and lat me ga   20
His breþer said bot ga we alle
In godds nam and sua we sall
Siluer inogh wit yow yee tak
And i yow prai for drightin sak
Quen yee funden haue your fang   25
Þᵗ yee duell not þan to lang
Bot gas warli thoru vncuth land
Godd hald ou[er] yow his holy hand
Þere breþer went out o chanaan
For þar was iacob wonnand þan   30
Þair yongest broþer left þai at ham
Beniamin þan was his nam
Þei heied þam on þair wai
Þat vntil egypte son com þai   35

Fairfax 14, Bodleian Library, Oxford

Betidde a time in litel quile
Iacob went walcand[e] bi þe Ile
He sagh apon þe wat[er]es reme
Chaf fletand[e] come wiþ þe streme
Of þat siȝt wex he fulle bliþe   5
and tille his sones talde hit squyþe
Childer he saide ȝe liste and lete
I sagh chaf[e] on þe wat[er] flete
Queþen hit come I con noȝt rede
Bot doun þe wat[er] hit come gode spede   10
If hit be co[m]myn fra ferre lande
Loke quilke of us sal take on hande
To do þis t[ra]uaile for vs alle
or ellis for hungre we mone falle
agayne þe flume to folow þe sloþ   15
and corne ȝe sal þen finde forsoþ
Ruben saide þen his reson
Lo I am alleredy boun
Our aller nedis vnder ta
Gif me my graiþe and lete me ga   20
His breþ[er] saide bot go we alle
In goddes name and so we salle
Siluer Inoghe ȝe wiþ ȝou take
And I ȝou pray for goddis sake
quen ȝe fondyn haue ȝour fange   25
Loke ȝe dwelle noȝt to lange
Gas warly þorou out vncouþ lande
God halde ouer ȝou his haly hande
Þes breþ[er] went out of chanaan
For þer was Iacob dwelling[e] þan   30
Þaire ȝongest broþ[er] laft atte hame
Beniamyn was his name
Þai hyed ham fast a pon þaire way
7 vn to egipt sone come þai   35

Göttingen MS theol. 107

Betid þan in a little quile
Iacob ȝode walkand bi þe Nile
he sau apon þe watris reime
Chaf cu[m] fletand wid þe streme

MAP I

CHURCH

kirk areas

chirch areas

church areas

cherch areas

Of þᵗ sight wex he ful blith   5
And til his sonis he tald it suith
Childer he said ȝe list and lete
I sau chaf on þe wat[er] flete
Queþe[n] it comis i can noght rede
Bot doun it fletis ful god spede   10
If it be come[n] fra fer land
Loke quilk of ȝu sal take on hand
For vs all take þis trauaile
Þarof es gode we ta c[on] saile
Agayn þe flum to folu þe chaf   15
Corn þare sul we find to haf
Ruben þan said his resun
Lo he said I am alredi boun
Vr aller nedis to vnderta
Gif me tresur and lat me ga   20
His breder said may we ga all
In goddes name and sua we sall
Tresur enohut wid ȝe ȝe take
And i ȝou pray for goddes sake
Que[n] ȝe funde[n] haue ȝour fang   25
Þat ȝe duell noght þar to lang
Bot gas warli in vncuth land
God hald ou[er] ȝou his hali hand
Þire bred[er] went vte of canaan
For þare was Iacob wonand þan   30
Þar ȝongest broder þai left at hame
Beniamyn þan was his name
Þai heyed þaim apon þair way
Þan sone to egipt com þai   35

MS R 3.8 Trinity College, Cambridge

Soone aftir in a litil while
Iacob ȝode bi þe watir of nyle
He say vpon þe watir glem
Chaf com fletyng wiþ þe streem
Of þat siȝte wex he ful bliȝe   5
And to his sones tolde hit swiþe
Childre he seide ȝe luste and lete
I saw chaf on þe watir flete
Wheþon hit comeþ con I not rede
But dou[n] hit fleteþ ful good spede   10

If hit be come[n] fro fer lond
Loke whiche of ȝou wol take on hond
For vs alle to t[ra]uaile
Herof is good we take cou[n]saile
Aȝeyn þe flu[m] to fynde þe chaue   15
Corn þ[er]e shul we fynde to haue
Ruben seide to his resou[n]
Lo I am al redy bou[n]
Oure aller nedes to take in place
Ȝyue me tresour and lete me pace   20
His broþ[er] seide go we alle
In goddes name and so we shalle
Tresour ynouȝe wiþ ȝou ȝe take
and I ȝou preye for godde sake
When ȝe fou[n]den han þ^t þing   25
Þ^t ȝe make not longe dwellyng
But gooþ wisely in vncouþe londe
God holde ouer ȝou his holy honde
Þese breþ[er] went fro canaan
For þ[er]e was Iacob wonyng þan   30
Her ȝongest broþ[er] þei lefte at home
Be[n]iamin was his nome
Þei hiȝed hem vpon her wey
Soone to egipte comen þey   35

British Museum Additional 36983; The "Bedford" MS.

Sone afftyr in a litell whyle
Iacob ȝede be þe watyr of nyle
he Se opon þe watyr gleme
Chaf come fletyng w^t þe Streme
Of þe Syght was he bliþe   5
And to hys Sones he tolde it Swiþe
Chyldre he sayde ȝe list and lete
I Se chaf on þe watyr flete
ffro whens it comeþ can I not rede
Bote dou[n]e it comeþ full gode spede   10
Ȝef it be come fro fer lAnde
Loke which of ȝow will take on ho[n]de
Of ȝow all to travayle
Here of ys gode to take cou[n]sayle
Aȝen þe flom to fynde þe chaf   15
Corne þe[n] schull we fynde to haue

Ruben sayde to hys Reson
Lo I am Redy bou[n]
Oure alþer nede to take in place
ʒefs mc tresour and lete me pas   20
Hys breþ[er] Sayde go we all
In goddis name so we Schall
Tresoure Inough wᵗ ʒow ʒe take
And I pray ʒow for goddis Sake
When ʒe founden haue þᵗ þing   25
Þᵗ ʒe make not long duellyng
Bote go wysely in oncouþe londe
God holde ou[er] ʒow hys holy honde
Þes breþ[er] went fro canaan
ffor þe[r] was Iacob duelly[n]g þan   30
Her ʒongest broþ[er] þey lefft at home
Beniamyn was hys nAme
Þey Sped hem Vpon þe waye
Sone to Egypte com þay   35

PHONOLOGICAL FEATURES

Of the few able to be dealt with here, perhaps one of the most obvious phonological discrepancies in the extract (corresponding to lines 4777–4810 of the EETS edition edited by R. Morris) can be seen in the following examples:

C(otton)	F(airfax)	G(öttingen)	T(rinity)	B(edford)	
⟨holy⟩	⟨haly⟩	⟨———⟩	⟨holy⟩	⟨holy⟩	(28)
⟨sua⟩	⟨so⟩	⟨sua⟩	⟨so⟩	⟨so⟩	(22)
⟨tald⟩	⟨talde⟩	⟨tald⟩	⟨tolde⟩	⟨tolde⟩	(6)
⟨fra⟩	⟨fra⟩	⟨fra⟩	⟨fro⟩	⟨fro⟩	(11)

Manuscripts T and B clearly tend to have ⟨o⟩ spellings for the root vocalic segments in these words, although there are some exceptions. One might suppose, therefore, that in the grammars of T and B there was an additional (innovatory) rule to the effect that:

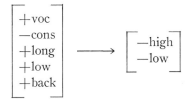

$$\begin{bmatrix} +\text{voc} \\ -\text{cons} \\ +\text{long} \\ +\text{low} \\ +\text{back} \end{bmatrix} \longrightarrow \begin{bmatrix} -\text{high} \\ -\text{low} \end{bmatrix}$$

The "exceptions" to this rule, C's ⟨holy⟩ and F's ⟨so⟩, suggest two possibilities. The first, and the most likely, is that these texts were copied from one that showed such an additional rule to its grammar, the orthographic consequences of which were sometimes and sometimes not "translated" into the spelling system of the copyist. The second is that in C and F the height-raising rule had only minor status—that is, it did not apply in all phonetic contexts, but was delimited to certain items in the lexicon containing long, low, back vowels.

Similar difficulties of interpretation are seen when another height-raising rule operates in environments where [—long] as well as [+long] vocalic segments occur before a nasal as in:

C	F	G	T	B	
⟨ham⟩	⟨hame⟩	⟨hame⟩	⟨home⟩	⟨home⟩	(31)
⟨nam⟩	⟨name⟩	⟨name⟩	⟨nome⟩	⟨nAme⟩	(32)
⟨land⟩	⟨lande⟩	⟨land⟩	⟨lond⟩	⟨lande⟩	(11)
⟨hand⟩	⟨hande⟩	⟨hand⟩	⟨hond⟩	⟨ho[n]de⟩	(12)
⟨lang⟩	⟨lange⟩	⟨lang⟩	⟨longe⟩	⟨long⟩	(26)
⟨can⟩	⟨con⟩	⟨can⟩	⟨con⟩	⟨can⟩	(9)

For the majority of the examples in T and B just quoted it can be formulated as follows:

$$\begin{bmatrix} +\text{voc} \\ -\text{cons} \\ +\text{back} \\ +\text{low} \end{bmatrix} \longrightarrow \begin{bmatrix} -\text{high} \\ -\text{low} \end{bmatrix} / \underline{\hspace{2cm}} \begin{bmatrix} +\text{cons} \\ +\text{nasal} \end{bmatrix}$$

For a rather similar raising rule before nasal consonants, see pp. 79–80 above.

This rule will not, however, enable us to generate the forms ⟨nAme⟩, ⟨lAnde⟩, and ⟨can⟩ in B, nor the ⟨con⟩ in F. We can, of course, say that we are again dealing with what is only a minor rule, whose occurrence is restricted by nonphonetic factors; however, it is perhaps more likely that (especially in F) the copyist has failed for some reason to "translate" his original into the orthographic/phonetic equivalent of his own dialect. The spellings ⟨nAme⟩ and ⟨lAnde⟩ in B are interesting, since they occur in line-final positions, rhyming with ⟨home⟩ and ⟨ho[n]de⟩ respectively. If the capital ⟨A⟩ symbol has any significance at all, it may be there to show a point where the scribe could have utilized a translation symbol ⟨o⟩ but chose not to. The question is: Why not? Perhaps his reluctance means nothing other than the fact that he tends to "translate" indiscriminately, yet it is strange that at this particular point where a rhyme is involved, such a discrepancy should have been allowed to exist. It may be, in fact, that the scribe is reluctant to change these words, since the nasal-raising rule may only have been a minor one in his grammar and on no occasion extended to items such as ⟨name⟩ and ⟨hame⟩, but possibly to ⟨hond⟩ and ⟨lond⟩. For him, ⟨land/hand⟩ and ⟨hame/name⟩ rhymes might not have been acceptable, a fact that he registers by failing in this context to change the ⟨lande⟩ and ⟨name⟩ of the text from which he is copying. In other words, for the scribe of *B,* the nasal-raising rule has a larger number of nonphonological context restrictions than it possibly has for the scribe of *F.*

It is interesting to notice too that the Modern English realizations of the underlying [aa] vocalic segment in words like ⟨home⟩ and ⟨name⟩ correspond to different Middle English dialectal treatments. Compare the derivations of these words in two Middle English dialects and their manifestation in contemporary British English regions:

	Dialect A	*Dialect* B
Input	[haam]	[haam]
1. Fronting	æǣ	inoperative
2. Vowel-raising	ee	oo
3. Glide Addition	ej	ow
Output	[hejm]	[howm]

Orthographic representations:

Middle English	⟨hame⟩	⟨home⟩
Modern English	⟨home⟩	⟨home⟩

Notice, however, the Northern and Scottish contemporary pronunciations [hejm], with the same vocalic segment as ⟨name⟩. In the above derivation, the Middle English dialect A form seems to stop after the application of the fronting rule, although the resultant segment later acts as input to vowel-raising and glide addition to produce the Northern modern forms. On the other hand, dialects with Middle English ⟨home⟩ have undergone rule 2, the output of which is later subject to glide addition to produce the modern Southern British form. Consider also the derivations:

	Dialect A	*Dialect* B
Input	[naam]	[naam]
1. Fronting	æǣ	inoperative
2. Vowel-raising	ee	oo

3. Glide Addition   ej   inoperative

Output   [nejm]   [noom]

Orthographic representations:
Middle English   ⟨name⟩   ⟨nome⟩
Modern English   ⟨name⟩

In this instance, it is the dialect A form that appears in Modern English, its Middle English equivalent being realized as [næææm], while
Middle English outputs with [noom] do not appear to have any contemporary equivalent.

Another example recurs in the *Cursor Mundi* extracts of what appears
to be the application of a minor rule in one dialect, but a major one in
another. Compare the occurrences set out below of the [—singular] forms
of the modal auxiliary ⟨shall⟩ :

C	F	G	T	B	
⟨sal⟩	⟨sal⟩	⟨sal⟩	⟨wol⟩	⟨will⟩	(12)
⟨sal⟩	⟨sal⟩	⟨sul⟩	⟨schul⟩	⟨schull⟩	(16)
⟨sall⟩	⟨salle⟩	⟨sall⟩	⟨shalle⟩	⟨Schall⟩	(22)

On many occasions there is, in the manuscripts of this text, a contrast
in the vocalic segment in singular and nonsingular contexts of this verb;
one finds, for example, the singular ⟨ic sall⟩ and the nonsingular ⟨we sull⟩.
One can, therefore, suggest the existence of rules of the following kind
for the ablaut variation in this verb:

$$\begin{bmatrix} +\text{voc} \\ -\text{cons} \end{bmatrix} \longrightarrow \begin{bmatrix} +\text{low} \\ +\text{back} \end{bmatrix} \Big/ [+\text{sing}]$$

$$\begin{bmatrix} +\text{voc} \\ -\text{cons} \end{bmatrix} \longrightarrow \begin{bmatrix} +\text{high} \\ +\text{back} \end{bmatrix} \Big/ [-\text{sing}]$$

However, it is a feature of our extract that in *C* and *F* on all occasions,
and sporadically in the other manuscripts, there has been a rule simplification or collapse (see above, pp. 176–177) such that:

$$\begin{bmatrix} +\text{voc} \\ -\text{cons} \end{bmatrix} \longrightarrow \begin{bmatrix} +\text{low} \\ +\text{back} \end{bmatrix} \Big/ [\pm\text{singular}]$$

This last rule appears to be a major one in the grammar of *C* and *F* (and
in Modern English), whereas in *G, T,* and *B* it only achieves the status
of a minor rule. Indeed, its validity for *T* and *B* may be minimal, since on
the one occasion one finds it operational in the extract (1.22), the vocalic

segment is made to rhyme with that in ⟨all⟩. Indeed, the ⟨s(c)hall(e)⟩ forms of *T* and *B* may be features, not of the dialect of the copyist, but of that of the text copied, translation from one to another being discouraged by the necessity to retain the rhyme.

The evidence so far produced suggests, if anything, a strong connection between the grammars of *T* and *B* as against all the others. Nevertheless, in some instances it is clear that *G* and *T* (at least) share common grammatical features. Compare, for example, the forms of the past tense singular of the verb ⟨to see⟩ as they appear in the extracts:

C	*F*	*G*	*T*	*B*	
⟨sagh⟩	⟨sagh⟩	⟨sau⟩	⟨say⟩	⟨Se⟩	(3)
⟨sagh⟩	⟨sagh⟩	⟨sau⟩	⟨saw⟩	⟨Se⟩	(8)

In the examples ⟨sau⟩ and ⟨saw⟩ in *G* and *T*, it would appear that there is an occurrence of an innovatory rule already discussed above (see "Spelling and Sounds," pp. 75–77). This rule states that a glide is formed (with frontness assimilation) in contexts before an underlying (deleted) [—sonorant] consonantal segment:

$$
\begin{bmatrix} -\text{voc} \\ +\text{cons} \\ -\text{sonorant} \end{bmatrix} \longrightarrow \begin{bmatrix} -\text{voc} \\ -\text{cons} \\ +\text{sonorant} \\ \alpha \text{ back} \end{bmatrix} \Big/ \begin{bmatrix} +\text{voc} \\ -\text{cons} \\ \alpha \text{ back} \end{bmatrix} \underline{\quad\quad}
$$

The spelling form ⟨sagh⟩ of *C* and *F* suggests that one has here a vocalic segment followed by a nonsonorant, back, high consonant. The ⟨say⟩ and ⟨Se⟩ forms of *T* and *B* present some difficulty. They may, in their contexts, be interpreted as [—past] and, therefore, not meet the conditions for the operation of the glide-formation rule. In all manuscripts, however, forms such as ⟨sei⟩, ⟨seȝe⟩, and ⟨seye⟩ can be found where the tense would appear to be unambiguously [+past]:

> ⟨he es þe sel cuthest man
> þat euer yeit we sei⟩   (Morris [1893], l. 16214)

> ⟨he was agaste quen he þat seye
> 7 to þe rote he keste his eye⟩   (Morris [1893], l. 1345)

One tentative explanation for such forms might be that in the grammars that produce them, one may have to allow for some low-valued simplification rule of the type suggested above for the ⟨sul/sall⟩ data, such that there is no alternation in height of the vocalic segment to mark [+past] from [—past]. Alternatively, for the form ⟨say⟩ at least, it could be suggested that the ⟨y⟩ symbol represents a glide, but is orthographically ambiguous as a marker of its relative degree of frontness or backness.

The formation of glides (that is, where the second, nonsyllabic vocalic segment of a long vowel undergoes a change of articulatory position from the first segment) is an important means of differentiating between some of the versions of the *Cursor Mundi*. Consider the forms of the *Part* of the verb ⟨to find⟩ :

C	F	G	T	B	
⟨funden⟩	⟨fondyn⟩	⟨funde[n]⟩	⟨fou[n]den⟩	⟨founden⟩	(25)

In the chapter on "Spellings and Sounds" it was suggested that underlying the variation in the height of the vocalic segment in the first syllable of the "strong" verbs in certain apparently nonphonological contexts (for example, *Pret$_2$* and *Part*) was a vowel-harmony rule of the type:

$$\begin{bmatrix} +\text{voc} \\ -\text{cons} \end{bmatrix} \longrightarrow [\alpha \text{ high}] \Big/ \underline{\quad\quad} C_2^2 \begin{bmatrix} +\text{voc} \\ -\text{cons} \\ \alpha \text{ high} \end{bmatrix}$$

Such a rule enabled us to account for the variation in height in the vocalic segment of the first syllable in such forms as ⟨chusen⟩ (*Pret$_2$*) and ⟨chosen⟩ (*Part*). It was also suggested that the [—high, —low] vowel of the *Part* (and the *Pres*) could be raised one degree of height whenever it appeared before a nasal consonant segment, hence the Middle English *Pret$_2$* and *Part* form ⟨funden⟩. Such a raising rule will be present in the grammars of *C* and *G;* but if one takes the evidence of *F*'s ⟨fondyn⟩ at its face value, it would seem to have been deleted from that scribe's grammar. On many occasions, however, the scribe of *F* is more consistent in his substitution by the symbol ⟨o⟩ preceding the minim strokes of the nasals ⟨n⟩ and ⟨m⟩ for the "original" ⟨u⟩ in such words as ⟨son⟩ (⟨a son⟩) and ⟨come⟩ (⟨to come⟩). As already seen above (see pages 30–31), such an orthographic innovation has no implications for the phonology.

Again if the orthographic evidence is given an autonomous phonemic interpretation, it seems that the grammars of *T* and *B* show an important innovation in such forms as ⟨founden⟩ compared to other manuscripts of the *Cursor Mundi*. Since the consonantal group [nd] is an environment before which vocalic segments become long (see pp. 71–72 above), it is possible that spellings such as ⟨funden⟩ show a [+long] vocalic element in the first syllable—[uu]. Compare the following derivations:

Input	C, G [fond-]	F [fond-]	T, B [fond-]
1. Nasal-raising	u	inoperative	u
2. Lengthening	uu	inoperative	uu
3. Glide Addition	inoperative	inoperative	uw
4. Vowel-lowering	inoperative	inoperative	ow
Output	[fuund-]	[fond-]	[fownd-]

T and *B* are distinguished from *C, G,* and *F* by the application to them only of rules 3 and 4, whereas *F* is distinct from *C* and *G* by its failure to add to its grammar the nasal-raising rule, which, in turn, blocks the application of all the other rules in the derivation.

The spelling evidence need not, of course, be so interpreted. Is one justified in assuming that an ⟨ou⟩ digraph represents a phonetic diphthong feature, or should the second graph be interpreted merely as a mark either of the blackness or the length of the vocalic segment? At the same time, can one always conclude that a single graph ⟨u⟩ in fact represents a vocalic segment [uu] and not a diphthong, since the scribes of *C, F,* and *G* may, in this instance, have been using a morphophonemic spelling system? Compare, for example, the spellings of the word for ⟨down⟩ in the five manuscripts:

C	F	G	T	B	
⟨dunward⟩	⟨doun⟩	⟨doun⟩	⟨dou[n]⟩	⟨dou[n]e⟩	(10)

In this instance, *F* and *G* appear to have the lowering and diphthongizing rules. Perhaps all one can say is that either one is not able to recover the full extent of such rules from the spelling system because of its morphophonemic nature, or one can conclude that (on the very limited evidence looked at here) our rules were present in the grammars of all the manuscripts (except *C*); only they seem to have been delimited by different nonphonological factors (that is, they may have been restricted to certain items in the lexicon) in each particular case. The solution to this problem could be approached only after a considerably greater sampling of the data from the five manuscripts, as well as from others earlier and later in date, in addition to achieving a fuller understanding of the nature of each scribe's spelling practice.

One should perhaps never expect a given scribe's orthographic usage to be consistently either autonomous phonemic or morphophonemic at any one time; if one were to ignore this, one might arrive at some rather curious conclusions. Compare, for example, the following spellings of the imperative singular of the verb ⟨to give⟩ :

C	F	G	T	B	
⟨giue⟩	⟨Gif⟩	⟨Gif⟩	⟨ȝyue⟩	⟨ȝefs⟩	(20)

A rigorously applied autonomous phonemic interpretation would suggest that the rule for the voicing of voiceless obstruents in voiced surroundings:

$$\begin{bmatrix} -\text{voc} \\ +\text{cons} \\ +\text{obst} \end{bmatrix} \longrightarrow [+\text{voiced}] \Big/ [V] \underline{\quad\quad} [V]$$

had been deleted from the grammars of *F, G,* and *B* perhaps because there the voiced context is no longer present. But it is difficult to see what is not voiced about a context like ⟨þou ȝif vs nv þe Iugement⟩ (*C, Morris* [1893], l.13714) or why the scribe of *G* has also spellings like ⟨giue⟩ and ⟨giues⟩. Rather than conclude that two different pronunciations are involved in such cases, it is perhaps more reasonable to assume an inconsistent use of both orthographic principles described above. This impression is furthered when one finds spellings of the verb ⟨to have⟩ within two lines of each other in the same manuscript: ⟨Que[n] i haue nede⟩ (*C, Morris* [1893], l.70) and ⟨i quilu[m] haf ben untrew⟩ (*C, Morris* [1893], l.73).

An overall willingness to interpret the spelling system in too rigorous a way can, therefore, lead to the making of statements about dialectal (and other) differences that might never have held. In the extracts chosen, it seems immediately obvious that *G* is distinguished from all the others by the fact that it appears to have a rule in its grammar that makes voiced consonantal obstruents noncontinuant:

C	F	G	T	B	
⟨breþer⟩	⟨breþ[er]⟩	⟨breder⟩	⟨broþ[er]⟩	⟨breþer⟩	(21)
⟨wit⟩	⟨wiþ⟩	⟨wid⟩	⟨wiþ⟩	⟨wᵗ⟩	
⟨breþer⟩	⟨breþ[er]⟩	⟨bred[er]⟩	⟨breþ[er]⟩	⟨breþ[er]⟩	

so that:

$$\begin{bmatrix} -\text{voc} \\ +\text{cons} \\ +\text{obst} \end{bmatrix} \longrightarrow [-\text{continuant}] \Big/ \begin{Bmatrix} [V] \underline{\quad} [V] \\ \underline{\quad} \# \end{Bmatrix}$$

Yet even in our short extract there is an apparent "exception" to this rule:

C	F	G	T	B	
⟨suith⟩	⟨squyþe⟩	⟨suith⟩	⟨swiþe⟩	⟨Swiþe⟩	(6)

The case is further complicated by the fact that in all five manuscript versions one finds such forms as ⟨fade/ur⟩ and ⟨moder⟩, except in *G,* where it is not uncommon to find ⟨moþer⟩; compare Morris (1893), ll. 77, 78, and 1254. Perhaps the only safe conclusion one can draw here is that the scribe of *G* saw no reason to represent the phonetic value of the intervocalic consonantal segment in such words as ⟨broder⟩ and ⟨moder⟩/⟨moþer⟩, since for him the graphs ⟨d⟩ and ⟨þ⟩ could, in these contexts, be used interchangeably (even though it is likely that the surface phonetic form they "represented" was [ð] in both cases).

Many scholars have, in the past, on the basis of a "systematic" spelling difference between dialectal manuscripts, made categorical statements about the phonetic differences these imply. On the basis of the very clear-cut preference for either ⟨qu⟩ or ⟨wh⟩ in manuscripts like the *Cursor Mundi,* it has been suggested that there existed in Middle English a rather similar distinction in the pronunciation of the initial consonantal segment of a word like ⟨when⟩ as there does today between, say, some Scottish ([hwen]) and Southern British English ([wen]) dialects. In our extract we find:

C	*F*	*G*	*T*	*B*	
⟨quile⟩	⟨quile⟩	⟨quile⟩	⟨while⟩	⟨whyle⟩	(1)
⟨Queþen⟩	⟨Queþen⟩	⟨Queþe[n]⟩	⟨Wheþon⟩	⟨whens⟩	(9)
⟨quilk⟩	⟨quilke⟩	⟨quilk⟩	⟨whiche⟩	⟨which⟩	(12)
⟨Quen⟩	⟨quen⟩	⟨Que[n]⟩	⟨When⟩	⟨When⟩	(25)
⟨suith⟩	⟨squyþe⟩	⟨suith⟩	⟨swiþe⟩	⟨Swiþe⟩	(6)

It is certainly interesting and important that *T* and *B* consistently prefer ⟨wh⟩ spellings in contexts where the other manuscripts have ⟨qu⟩, but whether one can go on to conclude that the northern manuscripts, therefore, "have a greater degree of initial aspiration" than the others is another matter. The only thing one can say with any certainty is that one digraph is more popular in the orthographies of scribes writing in given geographical standards than another. In themselves such spellings do not enable one to recover their phonetic values (and one cannot assume that there were only two); but, as will be seen below, one can perhaps make a more accurate assessment of a manuscript's geographical provenance by treating such spellings *qua* spellings than one can by postulating reconstructions for its phonological systems.

MORPHOLOGICAL AND SYNTACTIC FEATURES

One is perhaps on surer ground in making comparisons between the syntactical and morphological differences between manuscripts composed in divergent geographical regions, although even in this area there are many difficult problems. It is impossible to give a detailed picture of such contrasts as are to be found even in the short extracts above, but a few important points stand out. One of the most obvious of these is the rule involving the generation of the inflectional suffix ending appropriate to verbs with the features [+singular, −past, +III].

C	F	G	T	B	
⟨com⟩	⟨come⟩	⟨comis⟩	⟨comeþ⟩	⟨comeþ⟩	(9)
⟨fletteþ⟩	⟨come⟩	⟨fletis⟩	⟨fleteþ⟩	⟨comeþ⟩	(10)

T and B share a rule mentioned in an earlier chapter:

$$\text{inflectional suffix} \longrightarrow \langle e\text{þ}\rangle \Big/ \begin{bmatrix} \text{Verb} \\ +\text{sing} \\ -\text{past} \\ +\text{III} \end{bmatrix} \underline{\qquad}$$

but G, at least in our extract, seems to require a rule:

$$\text{inflectional suffix} \longrightarrow \langle is\rangle \Big/ \begin{bmatrix} \text{Verb} \\ +\text{sing} \\ -\text{past} \\ +\text{III} \end{bmatrix} \underline{\qquad}$$

In their contexts C and F appear to utilize forms that are [+past], although F's present-tense inflectional forms are usually identical with those of G (as are those of Modern English).

C, F, and G are again contrasted with forms in T and B in the rules involved in the selection of the inflectional suffix for the imperative of verbs with the features [−singular, +II]:

C	F	G	T	B	
⟨gas⟩	⟨gas⟩	⟨gas⟩	⟨gooþ⟩	⟨go⟩	(27)

For C, F, and G such a rule would be of the form:

$$\text{inflectional suffix} \longrightarrow \langle s\rangle \Big/ \begin{bmatrix} \text{Verb} \\ \text{Imp} \\ -\text{sing} \\ +\text{II} \end{bmatrix} \underline{\qquad}$$

but in the same context, T would generate an inflectional suffix in ⟨þ⟩ ; and B, one manifested as zero.

Perhaps the most mentioned dialectal "test" in the morphology of the Middle English verb is that involving the inflectional suffix of the "present participle"—one of the markers of continuous verbal aspect. With one exception, the T and B manuscripts of the *Cursor Mundi* have a form that distinguishes them from the three others:

C	F	G	T	B	
⟨walcand⟩	⟨walcand[e]⟩	⟨walkand⟩	———	———	(3)
⟨flettand⟩	⟨fletand[e]⟩	⟨fletand⟩	⟨fletyng⟩	⟨fletyng⟩	(4)
⟨wonnand⟩	⟨dwelling[e]⟩	⟨wonand⟩	⟨wonyng⟩	⟨duelly[n]g⟩	(30)

A grammar for the first three manuscripts (ignoring F's ⟨dwelling[e]⟩ for the moment) would require a rule:

$$\text{inflectional suffix} \longrightarrow \langle \text{and(e)} \rangle \bigg/ \begin{bmatrix} Pres \\ Part \end{bmatrix} \underline{\quad\quad}$$

whereas in T and B its "equivalent" would be:

$$\text{inflectional suffix} \longrightarrow \langle \text{yng} \rangle \bigg/ \begin{bmatrix} Pres \\ Part \end{bmatrix} \underline{\quad\quad}$$

It might be argued that since F has a form ⟨dwelling[e]⟩, we shall have to include in its grammar a minor low-valued rule like the second one above. This would, however, be an unnecessary complication, since as has already been seen, the scribe of F often failed to "translate" some of the features of the orthography of the manuscript he was copying (written in a different dialectal spelling from his own), so that one tends to find in his written work items that would have been ungrammatical (or at least unacceptable) in his spoken dialect.

Although the most obvious differences between the five manuscripts chosen for examination lie in the morphology of their verbal usage, there is, nevertheless, at least one important and clear discrepancy in their surface nominal forms. Among the great changes in the pronominal system in the Middle English period was, as has been noted, the innovation of the plural form with the initial consonantal segment spelled ⟨þ-⟩. *cf. 189* This innovation seems to have appeared at first only in [+agent] case-sensitive contexts until, at a later date, this part of the grammar was simplified and ⟨þ-⟩ forms appeared in all cases in the plural. A rather interesting situation is to be found in our five extracts:

C	F	G	T	B	
[+*agent*]					
⟨þai⟩	——	⟨þai⟩	⟨þei⟩	⟨þey⟩	(31)
⟨þai⟩	⟨þai⟩	⟨þai⟩	⟨þey⟩	⟨þay⟩	(34)
[+*object*]					
⟨þam⟩	⟨ham⟩	⟨þaim⟩	⟨hem⟩	⟨hem⟩	(33)
[+*possessive*]					
⟨þair⟩	⟨þaire⟩	⟨þar⟩	⟨Her⟩	⟨Her⟩	(31)

With one exception, ⟨h-⟩ forms are to be found only in *T* and *B*, where they are restricted to [−agent] case contexts. All the other manuscripts have an initial consonantal segment spelled ⟨þ-⟩ in, it would seem, all case environments. The [+object] ⟨ham⟩ in *F* can, as might by now be expected, be put down to a failure of the scribe to "translate" the manuscript he copied (and that probably had ⟨h-⟩ forms at least in nonagent case contexts). In other words, there is some probability that he is copying from a manuscript that has a situation like that in *T* and *B*, although he has "translated" what on this assumption would have been an original [+possessive] ⟨h-⟩ form into ⟨þaire⟩. It is possible, of course, though less likely, that his source had only the initial ⟨h-⟩ in the [+object] environment with ⟨þ-⟩ in all others.

It is doubtful if one can say anything useful about the apparent variety that exists in the extracts in case-sensitive nominal inflection. It might appear that on some occasions several of the texts show a rule deletion of the type already mentioned (see pp. 99–108), so that, for example, an underlying ⟨e⟩ inflectional suffix is realized as ⟨Ø⟩. Compare *C*'s ⟨fra fer land⟩ (11), ⟨on hand⟩ (12), and ⟨at ham⟩ (31) with *F*'s ⟨fra ferre lande⟩, ⟨on hande⟩, and ⟨atte hame⟩. However, it is unlikely that one should treat word-final ⟨e⟩ in *F* as a case-sensitive inflectional suffix, still less as a "survival" of some earlier system of inflection. Rather, since the scribe of *F* will spell these words with final ⟨e⟩ in *all* nonpossessive case contexts and *C* likewise always has ⟨land⟩, ⟨hand⟩, and ⟨ham⟩, it is better to assume that neither grammar has a surface mark (in the form of an inflectional suffix at least) of nonpossessive case in the singular.

The same observations probably hold for the apparently random appearance of word-final ⟨e⟩ in adjectives in the nonagent and nonpossessive case contexts:

C	F	G	T	B	
⟨litel⟩	⟨litel⟩	⟨littel⟩	⟨litil⟩	⟨litell⟩	(1)
⟨god⟩	⟨god⟩	⟨god⟩	⟨god⟩	⟨god⟩	(10)
⟨fer⟩	⟨ferre⟩	⟨fer⟩	⟨fer⟩	⟨fer⟩	(11)

C	F	G	T	B	
⟨vncuth⟩	⟨vncouþ⟩	⟨vncuth⟩	⟨vncouþe⟩	⟨oncouþe⟩	(27)
⟨inogh⟩	⟨Inoghe⟩	⟨enohut⟩	⟨ynouȝe⟩	⟨Inough⟩	(23)

It is unlikely that there is any question of the presence or otherwise of "inflectional endings" in these examples; the above spellings probably represented the ones used universally by a given scribe in all circumstances and, it seems, in the singular as well as the plural. Our earlier observation (see p. 127) that adjectives and other determiners had a word-final ⟨e⟩ as a surface mark copying the nonsingular number of the noun with which they were in "agreement" with ⟨Ø⟩ in singular contexts, is probably of limited adequacy, especially in texts of a later date; such occurrences as C's ⟨O gode pertre coms god peres⟩ ⟨from good pear trees come good pears⟩ (Morris [1893], l. 37) are not uncommon.

III

One of the main concerns in this book has been with the reconstruction of sound systems from orthographic evidence in a language that is no longer spoken. Any success or failure in this attempt depended upon the sophistication of one's theory of what scribes meant by their spelling systems. Since this theory was shown, in fact, to be not particularly advanced, it is often impossible, for instance, to decide to what extent a particular orthography is autonomous phonemic, morphophonemic, or constructed according to some other set of principles. Consequently, all the reconstructed material provided could only be considered as very tentative indeed. At the same time, concern to recover spoken features meant that other kinds of very revealing dialectal evidence (compare the distribution of initial ⟨qu-⟩ and ⟨wh-⟩ spellings) have not been given the importance they merit. In fact, in many previous studies, the majority of scholars in the field of Middle English dialect research have approached the topic from the reconstruction point of view, with the result that their conclusions are very often less reliable or inclusive than one would like them to be. Although it is undeniably of great interest to be able to suggest how Middle English and its regional varieties sounded, one tends to miss a great amount of detailed information if one restricts oneself too rigidly to this end.

There has, however, recently been a reaction against the traditional methodology used by historical linguists in Middle English dialectal differentiation. This has come mainly from McIntosh, whose forthcoming *Survey of Middle English Dialects* (done in collaboration with M. L. Samuels) will suggest that it is equally possible to construct the system of a scribe's *graphemic* method as to make statements about the system of sounds he may have employed in his spoken language. In other words, since Middle English scribes seem to have been remarkably consistent in their orthographic habits and since there appear to have been regional or even individual "standards" of spelling, it should be possible both to give a detailed account of the principle underlying an individual scribe's method and to set up a comparison between it and the systems used by other scribes. The proposal put forward by McIntosh (1953, 1956) is that a given scribe's spelling *qua* spelling is as useful (if not more useful) a guide to the dialectal provenance of a manuscript as any attempted phonological reconstruction: "if there is a contrast ⟨bane⟩ ⟨bone⟩ between the North and elsewhere, then for our purposes it is best treated as a contrast in graphemes irrespective of the phonemic 'value,' or to speak in more mediæval terms, a contrast in *figurae* irrespective of the *potestas* of each."

McIntosh's technique involves treating the written evidence in its own right. Spelling becomes all-important and phonological "representation" retreats into the background; if scribe A uses the symbol ⟨qu-⟩ initially in given lexical items and scribe B uses ⟨wh-⟩ in the same context, then this in itself is an important piece of information irrespective of any "phonetic" values such symbols may have. If one is able to show that there are consistent spelling variants of this type (and McIntosh utilizes more than two hundred orthographic variables), then they can be plotted on maps. Although such evidence is incredibly complex, it is, nevertheless, sufficiently systematic for statements to be made about the area of composition or copying. If one has a sufficiently large number of documents (wills and charters) that are known from internal and external evidence to have been composed in certain geographical areas, then it is possible to describe systematically the orthographic or graphemic peculiarities of individual locations, provided a number of precautions are taken. In the first place, the scope of inquiry should be restricted to a relatively small time span—ideally less than one hundred years, since variation brought about by temporal factors should, as far as possible, be treated separately. Secondly, a sufficiently large number of forms with graphemic variation must be chosen. Earlier studies, such as Moore, Meech, and Whitehall (1935) are inadequate, since the range of spelling variants they examine is too small; consequently, their conclusions are too general. Lastly, forms that are sufficiently frequent in their variation should be utilized, because statistically rare variants can provide only a low information factor.

Graphemic variants can then be plotted on maps and isogloss lines (approximate boundaries between graphemic alternants) drawn. Map I is a sample of the possibilities of this technique for one feature only (although it is not to be seen as a final statement of McIntosh's views on the distribution of the selected item). Here it can clearly be seen that there are quite distinct areas where certain spellings of the Middle English version of

⟨church⟩ are more popular than others. Indeed, some of the forms with initial ⟨k-⟩ occur in locales well outside the area bounded by the general ⟨k-⟩ isogloss, as do spellings with radical ⟨e⟩ turning up near Bath, far away from their "normal" southeastern area. Such spelling "pockets" inside larger isogloss areas are often very important pieces of evidence when it comes to the localization of individual texts. So too are even such apparently minimal spelling differences as shown by those in ⟨kirc⟩ in the middle of the area dominated by final ⟨k⟩ realizations. McIntosh's technique, which is probably the most important contribution recently made to Middle Eng-

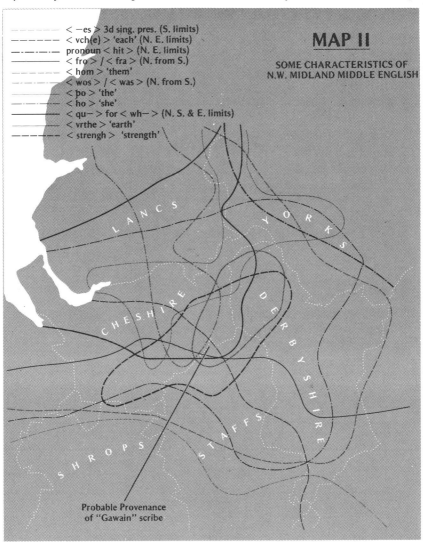

⟨ −es ⟩ 3d sing. pres. (S. limits)
⟨ vch(e) ⟩ 'each' (N. E. limits)
pronoun ⟨ hit ⟩ (N. E. limits)
⟨ fro ⟩ / ⟨ fra ⟩ (N. from S.)
⟨ hom ⟩ 'them'
⟨ wos ⟩ / ⟨ was ⟩ (N. from S.)
⟨ þo ⟩ 'the'
⟨ ho ⟩ 'she'
⟨ qu— ⟩ for ⟨ wh— ⟩ (N. S. & E. limits)
⟨ vrthe ⟩ 'earth'
⟨ strengh ⟩ 'strength'

MAP II

SOME CHARACTERISTICS OF
N.W. MIDLAND MIDDLE ENGLISH

Probable Provenance
of "Gawain" scribe

lish dialect studies, can rely heavily upon the accumulated weight of even such apparently minute variations.

Perhaps the greatest advantage to treating spelling systems in their own right, irrespective of any phonological "representational" value they may have, is that one has a much greater amount of information at one's disposal. For instance, graphs such as ⟨þ⟩, ⟨ð⟩, and ⟨th⟩ may, in certain environments, imply no phonological difference when found in manuscripts written in different dialects. Yet the fact that they will be consistently distinguished by scribes using different orthographic methods can be an important piece of information in the localization of texts. In addition, the McIntosh/Samuels technique has a very useful application. Maps as detailed as the one for ⟨church⟩ given above can be produced for over two hundred regular orthographic variants by using data from texts (and there are many such, especially wills and charters) that are known to have been written in certain areas and at particular dates. Texts for which there exists no external evidence for regional origin can then, by the use of as many of the same spelling variants as possible, be plotted or fitted onto the isogloss patterns provided by the already localized manuscripts. The place of composition of regionally unidentified manuscripts can in this way be discovered within a very small degree of tolerance. Once this has been achieved, their spelling data can then be added to the total localized material, in this way making all future *fittings* more detailed and more accurate.

A much simplified version of the general technique can be given here. On the basis of many different kinds of evidence—reconstructed phonological and syntactical, stylistic, and other—many scholars have for a long time believed that a manuscript containing some of the best-known late fourteenth-century alliterative poems—*Sir Gawain and the Green Knight, Pearl, Purity,* and *Patience*—British Museum *Cotton Nero A. x,* was written down by a single scribe living somewhere in the northwest Midland counties of England. This claim can be supplemented and made more specific by a comparison between the orthographic habits of the scribe of this manuscript and what is known about contemporary graphemic systems in the same area. In Map II only nine out of a possible much larger number of regular graphemic alternants have been selected and plotted for their isoglosses in this small area that includes Lancashire, southwest Yorkshire, Cheshire, Derbyshire, Staffordshire, and northern Shropshire. The features chosen are:

(1) Part of the national isogloss for texts with inflectional suffixes in ⟨es⟩ as against ⟨eþ⟩ in the third-person singular present tense of verbs. Texts north of the isogloss will tend to have ⟨es⟩; in *Cotton Nero A. x*

one finds ⟨he hewes⟩ and not ⟨he heweþ⟩, so, presumably, the scribe must be located somewhere north of this isogloss line.

(2) The initial vocalic segment of the word for ⟨each⟩ spelled with a ⟨v⟩ graph having its most northerly occurrence shown by our isogloss. The scribe of *Cotton Nero A. x* has ⟨vch(e)⟩ spellings most commonly (other Middle English versions include ⟨iche⟩, ⟨eche⟩, and ⟨euche⟩); consequently, he must be located to the south of this isogloss line.

(3) The pronoun with the features [+singular, —animate, +III] normally spelled ⟨hit⟩ in *Cotton Nero A. x,* in contrast to ⟨it⟩ spellings in areas to the North and East.

(4) The vocalic segment in the word for ⟨away from⟩ spelled in *Cotton Nero A. x* as ⟨fro⟩ and not ⟨fra⟩.

(5) The local isogloss for the pronoun with the features [—singular, +animate, +III, —agent, —possessive] spelled ⟨hom⟩. *Cotton Nero A. x* has both ⟨hom⟩ and ⟨hem⟩ forms for this item, but the fact that it has the former suggests that it should be placed within the boundaries of the mapped isogloss line, outside of which ⟨hem⟩ forms predominate.

(6) The verb ⟨to be⟩ with features [+singular, +past] with vocalic segment spelled ⟨a⟩ in *Cotton Nero A. x,* suggesting an area of composition south of the isogloss line.

(7) The vocalic segment of the definite article spelled with the graph ⟨e⟩ in *Cotton Nero A. x,* placing its scribe outside the area enclosed by the isogloss line for ⟨þo⟩.

(8) *Cotton Nero A. x* has ⟨ho⟩ forms of the pronoun with the features [+singular, +animate, +female, +III], whereas areas outside the isogloss line show ⟨heo⟩ and ⟨s(c)h-⟩ types.

(9) Spellings such as ⟨queþen⟩ and ⟨queþer⟩ suggest (although ⟨wheþen⟩ and ⟨wheþer⟩ also occur) that *Cotton Nero A. x* should be located somewhere within the isogloss line that includes initial ⟨qu-⟩ spellings.

(The next two variant forms are rather unusual in that they tend to go against the overall local regional spelling varieties and to constitute small pockets of atypical usage, rather like the initial ⟨k-⟩ spellings in the middle of what is a predominantly ⟨ch-⟩ area around Gloucester on Map I. If one were to ignore "details" of this kind (as earlier Middle English dialectologists have tended to), then, for example, not only would the variants (10) and (11) appear irrelevant to or impossible for manuscripts written in the northwest Midland area, but (perhaps more importantly) one would be prevented from making as detailed a statement about the scribe's provenance as the one given below.)

(10) In the area covered by Map II as a whole, the most popular spelling for the initial vocalic segment in the word for ⟨the earth⟩ is ⟨e⟩. In *Cotton Nero A. x*, however, alongside a proportionally large number of ⟨erþe⟩ spellings, one also (especially in *Pearl, Purity,* and *Patience*) encounters ⟨vrþe⟩ forms. Such information would completely lose its force if one did not include the evidence from localized texts in the area that show a small pocket of ⟨vrþe⟩ forms represented by the isogloss line.

(11) Similarly, the overall regional spelling for the noun ⟨strength⟩ is most commonly ⟨strenkþe⟩, and indeed this form is to be found also in *Cotton Nero A. x*. The same manuscript, nevertheless, contains also the spelling ⟨strengh⟩, which, like ⟨vrþe⟩ above, can be shown from contemporary localized materials to exist in a small enclave within the larger area of a rival spelling form.

If one uses what McIntosh describes as the *fit* technique, the selected forms in *Cotton Nero A. x* can be mapped onto the pattern shown by the localized regional isogloss lines. In this instance, one can conclude (although it must be remembered that since only a small percentage of the total known variants has been utilized, any conclusions must be rather tentative) that *Cotton Nero A. x* is likely to have been composed in the very small area in north Staffordshire shown on Map II. Once a manuscript has been localized in this way, its graphemic peculiarities can then be added to the bank of localized information to be used in future "fittings" for contemporary manuscripts for which areas of composition are sought.

BIBLIOGRAPHY

ANDERSON, J., and R. LASS, *Studies in Old English Phonology* (forthcoming).

CLARK, J. W. (1957), chapter 12, pp. 126 ff.

DE CAMP, D., "The Genesis of the Old English Dialects," *Language,* 34 (1958).

EKWALL, E., "Contributions to the History of Old English Dialects," *Lund Universitets Arsskrift,* N.F., Avd. 1, Bd. 12, Nr. 6, Lund, 1916.

GABRIELSON, A., *The Influence of w- in Old English as Seen in Middle English Dialects,* Leipzig, 1912.

JONES, C., "The Computer in Middle English Studies: A Note," *Canadian Journal of Linguistics,* 14 (1968).

KAISER, R., *Zur Geographie des mittelenglischen Wortschatzes,* Leipzig, 1937.

KING, R. (1969), chapter 3.

KRISTENSSON, G., "A Survey of Middle English Dialects, 1290–1350," *Lund Studies in English, 35* (1967), Lund.

KURATH, H., "Interrelation Between Regional and Social Dialects," *Proceedings of the Ninth International Congress of Linguistics,* 1964.

LOGAN, H. M., "The Computer and Middle English Dialectology," *Canadian Journal of Linguistics,* 13 (1967).

MCINTOSH, A., "A New Approach to Middle English Dialectology," *English Studies,* XLIV (1953).

———, "The Analysis of Written Middle English," *TPS,* 1956.

———, and M. G. DAREAU, "A Dialect Word in Some West Midland Manuscripts of the *Prick of Conscience,*" in *Edinburgh Studies in English and Scots,* London, 1971.

———, *An Introduction to a Survey of Scottish Dialects,* Edinburgh, 1961.

MACKENZIE, B. A., *The Early London Dialect,* Oxford, 1928.

MENNER, R. J., *"Sir Gawain and the Green Knight* and the West Midland," *PMLA,* 37 (1922).

MOORE, S., S. B. MEECH, and H. WHITEHALL, *Middle English Dialect Characteristics and Dialect Boundaries,* Ann Arbor, 1935.

NELSON, F. W., "Graphemic Analysis of Late Middle English Manuscripts," *Speculum,* XXXVII (1962).

OAKDEN, J. P., *Alliterative Poetry in Middle English,* volume I : *Dialectal and Metrical Survey,* Manchester, 1930–1935.

PATCH, H. R., and R. J. MENNER, "A Bibliography of Middle English Dialects," *Studies in Philology,* XX (1923).

REANEY, P. H., "On Certain Phonological Features of the Dialect of London in the Twelfth Century," *Englische Studien,* LIX (1925).

SAMUELS, M. L., "Some Applications of Middle English Dialectology," *English Studies,* XLIV (1953).

———, "Kent and the Low Countries: Some Linguistic Evidence," in *Edinburgh Studies in English and Scots,* London, 1971.

SERJEANTSON, M., "The Dialects of the West Midlands in Middle English," *Review of English Studies,* 3 (1927).

———, "The Dialectal Distribution of Certain Phonological Features in Middle English," *English Studies,* 4 (1922).

———, "The Dialect of the Earliest Complete English Prose Psalter," *English Studies,* 6 (1924).

SKEAT, W. W., *English Dialects from the Eighth Century to the Present Day,* Cambridge, 1911.

SUNDBY, B., *Studies in the Middle English Dialect Material of Worcestershire Records,* Bergen, 1963.

———, "The Dialect and Provenance of the Middle English Poem *The*

Owl and the Nightingale," Lund Studies in English, XVIII (1950), Lund.

WATSON, G., "Dialect Survival of Anglo-Saxon Inflections," *JEGP,* XXXV (1936).

WEINREICH, U., "Is a Structural Dialectology Possible?", in *Readings in the Sociology of Language,* edited by J. A. Fishman, The Hague, 1968.

————,"Languages in Contact," in *Psycholinguistics: A Book of Readings,* edited by S. Saporta, New York, 1961.

WRIGHT, J., *The English Dialect Grammar,* Oxford, 1905.

WYLD, H. G., "South Eastern and South East Midland Dialects in Middle English," *Essays and Studies,* VI (1920).

————, "The Surrey Dialect in the Thirteenth Century," *English Studies,* 3 (1921).

ZETTERSTEN, A., "Studies in the Dialect and Vocabulary of the *Ancrene Riwle," Lund Studies in English,* 34 (1965), Lund.

EDITIONS

CHAMBERS, R. W., and M. DAUNT, *A Book of London English, 1384–1425,* London, 1931.

GOLLANCZ, I., *Pearl,* London, 1921.

————, *Purity,* London, 1922.

————, *Patience,* London, 1913.

MORRIS, R., *Cursor Mundi,* EETS, O.S. 57, 59, 62, 66, 68, 99, 101, 1874, 1875, 1876, 1877, 1878, 1892, 1893.

TOLKIEN, J. R. R., and E. V. GORDON, *Sir Gawain and the Green Knight,* Oxford, 1963.

INDEX